AF573616

By the same author:
*The Hope of Glory*
*Wide Horizons*
*Exit*
*One Way Street*
*Dead End*
Non-fiction:
*Stopping the Clock*
*The disposal of terrorist bombs*
*Hotheads and Heroes*
*The Bristol Riots of 1831*

# MINUTES OF TIME

## Man in the Universe

by

Peter Macdonald

Christopher Davies

Published by
Christopher Davies (Publishers) Ltd.,
P.O. Box 403, Sketty,
Swansea, SA2 9BE.



ISBN 0 7154 0685 X

*Printed in Wales by
Dynevor Printing Company,
Rawlings Road,
Llandybïe, Dyfed.*

# CONTENTS

# INTRODUCTION

The aim of this book is to lead you along the rim of knowledge to the place where we think we now stand.

It is a difficult path. In some places you will stride along on firm ground, breathing clear air under a blue sky, understanding everything. In others you will have to step from stone to stone across a morass and under leaden clouds; there is so much that cannot be explained, that nobody comprehends. And as you pass along the rim, so it will move, for every minute things change, and so does our understanding of them.

The book is written in four parts. The first tells of the creation, of the evolution of men and women, of the ancient world and of the development of religions. It covers an enormous time span – from fifteen billion years ago to a thousand years ago. The second takes you through "the history book years" to the beginnning of the 20th Century, concentrating on events which affected mankind as a whole, and on the development of culture. The third tells of war and politics, the themes around which so many variations in people's history have been written. The fourth is about the great threats which face us – but also about our astonishing achievements and brilliant potential.

The book is not an encyclopaedia, it is one man's history of the universe and mankind's part in it. Because it is concise you may, if you wish, read it from beginning to end, but you may also read it a chapter at a time, to satisfy your curiosity about the world we live in. So that the story may continue without being interrupted by too many details some facts have been put into Appendices. These you can read or not as you feel inclined: their omission will not lessen the impact of the book though you will find the contents are well worth your attention.

The book may well change your life. When you have read it you will find yourself standing on the edge of an abyss, but understanding the world as you never have before, with a sense of wonder and a clear idea of how you came to be here.

*

## CHAPTER ONE

# THE CREATION

We live for a very short time. In comparison with the number of Earthly years which have passed since the creation of the Universe our lives are so short as to be almost nothing – though, to us, a year may seem a long time. Or even, sometimes, a day. Not surprisingly, it is impossible for us to comprehend the timescale of evolution: it is beyond belief.

If the whole of time since it began is measured as one thousand years, something like 660 of them passed by before our Earth was created. It was perhaps another 200 years before the first simple forms of life grew in the seas, and another 140 before creatures came out of the water on to dry land; that is, about sixty years ago. It is only twenty-five *days* ago that Mankind became recognisable as an animal species, one of the millions which had evolved – had burrowed and crawled and grown wings and leapt into the trees – and less than one day ago that men and women, in very small numbers, had migrated to most parts of the world. Only three hours ago the first civilisations left a record for us to read and about twenty seconds ago the 20th Century began . . . That is Time.

As for the size of the Universe, if you could travel at the speed of light, which is nearly 300,000 kilometres a second, or six million million miles a year, it would take you more than four years to reach our Sun's nearest star – and by Concorde more than two million years! Even at the speed of light it would take hundreds of years to penetrate deeply into our own great galaxy of stars, let alone beyond them to the more distant ones we can see above us in the night sky.

Some people spend their whole lives trying to discover new information about the universe and make sense of it. They glean seeds of knowledge, interpret them and present them, yet all the time are aware that they are like blind people tapping their way along a pitch black street. However, as there is no-one else to whom we can turn we must see what they have to tell us. If it makes no sense it is because nobody really understands what happened, or why, or how to interpret what is known. How can scientists explain in human terms things which are beyond human comprehension?

In the beginning there was nothing at all. No time, no space, nothing. Only a tiny, fantastically hot fireball. Around fifteen billion – fifteen thousand-million – years ago this fireball started to expand with fantastic force. In that instant time began, space was created and so were the basic materials for everything in it.

As the fireball expanded it cooled. After three minutes or so it was possible for the centres (nuclei, electrically charged particles) of what would become atoms to cling together. After half an hour the temperature had fallen to 300 million degrees Centigrade, fifty times hotter than our Sun. For about a million years the dispersing fireball continued to cool until the nuclei were able to capture free electrons which were hurtling through space and make atoms – but only the very lightest ones, Hydrogen and Helium. These started to cling together and as their mass became larger and larger it reached such a high temperature that the atoms broke up again, releasing high speed particles which broke up other atoms, which released particles which split other atoms and so on. Nuclear reactions began; stars – suns – came into existence.

As the stars burned they created heavier elements such as Carbon and Nitrogen. When all the atoms that could be used as fuel had been burnt the larger stars exploded, making even heavier atoms such as Iron in the process and scattering all their atoms and energy particles into space. (The heavier atoms vital to life were made at this stage, not at the first instant of creation – many of the atoms in our bodies and around us were not made when time began but one or two billion years later, by the nuclear reactors in the sky.)

The explosion of stars filled space with tiny dust particles (about the same size as the particles which we see as cigarette smoke) made of Carbon, Iron, ice, stone and many different types of chemically active clusters of atoms such as Formaldehyde. (Which, today, is used to embalm human bodies, and sometimes to make high explosives!) Some of these particles clung together and began to spin around, creating gravitational forces which drew more and more particles together. New suns were formed, and planets, which went into orbit around the suns, and meteors and comets – small clusters of matter which loop in orbit around a star, which holds them by gravitational force. There are a billion comets in and on the edge of our Solar system, seventy of which appear regularly in our sky at intervals of between three and a thousand years, coming into sight as they approach and then looping away again on their long orbits. Nobody knows for certain what is at the centre of a comet but it would seem to be rock and ice surrounded by a halo of dust and gas that tails away behind it; and that it will eventually disappear altogether as the tail drags matter away from it on its journey. (Halley's Comet comes towards Earth every 76 years and passed by in 1985/1986.)

In groups, called galaxies, all these varieties of stellar objects continued to be projected outwards. (There must be planets in the galaxies but because they are too small, too far away from Earth and, unlike stars, give off no light or radiation, we cannot "see" them, so we have no positive evidence that they are there. However, very recently American astronomers claim to have evidence that there is a huge planet (fifty times as big as Jupiter, the biggest planet in the Solar System, which is itself eleven times the diameter of Earth) circling a small star which is twenty-one light years away from us.

Perhaps ten billion years ago a galaxy we call the Milky Way, was formed. It is only one of millions of galaxies in the Universe, contains perhaps 100 billion stars and is shaped like a flattened spiral, a disc. About five billion years ago our Solar system grew out of free particles in the Milky Way. It has nine planets orbiting around a star, our Sun. Mercury and Venus are closer than we are to the Sun but Mars, Jupiter, Saturn, Uranus, Neptune and Pluto are further away. Some of the planets, like Earth, have moons in orbit around them.

Because distances in the universe are so vast light years – the distance light travels in one year – are used as the yard-stick to concentrate miles or kilometres into measurements that have fewer noughts. The Sun is a brief eight light minutes away from Earth and the distance across the entire Solar system is only eleven light hours but the disc of the Milky Way is 80,000 light years across and about 20,000 light years thick.

Distances within the Solar system can be measured by radar ranging, and distances to nearby stars mathematically by checking their position from different places on Earth. The brightness of light given off by a star can also be measured; if that is then compared with the brightness of stars whose distance is accurately known, it is possible to estimate how far away it is. However, distances deep into space can only be guessed at.

The Universe is constantly changing. Out there in space stars are forming and growing and dying; there are stellar winds which blow atomic particles around in space; there are gravitational forces which act on each other, changing the way in which galaxies and stars and planets move in orbit. But very slowly. The changes take millions of our years, though in cosmic time they may be a tiny fraction of the whole continuing process of creation.

Stars go through a pattern of change which is repeated over and over. They form and start to burn, Hydrogen mostly – 99% of the atoms in the Universe are Hydrogen and Helium – and begin to swell and turn red. Some then expand so much – up to two hundred million miles in diameter, whereas our Sun is less than one million miles in diameter – that they break apart and become clusters of stars – nebulae. Some stars fade out, cease to shine and eventually become a cold black globe: their nuclear reactions cease and what is left of them collapses under its own gravity into tightly packed masses of inert particles. Others may flare up in a great outburst of energy which makes them shine with many times the brightness of our Sun. But whatever the sequence the matter – the atoms and energy particles – they were composed of is taken up into another sequence again: it starts to circulate, becomes a mass, starts to burn, expands, flares up or dies, and so on. And, fortunately, all of this in complete silence. Since sound cannot travel through a vacuum and there is no atmosphere in space we cannot hear all these fantastic explosions.

Stars exist in various sizes; at their heaviest blues, which can be 100,000 times brighter than our Sun, and at their smallest red dwarfs, celestial glow-worms with a surface temperature only slightly more than half that of the Sun, a yellow star which has a surface temperature of about 5,500 degrees Centigrade and an internal heat of around fourteen million degrees. Large stars burn up very quickly, medium stars such as the Sun a hundred times less quickly and small stars very slowly. Our Sun is destroying itself at the rate of four million tons a second. Now and then it flares up, or it cools in spots which show up as black dots on its surface (and are as big as our planet) and which in some way affect our weather. At some time in the future, about five billion years from now, it will heat up, expand, become a Red Giant and fry up the Earth.

Some two-thirds of all stars exist in pairs but our Sun seems to be one of those that lives alone. Some astronomers think that single stars in the galaxies are those which have planets, matter which somehow never came together to form a star and which, over millions of years, instead formed satellites around another. Others have recently suggested that perhaps the Sun has a dim companion star, so far unseen by human eyes, which comes to within two light-years distance from Earth every few million years, exerting a gravitational force on the comets it passes and scattering them in all directions, some of them towards us. That theory would explain why geologists have found evidence of cataclysmic collisions between comets and Earth every twenty-six million years or so. But in the timescale of human life, like the future expansion of the Sun, it does not really matter. Mankind's history is so short and our evolution has been so fast that nobody can foretell what may happen to us in a hundred years, let alone a million.

Earth is not perfectly round – there are small depressions at the top and bottom, slightly bigger ones in other places and a bit of a bulge around the equator. It spins, and we with it, at between sixteen and twenty-seven kilometres a minute, depending on where you are. (If you live in Europe or North America you are moving at about twenty-four kilometres a minute.) Also, the whole Earth is moving through space around the Sun at nearly 1,800 kilometres a *second*. We are all space men and women, not only because we travel through space at high speed but because our bodies are composed of atomic particles which were once space dust or parts of suns and comets.

The Moon, which reflects the Sun's rays and emits no light of its own, is our own dead satellite and travels around us every twenty-seven and a quarter days. (It is only one and a quarter light seconds away, though it takes a man-made space vehicle three or four days to get there.) The whole Solar system lies near one of the edges of the Milky Way and takes 225 million years to move around the centre of it. That too does not matter. What does is that Earth has an atmosphere, a very thin film of gases, including Oxygen. Human beings evolved from creatures who breathed Oxygen.

*

From the very earliest times Man has stared in wonder at the night sky; there were observatories in the Middle East thousands of years ago. Nevertheless, for most of our recorded history people were certain that the Earth was flat. It was only 300 years ago that optical telescopes gave proof that it is not, that we are not the centre of the Universe and that we move through space. And it was only sixty years ago that giant telescopes enabled observers to penetrate 230 million kilometres into the sky and bring the true awesomeness of it all home to us. Thirty years ago, with the use of electronic telescopes which record radiations from space – sometimes from things which cannot be seen – and Infra Red telescopes which measure IR radiation, more and more galaxies were found. And new things too . . .

Quasars, about as far distant as we can reach out, which are thought to be enormous sources of radiation created by the remnants of stars which have exploded. (One particular quasar gives off 200 times as much radiation as the whole of the Milky

Way.) Pulsars, which eventually stop spinning and become undetectable but which, while they exist, send out directional radiations so that a beam appears to be flashing up to 650 times per second! And Black Holes, which exist in all galaxies, are surrounded by Quasars and are believed to be collapsed stars, so densely packed with particles of matter that those which were once many times the size of our own Sun are now only a few kilometres in diameter. They do not reflect radio waves and have such enormous "pull" that they suck into themselves any meteors or small planets that come within reach. And even light waves. What a thought . . .

On a clear night you could count perhaps three or four thousand stars in the sky; with a light telescope you could see fifty million and with a radio telescope up to one *billion*. In 1983 a space satellite was launched which carried a radio telescope out beyond the haze that encircles Earth. The information it sent back has caused astonishment because it reveals so many new things: Infra Red "clouds" in space; radiation from nowhere; new stars forming. And so it goes on. More search for knowledge. More discoveries. More questions not answered.

It seems unlikely that we are the only populated planet but if others are, then the "people" there will not be like us. They will have evolved in a totally different environment, with a different cycle of night and day and seasons. Or maybe none of those things. They could live for a thousand of our years, be light years ahead of us in development or just starting out on the long road to intelligence. But if they are there, it is very surprising that we have not heard from them. Our television transmissions are moving through space at 670 million miles an hour. Those we beamed out thirty years ago are now thirty-two light years away; Sergeant Bilko's antics may one day be gazed at with amazement by other eyes. Yet we detect nothing emanating from space, there is only a Great Silence.

An astonishing thing to contemplate is that when we look up into the night sky we are not seeing anything as it actually is. The light from some of the stars we see left them four thousand years ago, when the first Pharoahs ruled in Egypt, or two thousand years ago, at the time of the Roman Empire. If one of the distant stars had exploded long ago we might not learn about it for another thousand years. The rays from the Sun take eight minutes to reach us but the energy emissions from the outer edges of the known Universe "seen" by infra-red telescopes left the stars and galaxies which generate them so long ago that we are now receiving information about what happened quite soon after the moment of creation . . .

Nobody knows if there is a limit to the size of the Universe or if it goes on for ever, but if there is a limit – as some people believe – then what is on the other side?

*

Earth began as a mass of gas at great temperature. When it started to cool the gas became a ball of molten lava, mostly made of iron. A layer of rock formed around the lava – the mantle – then a crust cooled around that. After many millions of years the crust was ten kilometres deep and a halo of thick cloud enveloped us, formed from gases which had spewed out of Earth's core through ruptures in the mantle and crust. It started to rain, and continued to do so for about fifty thousand years. When it stopped our atmosphere was a choking mixture of toxic gases, seven-tenths of Earth was covered with water and there was just one part of the crust, one huge continent, above sea level. As ages passed it became thicker than the crust under the oceans. Slowly, very slowly, great stresses built up and the surface moved. Gigantic areas of it split into smaller continents, which slid over the mantle, oiled by molten lava erupting through great fissures.

Over millions of years the continents parted company, twisted around and changed direction. There are deserts and pastures now where there used to be oceans: for example the Sahara was once at the South Pole and there are fossilised ammonites, coiled sea creatures, in the clay under the green fields of central England. The Mediterranean was an empty basin until the Atlantic burst through the Straits of Gibraltar, filling it and leaving it dotted with islands. Huge mountain ranges were thrust up on land, and vast depths were created in the oceans: Everest, at 8,848 metres, is the highest mountain in the world but the Mariana Trench in the Pacific is deeper than Everest is high – 11,033 metres. There are great "faults" where slabs of the crust collided and rubbed against each other – and still do. It is along the line of faults, where there is a weakness in the surface, that earthquakes occur and volcanoes erupt, throwing out the molten centre of our planet with frightful force. (Continental Drift is still going on. In a few thousand years from now most of Western Europe will be under water, and so will California. In fifty million years North and South America will have separated, Africa will have split in two and the Persian Gulf will have filled up and been replaced by hills.)

Lightning flashed in the sky for centuries and electricity sliced into the atoms swirling in the swamps and seas, changing them. Chemicals which could reproduce themselves, the very beginnings of life, came into existence: bacteria, single-cell microscopic organisms, and algae, plants which mostly grow in the sea and make their own food by converting the energy from light rays. (Bacteria exist in unbelievable numbers: a spadeful of soil contains as many as there are people in the world.) Then some algae evolved into chlorophyll, a substance which, amongst other things, releases Oxygen. This was crucial because Ozone, a form of Oxygen, rose to the upper atmosphere and created a shield through which Ultra-Violet rays could not penetrate in lethal strength. Life became possible on land.

Already, because water had acted as a screen against Ultra-Violet rays, the very first forms of life had begun in the oceans, around three and a half thousand million years ago. After a hundred million years had passed fish adapted themselves so as to be able to breath the Oxygen in air instead of extracting it from water; amphibians walked upon the land. In another twenty-five million years reptiles evolved which laid their eggs on dry land, as their predecessors had done in the sea.

Creatures had started on the long road which was to lead through insects, birds and mammals to Computer Child, the miracle of them all.

*

We are atoms, and so is everything around us, including the air we breath. Life is Carbon compounds suspended in water! But life is many other things too: it is compassion, and cherishing what is good; it is thinking, and the will to create. But at its most basic, chemical, level, life on Earth depends on everchanging combinations of atoms.

Atoms are infinitesimally small particles at the centre of which is a nucleus of protons – with a positive electric charge – and neutrons, which are electrically neutral. Powerful attractions normally bind the parts of the nucleus together. Around the nucleus are electrons – negatively charged particles – which circle around the nucleus as Earth circles around the Sun, and our moon around us. The composition of nucleus and electrons, the numbers of each, determines what the atom is – Oxygen, Iron, Carbon, Copper, Magnesium, whatever. The electrons of some atoms can switch into orbit around the nuclei of other atoms, linking them together and so creating molecules – that is, groups of atoms. The way in which molecules are locked together determines whether they can be part of you or the chair you are sitting on. If molecules are heated, the bonds linking them are agitated and they break apart. That is what happens when we cook something – its chemical structure is changed: the runny part of an egg becomes hard, the hard fibres in a piece of meat become soft.

"Infinitesimal" is the only appropriate word to use when describing atoms. Just as the Universe around us is vast beyond comprehension so the structure of atoms is miniature beyond belief – a single drop of water contains more than a thousand billion-billion molecules of Hydrogen/Oxygen links! There are eighty-one different chemical elements which are completely stable and another 193 isotopes of them; that is, atoms of the same element which are different in composition and hence in weight. As well as neutrons and electrons each atom contains particles which are so small that they cannot be seen even with the most powerful electron microscopes: they are assumed to be there only because of the disturbing effect they have on other particles around them. (Electron microscopes photograph deflected X-rays which have hit objects which are so small that they cannot be detected in any other way.) Some particles live for only the briefest of moments, tiny fractions of a second. And as some particles are small beyond belief so the distances between them compared to their size are vast. The atom is like a Solar system in miniature; its nucleus the Sun, its electrons the planets, and the unseen particles the comets and space debris and dust that surround our Earth – some of them appearing briefly then vanishing, just as shooting stars do: meteors – small chunks of rock moving freely in space – that enter Earth's atmosphere and are burnt out by the friction of the atoms they encounter at high speed.

Nothing is ever still. Not the calmest sunny day nor you, while you are asleep. In space there is nothing at all except the occasional molecule of gas or a loose atom but in our atmosphere, made mostly of Hydrogen, Oxygen and Nitrogen, atoms are forever moving about and colliding together at great speed to make new molecules; trees and plants are using the energy from the Sun's rays to make new cells within themselves and are releasing new molecules into the air; animals are breathing in Oxygen and breathing out Carbon Dioxide; cars are drinking Hydrogen-Carbon mixtures and breathing out Carbon Monoxide. In our bodies clusters of molecules which cause other chemicals to change their shape, for example in order to feed us, react at astonishing speeds; they can identify a group of molecules in something we ate for lunch and change them into something else a thousand times a second!

Though scientific knowledge has advanced to the point where people know how living bodies go on living nobody knows precisely how life began. It seems that it was a random coming together of molecular structures which were capable of reproducing themselves, but there is not enough evidence to say whether life in

Earth's environment was almost a certainty, given time, or a very unlikely event. Or even a miracle. Indeed, life may have begun somewhere else in the Universe and somehow reached Earth. Its origins are as unfathomable as the origin of the fireball which was the start of everything. Nevertheless, we are here.

Though some of the animals on Earth have recreated themselves for hundreds of millions of years Man, as a species, has existed for less than a million. The evidence of Man's evolution is sketchy but proof of the evolutionary process is positive.

In essence, species adapt over thousands of generations in order to be able to go on living in a changing environment. If they do not, they die out. But though more than a million types of animal exist today tens of thousands which once lived have disappeared. (And go on disappearing: dozens of species a year cease to exist, die away forever; including plant life, about 250 different species.) About 135 million years ago dinosaurs, which had dominated the world for millions of years, became smaller and smaller in numbers until they vanished altogether, probably because a giant comet collided with Earth and threw up a dense cloud of dust which brought night for a hundred years: most things, including the vegetation many dinosaurs lived on, died.

Despite that cataclysmic event some of the descendants of creatures who lived as long ago as the dinosaurs, or even longer, are still with us. The Vermes, the worms, 450 million years old, coelacanth fish, 400 million, scorpions, 350 and turtles, 300. And horseshoe crabs. If you go to Delaware Bay in the United States of America when the season, the phase of the moon and the tide are just right you will see the crabs come out of the sea in their thousands to mate on the shore as they have done for the last 400 million years or so.

There is evidence of adaptation everywhere: coelacanths, which began to form legs as if to come out of the water and then changed their minds and stayed where they were; scorpions, which learned to defend themselves from being eaten alive by growing a tail with a deadly sting in it; turtles which swim around covered by a hard, uneatable, shell. (Worms are worms and have not needed to change very much.) Every type of creature is a development, a mutation, from its earliest ancestors, and goes on changing as generation follows generation. Many mammals grew until their size was in balance with their environment – the physical attributes they needed to survive in competition with other creatures were balanced against the available intake of food: horses and hippos were once the size of a big dog.

The rate at which a species changes depends on the pressures it is under to survive; if it lives peaceably in no danger then it will ruminate forever. If it must change it will, for if it loses the race it will die out. There is no apparent end-purpose in nature's selection of new characteristics, only a locked-in compulsion to survive which seems to exist in every species, a blind response to the danger of a threatening environment. Those attributes which enable a creature to cope well with life are the most likely to continue in future generations.

Our ancestors changed because they lived in a hard world. Hounded by flesh-eating animals they took to the trees. Slowly, over a time span of thousands of generations, they became quick-witted enough to spend more time on the ground. Then they stood up and began to think.

Between twenty and fifteen million years ago creatures which had developed as tree-dwelling, fruit-eating animals seem to have produced three different lines of succession. One was a ground ape which failed to adapt and died out: they did not think enough. The second, we now see in the tree apes – gorillas, chimpanzees, baboons, monkeys, orang-utangs and gibbons – of which there are 123 different varieties. The third became a thing we call Ramapithicus, which, because it had to find its food on the ground and not in trees, became a flesh eater.

Four million years ago this animal became Australopithicus, which walked on its hind legs some of the time and used primitive bone clubs. After thousands of generations, nearly a million years ago, Homo Erectus, Upright Man, a creature who knew how to make stone tools and discovered Fire, eventually appeared on the scene. (Fire was made by striking a spark off a flint into dried grass or leaves and blowing until a flame burst. Once made, it was very important to keep the warmth alive. Infants and their mothers constantly fed it with fuel.)

100,000 years ago Neanderthal Man, a spearman,lived in Europe and Asia.(So named after a village near Dusseldorf on the the Rhine, where the remains of this creature were first found.) As time passed a variation of him, Cro-Magnon Man, evolved, then, between fifty and a hundred thousand years ago, Homo Sapiens, Wise Man, Man who could think, lived and mated. It took a long time but in comparison with other species Man has changed at a unique and amazing speed.

Australopithicus had a brain less than half the size of ours but it was not the brain that started it all, it was the hand. The hand made it possible for the ape to grasp trees and live in them, for the ape-man to make things, and for Man to write. Using the hand drove the brain to think, and the tongue to find ways to communicate thoughts. Thinking and speaking found new ways in which to use the hand. Now the brain drives the hand.

*

It is most probable that our origins were in what we now call Africa, for that is where the right jungle conditions existed for the evolution of the tree ape. However, because of the nature of the forest and its flesh-eating inhabitants no remains of our ancestors have been found there: the bones were crunched up by carnivores or eventually rotted away. In other places, though, as small groups of ape-men and their descendants moved first south and then north and then east, their bones were covered by dust or sank into mud, and after thousands of years became parts of a layer of rock in which they fossilised and have since been found. (Minerals slowly replaced, hardened, and took the form of the dead creatures.) Not many ape-man fossiles exist, but enough to see the pattern of development: Ramapithicus in India, Australopithicus in southern Africa, Homo Erectus in China and Neanderthal Man in Europe and Asia. In 1983 the remains of Cro-Magnon men and women were found in Sicily. Man's predecessors had slowly spread, but in very small groups. The entire world population of so-called Wise Man and his mates and children was probably not more than half a million.

It was between fifty and a hundred thousand years ago that the racial characteristics we know today began to emerge as our remote ancestors slowly adapted to the climatic conditions in which they found themselves.

Variations in colour came about because a particular pigment in the skin acts as a shield against the harmful effects of Ultra-Violet rays: the more there are, the more pigment is needed. Similarly, pigmentation affects the colour of the eyes: naturally brown, they became "bleached" and blue in those places where for ages generations lived under cloudy skies. Hair too changed, from the tight curly mat which protects the head of the African from the Sun's heat to the fine blond threads which are adequate for the northerner. Body hair almost disappeared from the African but was retained by some other races as a token protection against the cold, although men and women soon learnt to clothe themselves with the furs of the animals they killed. Facial shapes also changed, and the nose and lips, though the reasons for this are less obvious.

There was much in-breeding. The small numbers of savage beasts, many of them cannibals, who wandered aimlessly in pursuit of food, whether on the hoof or growing wild, may not have encountered other tribes for decades, and if they did would not have welcomed them, fear of strangers being a condition they had inherited from their forbears. People mated with those who were healthy and virile, and therefore appealed physically to them. Thus characteristics which had helped people to be healthy and virile and survive, or which for some reason became fashionably attractive, tended to be reproduced over and over again, generation after generation, breeding out less dominant, weaker ones.

So it came about that groups developed round faces, long faces, short noses, long noses, thick lips, thin lips. Distance and isolation retained such basic physical characteristics once they had become established but where the three main types, the Black Negro, the

White Caucasian, and the Yellow Mongoloid, met they interbred, and where they did the physical attributes have become blurred. However in size, physique and brain capacity the differences between us all are not great.

There is no proof yet, and there may never be, but it seems likely that Man's progression was from Africa to the Mediterranean to Europe and then north-east, where the Mongoloid race developed folds of skin over their eyes to protect them from the blinding glare of sunlight on great fields of snow. As they went further east and then south the slant eyes of the Oriental were inbred and then, merging with peoples from India, their skin colour altered, mixing a little more brown with white.

These were the main migrations but there were minor ones which were to have lasting effects. Mongoloids moved east across an existing land bridge through Alaska and into the far north of the American continent, then south into great, empty, totally unpopulated spaces – there were few mammals of any sort there and no men at all. Eventually they reached another, hotter, bridge and, moving ever onwards, thinly populated the southern hemisphere. American Indians had arrived. In the north a few hardy people stayed in the Arctic wastes, the Eskimos. Not knowing there were better places they, and the Patagonians, who had kept moving south until there was nowhere left to go, accepted what they had and adapted to the conditions: their noses became flattened and thick so that there was more blood circulating, they were less likely to get frost-bite and cold air was warmed before it reached their lungs; in the Andes people slowly developed larger-than-average lungs in order to be able to survive in high-altitude air, which has less Oxygen in it than air at lower levels.

Very early on some Africans had moved east too, into India and beyond and then south until, despite all the odds, they somehow reached the islands in the Pacific ocean, perhaps during the last Ice Age when the water level in the oceans dropped and chains of islands were threaded like a necklace, allowing small groups of primitive people to migrate to places where they had not been able to go before. There they stayed, unchanged, until a few hundred years ago, or even less, when white men appeared over the horizon. (In 1930 some Australians discovered human beings living in very remote parts of New Guinea: there were nearly a million of them and they thought their valleys were the whole world, and that they were the only people in it.)

*

Ten million years ago, then, the apes started to change. One million years ago Man began to climb the long ladder to the moon. Less than a hundred thousand years ago we could have recognised ourselves, albeit as brutish people, ugly and without sensitivity. Thirty thousand years ago men and women in many colours had spread to every continent except Antarctica, and had learned how to use metal. For good or ill, we were here.

*

## CHAPTER TWO

# MAN

Thirty thousand years ago many parts of the world were very different. Because the human population was so small – perhaps two million primitive people – it made no significant impact on the environment. People lived on the Earth not off it; sharing, not dominant; one of millions of species for which Earth was home.

The climate was generally hotter, so that animals now found only further south roamed across Europe and Asia: elephants lumbered about in Russia, panthers prowled around Spain and Italy while further north the lynx and the lion and the leopard stalked their prey where badgers, foxes and rabbits now live. Forests thickly covered land that now is parched and barren: there was sweet water and shade. Then another Ice Age came, the third or fourth. Glaciers slowly gouged great clefts in the land and men and animals retreated south to survive.

Many creatures fed on foliage and grass but then, as now, others fed on them: the carnivores, of which type Man was and is. Animals tended to mark their territory and stay in it, defending it against their own kind who intruded and threatened their food supply, but even the flesh eaters did not kill their own species, let alone eat them. Man did, when other sources of food failed or, in later times, after a battle, when it was believed that eating the flesh of the vanquished and drinking his blood out of his skull made the victor stronger. (The ability to think did not get off to a good start!)

At first Man wandered, in the right season finding fruit and berries, at other times cornering and clubbing to death the evening meal. It was probably women, bored while their men were away hunting, who first grew things from seeds, a discovery that changed people's lives entirely, for where their crops grew there they had to stay. And where they grew the food supply increased enormously in comparison with the hit-or-miss pursuit of game. As much as a hundred times more food became available and with adequate nourishment the population began to increase significantly. Man became a gardener instead of a hunter, and has remained one in most parts of the world ever since, sometimes in a good place, sometimes having to struggle for existence all the time.

When the Earth was a molten ball, and for millions of years after as the crust heaved and broke apart, atoms, and the molecules they become when they join together, were subjected to gigantic pressures and temperatures and changed into minerals. As thousands of years passed and vegetation rotted, was compressed and sank deeper and deeper, oil and coal were formed. Pockets of gas were tightly held, locked in folds of rock. But all of these things were hidden away out of sight. The nature of the visible land depended on two things: the type of ground and its position in relation to the sun and sea.

The type of ground people walked upon was also the result of the upheaval of the crust. In some places there were hard rocks, granites and marbles which had been forced up out of the depths of the Earth and would one day make fine buildings, while in others there were soft ones like limestones, the compressed remains of countless billions of tiny sea creatures. Some places were carpetted with crumbling loam in which roots can grow deep, while others were covered with clays in which it is hard for plants to get a grip.

Ten thousand years ago the last Ice Age ended and the climate became much as it is today, though there have since been cycles of hotter and cooler weather. (No-one is quite sure why the ice came or why it went. Only a small drop in average temperature will create the conditions in which more ice forms at the Poles, furthest away from the heat of the Sun. Conversely, an increase will cause melting of the ice and a rise in sea levels.)

Space is ice cold because the Sun's rays do not create heat until they make contact with atoms and agitate their structure, thus raising their temperature. When they warm water, molecules of Hydrogen and Oxygen are detached, rise into the atmosphere, cool as they go higher, change from invisible moisture into drops (at the centre of each one of which there is a speck of dust – a little cluster of inert atoms – around which the Hydrogen/Oxygen links cling) and fall again to Earth. The motion of the Earth moves its atmosphere so that in a particular place winds generally come from the same direction, though there is local turbulence due to the effects of the Sun's heat on the land and sea, the mass of cold air above the Poles and the deflection of air currents caused by mountain ranges.

Man did not know about the minerals or the soil, or that the amount of rain, wind and sunshine that so greatly affected his life depended on where his home was in relation to the land mass and the oceans that surrounded it. Man was concerned only with the day-to-day cycle of hunger, hunting, eating, mating and sleeping. Some days there would be accident, injury and death, others would bring new life. Nearly every day there was blood, which he feared because it often meant death, but which he accepted as a natural part of life. As he did everything else. As other animals do today. He knew not, neither did he care.

He did not know that in the great rending of the Earth during its formation things had been created which would shape the future; that where he chose to settle, purely by chance, the land and its climate would determine how his descendants would evolve and live. Whether they would have wool or cotton for their clothing, or even silk. Stone with which to make strong shelters or, perhaps, as in Africa, only thatch for a hut. Rice to eat if they lived near muddy fields where it could be cultivated, or bread, if their home was on sun baked, rain moistened plains where wheat would grow as far as the horizon. And if they were very fortunate they would choose to build their homes on top of minerals which would one day bring wealth, shape Man's future and then, in time, take him far away from Earth.

He was rich – but his credit was not limitless.

*

If you live in a society which has preserved a record of births, marriages and deaths you can, without much difficulty, trace your ancestors back for two hundred years or so; about seven generations. If you are descended through the European nobility you might be able to go back a thousand years. Otherwise you are unlikely to know who your great-grandfather's father was. Where he lived or what he did, and still less what he looked like.

A thousand years, then, is a long time in heredity. Four and a half thousand years before that, one hundred and fifty generations back, and we are at the start of known history, when the entire world population was still only perhaps a hundred million. Because such a small number of people are the nucleus from which we are all descended, within our own racial group most of us are distantly related. This applies particularly to those people who until recently were cut off from the rest of the human race by geographical isolation – Australian aboriginals, New Guinea headhunters, African Bushmen, Amazonian Indians. In particular, one primitive tribe, in Tasmania, had developed apart from all others since the beginnings of the human race. They were unique, of unmixed blood, but by the end of the 19th Century had been totally exterminated by the white settlers who migrated there from Australia to take over the country using the sweated labour of prisoners who had been convicted of crimes on the other side of the world.

In addition to the differences of physical appearance which emerged because of climatic conditions there were other characteristics which became inbred in us during hundreds of generations. Some we had inherited from the beginnings of time, others had evolved more recently, new ones developed as people went through life like infants – puzzling, enquiring, learning, inventing.

At the start men had banded together because numbers gave protection. Because of their physical strength and confident nature some males emerged as leaders, while others were content to be led, or were too weak physically to beat the leader. Speech became vital for the coordination of the group and therefore its continued existence. Loyalty to the leader meant a united purpose, which added strength to numbers. Aggression made success more likely because the meek did not inherit the Earth, they were trodden down into it: timid individuals, leaderless, died; females, a fertile bed for the seed of men, physically weaker and naturally submissive, were carried off or killed. An aggressive band, loyal to a strong and intelligent leader, won the day, so that aggression, banding together, the acceptance of direction, became scored into our existence – to which could be added a distrust of strangers, because they posed a threat, and fear of anything that was different, and therefore not understood.

When the leader died the led felt lost. In the hope that he could continue to protect and help them his people buried him with the things he would need in an after-life, thus presuming that there was one. Primitive people tried to call back the spirits of the dead, and as time passed began to make totems and and appoint special people through whom they could direct their appeals for help. Religion, the belief in supernatural powers, had arrived.

Five million years ago Man's first skills were to break stones and use the sharp edges to cut things, and the leg or jaw bone of his source of food as a club or hammer. He fished and farmed and hunted. After he found out how to make fire his cooked food became easier to eat and as the generations passed teeth and jaw changed: no longer did men and women look very like monkeys. Thirty thousand years ago a few of them scraped the outline of pictures on cave walls and rubbed earth into the marks to colour them. (Ochre is still a much-used painting pigment.) There were sculptors then too: an Earth-mother figure from that time has been found in what is now called Austria, and a pottery boar's head in Czechoslovakia.

The age of such things can be established in a number of ways. There is an isotope of Carbon (a slightly unstable variation of the Carbon atom) which gives off radiation for up to 50,000 years and is found in the remains of many creatures and things. Scientific analyses of the Carbon atoms present in an object will establish with fair accuracy the date within the last 50,000 years at which it came into existence, i.e. when it absorbed the Carbon. The rate at which radio-active potassium decays into argon, the analysis of pollens found in archaeological remains, the amount of fluorine absorbed by bones out of the surrounding soil – all these techniques can be used to determine the progress of Man.

Twenty-five thousand years ago rafts were made in South East Asia, and fifteen thousand years ago there were spearmen in Europe. Four thousand years later they had bows and arrows – at which time dogs were first allowed to warm themselves beside the fire. At around the time when the ice sheets retreated and people migrated north again, ten thousand years ago, the hand cultivation of crops became widespread and some people kept flocks of sheep. Copper ore was being fashioned into metal tools in several places and in Japan pottery was made for the first time. (But not "thrown" on a wheel: that was not to come for another five thousand years, and then half a world away.)

9,000 years ago – when the first town of which any remains exist was built, Jericho, in Jordan – wheat was being cultivated and bricks were being made. 8,000 years ago the loom was used to make woven fabrics in the Middle East and Aboriginals threw boomerangs in Australia! There were irrigation canals in Iraq and maize was grown in Mexico. Not long after that, the honeybee had been invited to work for men in Eurasia and Africa, and cattle had been domesticated in France. (It was to be another thousand years before men contrived to get cows and a bull or two across the Channel to England, where they could keep company with beavers, bears, boars, elks and wolves.)

6,000 years ago there were boats on the Nile and bronze sickles were cutting the crops growing on the land beside it. Negro fishermen were landing their catches on the beaches of Nigeria. In South America potatoes were being grown and in the Middle East flax, for the making of linen garments.

5,500 years ago, for the very first time, people could see after the sun had set: oil lamps were treasured in Iraq. By day the people there were making donkeys carry loads, and potters were turning clay on a wheel to make symmetrical jugs and plates. A thousand years on, in the same place, a clever fellow invented the plough, pulled at first by a man or his wife and not until later by a harnessed animal: now men could become farmers as well as gardeners. Perhaps it was his wife who figured out the four steps needed for the making of cloth: cleaning and straightening its fibres; twisting them into threads; weaving the threads to make fabrics, then dyeing them in pretty colours.

Not everyone everywhere was doing these things but as time passed the knowledge did too: words in different tongues were used to communicate and describe. Man was ready to make his mark and begin to write his history.

*

What had nature and evolution given us?

The human body is covered with twenty square feet of skin, out of which grow between four and five million hairs. Inside the skin there are 650 muscles, 206 bones (jointed 100 times), sixty thousand miles of arteries, veins and capillaries, between six and ten pints of blood, ten billion nerve cells and more than a billion brain cells: which are not replaced by new ones when they die – as they do continually – unlike other body cells which are. ( A snail has 20,000 brain cells. Whatever for?)

The skull cavity of the male has a capacity of 1,500 cubic centimetres, that of the female 1,300. The average brain weighs three pounds. (Cro-Magnon man's brain cavity was 1,800 cc, but obviously not much was going on in there. The skull capacity is therefore not the sole indicator of mental ability.)

The tongue has twenty-four muscles in it, evolved over hundreds of generations so as to enable people to communicate in the many languages their ancestors invented.

Males can throw a stone at 160 kilometres an hour, jump seven feet off the ground and for a very short distance attain a speed of forty kilometres an hour – but there are not many who can do this and none we know of who can do all three. Their tendons have great power, equivalent to a force of eight tons per square inch, and their thigh muscles are more efficient, in terms of energy produced, than most modern metal engines. Women have only 55% of a man's muscle power and 67% of their endurance, but can usually see and hear better than a male.

World-wide,the average height of the male is five feet five inches, while the female is two inches shorter. In Europe the average height of a male is five feet eight inches, the female five feet three and a half inches. (Two hundred years ago European men were only five feet four inches high and weighed 130 pounds, as against 162 pounds today, while their womenfolk were less than five feet high and weighed about 112 pounds, compared with 137 pounds today.)

The living being constantly generates the same amount of heat as a 75-watt electric light bulb; which is not surprising, since blood is as hot as a summer day in the Mediterranean.

People who are able to eat as much as they want consume their own weight of food every three months. Women need less food-fuel than men – and if they eat as much become fat! During a day a human being will produce around two pints of saliva to assist in the digestive process.

In a 70-year life we use our 9,000 taste buds during the consumption of seventy tons of food and drink – most of which is released again! And in such a lifetime our hearts would beat 2,500 million times and we would take 500 million breaths.

Evolution has not been entirely successful. The high incidence of back-ache and abdominal ruptures in modern times is due to the fact that Homo Sapiens is not quite used, even now, to standing up straight. And we are not the greatest in all things – a rabbit can see movement as slow as that of the Sun across the sky, some creatures can detect the magnetic field of the Earth and so find their way, flies have all-round vision, and so on. But taken as a whole, men and women have incredible attributes and are the toughest animals in creation. Not least mentally. The brain is the real miracle.

*

The human brain is said to be the most complex structure so far discovered in the universe. Though only 3% of the body's weight it is more sophisticated, has more "connections", than the entire world telephone system. It is of such complexity that very little is known about how it functions.

It fills the skull completely, indeed has evolved in such a way as to make maximum use of the volume available. The cortex, the outer layer, the visible part that looks like overlaid coiled grey tubing, is full of fissures which increase its surface area and cell formation, thus reducing the need for more cranium space.

Put simply, the brain evolved upwards and forwards from the top of the spine. At its root are the parts which control the basic, animal functions of the human body, including aggression and the sexual urge. Balance and movement are there too. Then comes sight and sound and touch. Further forward is the part which controls dexterity and, in front of that, speech. But the grey matter which lies behind the forehead is what really makes men and women different from other animals. In it is the ability to show compassion, unselfishness and affection, to think in abstract terms not linked to immediate happenings, to figure things out mathematically and to know beauty when we see or hear it. And to apply those sorts of judgments to what is done by our animal nature. (Hence human beings are the only creatures intelligent enough to systematically destroy their own species, and the only ones able deliberately to prolong the sexual act and extract every nuance of sensation from it – to the point where, for some of Earth's inhabitants, it has assumed an importance out of all proportion to its natural function.)

Brain tissue has no nerves, and is therefore insensible to the pain that heat, pressure or tearing would cause in other parts of the body. It is an astonishing tangle of interconnecting cells and fibres which respond to electrical impulses which do not vary in strength but do so in the frequency with which they are generated; in some cases one thousand times a second! The faster the frequency of impulse the more imperative is the need for reaction! Every cubic inch of the cortex contains sixteeen thousand kilometres of nerve fibres. It is no wonder that, at present, scientists cannot determine exactly what goes on in there, although the general principles are known.

As you would expect, the number of cells allocated to a particular function are proportional to its importance to the body: for example, the eyes, the mouth, the thumbs have more cells working for them than have the shoulders or the shins.

Perception, the way the world appears to our brain, and therefore to us, is the outcome of all the information continually being relayed through our senses, which are stimulated by the energy radiated by objects around us, or by their solidity. We receive the energy (electrical or chemical) radiated by light or sound, taste or smell, or we touch something: our retinas, ear drums, taste buds or nerve endings code the information into electrical impulses which convey the form of activity to the appropriate part of the brain, which then transforms what it has been told into something we recognise – a picture, a sound, a taste or a feeling. It is miraculous, especially as we are not physically aware of any of the processes going on and take them all for granted until something malfunctions.

The cerebrum, the main part of the brain, is in two halves, which are joined by white matter – up to three hundred million nerves in what is called the corpus callosum – which passes signals between the two. The left half of the cerebrum controls the right side of the body, and usually processes word-handling, logic and analysing, and the right half controls the left side of the body and processes mathematical reasoning and pictures, patterns and shapes – artistry. It is also responsible for the body's immune systems which expel or smother invading disease-carrying organisms.

Men generally have better spatial ability (and therefore are more capable of hitting a target with a rifle or driving a car) and are more skilled at mathematics and the arts, whereas women are better at languages; only exceptionally have great visual artists or composers been women, whereas they have been more successful at processing words or the physical manipulation of musical instruments. A possible explanation is that the brain of an unborn child is affected in the womb by a hormone called testosterone, which nourishes the right side of the brain, in which is spatial and mathematical ability (the composition of music is largely a mathematical function, enhanced by emotional sensitivity.) Because boys are dosed with more testosterone during pregnancy than girls, the right side of their brain becomes dominant – and may even take over some functions normally done by the left. Hence more boys than girls are left-handed. And more boys than girls suffer from asthma and other allergic diseases, presumably because their over-dominant right brain upsets the balance of the immune system. If they are very bright they often have, for example, breathing or skin problems. They pay for their talents.

Nobody knows why, but a woman's corpus callosum is bigger than a man's – they have more nerve fibres connecting the two halves of their brain. Perhaps their quick, so-called intuitive, reactions result from a faster exchange of information between the two parts.

Environment has a great deal to do with the development of a person's abilities. It has been proved in recent years that an enriched environment can develop an enriched brain, one with the capability to use more of its cells. (Even the most intelligent individual uses only a very small proportion of the cells available.) Put simply, if people are brought up in an environment in which they hear stimulating conversation, in which there is an appreciation of things not directly related to the business of living, such as the arts, and, where, above all, they are expected to think, then they will do so, and enrich themselves and those about them.

*

Several times in the last five thousand years small groups of human beings have suddenly shown tremendous collective energy, creativity and inventiveness. A few individuals, exchanging thoughts and ideas, and spurred on by vain leaders with ambition and money, have moved humanity forward at great speed. Then for a time there has been no progress. Very often it was war that brought about the incentive to invent and make and do, and the aftermath of it that drained all energy out of the same people: all they wanted was a quiet life.

So it must have been with the Sumerians, who created the first civilisation. The clay tablets on which they wrote tell us what the human race was capable of thousands of years ago but they also record the flaws.

*

## CHAPTER THREE

# THE ANCIENT WORLD

Chapter One moved at the speed of light from fifteen billion years ago to thirty thousand years ago. Chapter Two went cautiously forward until Man as we know him suddenly began to write history fifty-five centuries ago. Now we will go on step by step another forty-five centuries until we are almost within sight. A thousand years from where we now stand.

Though a lot was achieved during this period, four-fifths of Man's recorded time on Earth, during which the entire world population of human beings grew from perhaps 100 million to around 280 million, progress was very slow. While some people in some places discovered an incredible amount in a very short time, say three or four generations, in other parts of the world hundreds of years passed and millions lived and died without learning anything new at all.

There were many civilisations during those long ages. Some were important in the history of mankind and left lasting legacies, others made their mark then went the way of all flesh. Some lasted for thousands of years until they died out, were absorbed by others or suddenly ceased to exist. A few who are able to trace their culture back into those distant years are still with us.

The longest-lasting is the Indian, which in its present form was in its infancy 4,400 years ago. It existed 800 years before the Chinese were brought under centralised control by an emperor, though long before that they, like the Dravidians in the Indus valley, had had farming and village communities. But four others which died out, the Sumerian, the Minoan, the Hebrew and the Phoenician, pre-dated both the Indian and the Chinese. A fifth which still exists, the Egyptian, has evolved so much that it bears no resemblance to what it used to be.

Though some civilisations overlapped they were not all at their peak at the same time, so to make progress simpler to follow they will be brought to these pages in the order in which they shone most brightly. Lights twinkled here and there in the darkness, life was briefly illuminated and then night came again, people walked on to the stage and off again, the hand holding the stylus let it fall. But all the time Earth whirled through space, dawn followed night and men and women lived their lives, fortunate or ill-fated, in the societies into which they had been born.

*

Civilisation is not easy to define, for it is many things. It is, at its most basic, the difference between a human being and an animal, but it is also the birth of new ideas and ideals and the ability to create new things. It is compassion, consideration and kindness. It is the condemnation of cruelty and brutish behaviour. It is even, to some people, good food and wine: over-indulgence transformed into an art form.

Judged in this way there has never been a completely civilised society but there had to be a start and that was made by people called Sumerians who lived in Mesopotamia, "the land between the two rivers", in what is now Iraq, 5,500 years ago.

It is astonishing that quite suddenly, out of an empty infinity of time, after all the long but unrecorded developments which had brought Mankind through the ages, almost without trace, from the time when we were apes, people should appear who were recognisably us, whose basic nature and characteristics are the same as those with which we live today, but that is what happened. From out of the very long past a book was opened and there on the page was civilisation.

In the beginning the script the Sumerians used to record it was a representation of objects drawn on moist clay tablets which were then dried in the sun, but later these pictures were shortened into abstract forms which meant words. The very first form of writing had to be invented for the compelling reason that they needed some means by which to remember their business transactions: "files" of tablets were kept which listed purchases and sales.

But they did more than write. In addition to simple arithmetic their mathematicians discovered the essentials of algebra and geometry, which were used by their architects – who invented the arch – and astronomers. There were Sumerian sculptors, potters, weavers, seamen and ploughmen – and doctors, who were punished if they got it wrong and the patient died, as were builders if their houses fell down. And there were brewers. Sometimes workmen were paid in ale instead of wages and in some towns half the harvest of grain was used to make beer.

The shaven-headed Sumerians mixed tin with copper to make bronze, understood the rudiments of anatomy and surgery and constructed lasting stone buildings as well as their more common mud-brick ones. They irrigated their fields with water brought from the two rivers and used their women and asses to do the donkey work. They kept sheep and goats, and cattle to pull the ploughs, and they invented the wheel.

In a sense they invented war too, for whereas until then there had been only tribal skirmishes in the various parts of the world in which men and women had settled, the Sumerians had an organised military command structure and fought many battles with weapons which were to continue to be used for hundreds of years: spears, swords and shields. They enacted laws and established scales of punishment, the basis of which was "an eye for an eye".

The Sumerians believed that their only purpose in life was to serve the gods they had invented, and because of this their priests ruled the land. When they and their wives were buried so too were their courtiers and attendants, richly dressed and ornamented with gold and silver jewellery. One queen took with her 68 women servants who had, apparently – their skeletons show no signs of any physical injury – taken poison voluntarily. Already, it seems, another basic human characteristic had been well established – credulity: the willingness, almost an eagerness, to believe anything.

The reason for the many wars in Sumeria was that it consisted of a number of "city-states" which contested the right to use the water of the two rivers which was vital to their existence. (They were not cities or states in our sense but towns and their surrounding areas up to half a day's walking distance away.) However, it would be wrong to think that they were always fighting, for there were long periods of peace and progress. One of the direct links we have with them now is that as well as calculating in decimals they used Sixties: hence there are sixty seconds in our minute and sixty minutes in the hour.

After hundreds of years they were invaded by some of their neighbours from the north, long-haired Semites (named after Shem, the eldest son of Noah) who had migrated out of Arabia and for more than two thousand years were to become the dominant people throughout that area. One of the new kings conquered the city-states, made a nation of them, expanded it and created the world's first empire. Five hundred years later Assyrians, another, more aggressive, Semitic race arrived, and brought new energy, brutality, skills and ideas. One was to use the 7-day week and the 28-day month and another was to harness horses to chariots. (It was to be a long time, though, before men rode horses. It was one thing to make them pull a two-wheeled cart, quite another to stay on top. Only men in central Asia got the knack of bare-back riding early on.)

Three thousand years after the first shoots of civilisation had thrust up out of the ground, and not long after the Persians had conquered them, the 80,000 inhabitants of fabulous Babylon dwindled in numbers until eventually those who remained abandoned the place altogether and scattered in search of food. They had not realised that it is necessary to return to the soil the nourishing chemicals which are eaten by crops, and so the land had become barren. Dry heat slowly crumbled the 250-room blue-tiled palace, the hanging gardens up to which water had been pumped and the dusty shops behind the doors of which women with clever fingers had fashioned delicate fabrics and craftsmen had created gold and silver jewellery. And, too, the sun beat down on brittle shreds of skin, flayed from living, shrieking human beings, which had been nailed to the city gates as a warning to other rebels who might rise against the government.

It had been brilliant but bloody and ended because the empire was over-extended, and therefore ungovernable, because captive people demanded freedom, because the wars had cost too much and because out of ignorance the farmers had milked the earth dry. As with so many things – thought, invention, skill, kindness, brutality, bullying and a sense of beauty – the first civilisation pointed the way to the future.

The Sumerians also showed other characteristics which have not changed – insight into human nature and a sense of humour. On one of the clay tablets on which they scratched their symbols with a stylus someone inscribed "A restless woman in the house adds ache to pain", and on another, "The man to fear is the tax collector."

*

Not very far away another society which was to last even longer had begun only a short time after the Sumerians'. Like theirs it depended for its existence on river water, that of the Nile.

Whereas the Sumerians had been wide open to invasion the Egyptians were protected by desert on two sides, by sea to the north and had only a scattering of very primitive negro people in the empty lands to the south; for century after century their civilisation developed unhindered by interference and unchanged by other people's ideas.

Their greatest achievement was that they organised the efficient control of irrigation, by means of which they brought the waters of the Nile to land on either side of it and converted desert into fertile pastures; because the population was small there was plenty for everyone. Also they invented a form of written record, though they never had an alphabet. Seven hundred different signs were used to convey meaning, drawn only by priests on the dried leaves of a reed (papyrus, hence our word "paper") with ink made from carbon crusts collected from the wicks of oil lamps, or chiselled by them on to stone. Later, another set of hieroglyphs was invented for use by lesser people, thus keeping religious communications separate and secret.

About 4,800 years ago the Old Kingdom of Egypt developed. It was one of great splendour – thanks to some extent to the work done by negro slaves brought from the south – and prospered despite the fact that for centuries men could only multiply and divide by two. (Women were not expected to do either.) The men did, however, use decimals to add and subtract, probably because, as the Sumerians had already found, evolution had been kind enough to provide them with five digits on each hand.

There followed a long period of wars between competing towns, each supporting different versions of a complex religion, and then, 1,600 years after the founding of the nation, there was another time of dynamic progress when the Egyptians became aggressive and pushed military expeditions as far as Sumeria. They also invaded Palestine where, at Megido, they fought Semites in the first battle in which military tactics were accurately recorded.

Egypt was a priest-ridden society, bound up in compulsive rituals and a fearful belief in magic; if the rules were not obeyed retribution would be meted out by unseen and inexplicable forces. Because certain animals, including the inscrutable, secretive, nocturnal and beautiful cat, were thought to be in possession of some of these forces they were regarded as sacred. At the pinnacle of the whole edifice of society was the king, the Pharaoh, under him the priesthood, under them the courtiers, army officers and courtesans then, far below, the townspeople, soldiers, fishermen and farmers. Lastly, at the very bottom of the pile, were the slaves. It was a social stratification of human beings which has endured, with some variations of nomenclature, throughout history.

The Egyptians devoted much thought to Man's condition on Earth and were the first to put into words five concepts which were often to reappear in later times: resurrection, heaven, judgment, reincarnation and immortality. They believed that one of their gods, Osiris, the god of Day, had died and come to life again and that he would enable his worshippers to do the same, receiving them in a green paradise "somewhere in the West". They thought that death would be followed by judgment, and that only those souls whose good deeds outweighed their bad ones would be allowed to enter Osiris' kingdom. The souls of the wicked would pass into animals and after 3,000 years, having lived once in every species, would return again as human beings for a second chance. As to immortality, it was achieved by such a change of living form or by resurrection. (The primitive ancestors of the Egyptians, who lived about 7,000 years ago, ate flesh from dead bodies, thus continuing the life of that flesh and making it immortal. They also, like cave-men, believed that they could absorb the physical strength and spiritual power of those who had left them.)

To priests and people the Pharaohs were the living incarnation of the sky-god Horus. (One of them, Pepi II, reigned for ninety years, longer than any other monarch has anywhere, at any time. He must have known something the others didn't.) Since they were gods, Pharaohs obviously could not mate with mortal people so the succession passed to their children born of their sisters. Or sometimes, if they had no issue, to their sisters. Incest was a way of life.

To visibly show their religious dedication the Egyptians used most of the nation's resources, wealth and labour, and the lives of thousands and thousands of slaves, to construct massive stone temples and gigantic and completely useless tombs in which to hide the bodies of their dead kings. But it was their belief that the great pyramid into which he was put became the king, who would thus be immortal – and so, moreover, would all those who had worked to build his immortality. Like the Sumerians, and pre-historic men before them, the Egyptians could not bear to think that when they died it was the end of all existence, so they turned their Pharaoh into a pile of stone, embalmed his dead body to preserve it for the new life, then entombed it with the riches he would need if he were to live in the style to which he had become accustomed: the gods of the dead were bribed with gold, silver, alabaster and precious stones. Since life before death is undoubtedly of short duration but life after death could be everlasting much more time and effort was devoted to the tomb and its contents than to the people living around it.

The oldest stone monument in the world is the Step Pyramid at Memphis, built more than four and a half thousand years ago to point the Pharaoh to the sky. Another, the Great Pyramid at Gizeh, weighs nearly five million tons, all of it dragged into place by panting human beings, the stones lubricated by sweat, the labourers encouraged by the lash. (Or so it was thought until recent times. Now a theory has been put forward that most of the "stones" are a form of cement, made by pouring water on to sand held in wooden moulds and then letting it be baked and hardened by the sun. Either way there are still millions of tons of it.) To help them achieve symmetry and balance in their buildings the Egyptians used standard measurements, which also assisted them in the construction of the first water dams. But all was not work. Women had metal mirrors in which to see the reflection of their pretty painted faces, and locks and latches with which to keep their doors barred when the need arose. They used a pessary made of crocodile dung as a contraceptive.

Obsession with the spirits led the Egyptians to star gaze; an observatory was built, partly in a quest for knowledge about astronomy but also from a wish to ascribe control of what happened on Earth to what was going on in the night sky above it. Out of those early studies and deliberations grew the use of the 24-hour day and the 365-day year – and astrology and horoscopes: a down-to-Earth system of marking the passage of time and a celestial mythology of nonsense.

The first two civilisations, like those of later times, showed both sides of mankind's nature: the love of beautiful things and peaceful progress and the pleasure taken in destruction and the creation of chaos. Today, tourists stand under the blazing sun gazing with astonishment at the magnificent buildings and sculptures the Egyptians made and wondering at the luxury in which some people lived so long ago. Yet under that façade men were brutal and violent. A surprisingly large number of female skeletons found in ancient graves had once had a broken arm, as if it had been raised to ward off a blow to the head.

*

Even before the Old Kingdom of Egypt had been founded a few Semitic nomads, Canaanites, had migrated north and settled on the coast of the Mediterranean Sea (in what came to be known as Palestine and Lebanon) and begun to trade with Minoan people living on the island of Crete: 4,000 years ago Phoenician ships left the harbours of Acre, Tyre and Sidon and sailed upon the sparkling sea.(It was they who mixed Egyptian pictures with Sumerian signs and then simplified them to make a 22-letter alphabet. The Greeks changed it and the Romans added four letters; hence this book.) The Minoans had been sailing ships long before the Phoenicians, and had traded with Egypt from the earliest times. Perhaps, indeed, the Cretan civilisation is even older than the Egyptian; at present no-one is sure.

The Minoans took two thousand years and more to build their way of life, only to have it snuffed out in a few days. Living on a beautiful island in a blissful climate and secure from any enemies they lived for generation after generation in peace and prosperity. Knossos, their unfortified capital, at the peak of its greatness, had a population of a hundred thousand people, an astonishing congregation for those days, who enjoyed the benefits of aqueducts, baths, piped water and drains. Their king, the Minos, had a palace which spread its stones over six acres. Minoan paintings, pottery and sculpture reflect the devoted skill which comes from tranquility, much thought and an unhurried existence. The people also had time to develop a system of writing which baffled European experts for decades. (When at last, in 1954, some of the tablets were deciphered they yielded up not the astonishing secrets of an ancient world but lists of stores and what they cost. When all is said, the daily business of living has to take precedence over theories.) Religion centred on a mother-goddess, full-breasted, bare breasted, but the Minoans were not obsessed with spirit worship, as were the Sumerians and the Egyptians. Festivals in the sun appealed to them much more; and the gymnastic contests in which young men leapt over the tossing, pointed horns of a charging bull. That pastime went to Spain and, with some alteration, stayed there.

Another Semitic tribe from Arabia, the Hebrews, walked from Mesopotamia to Palestine a thousand years after the Canaanites but because of famine had to move westwards into Egypt, where they became slaves. In England and in Brittany at about this time great stone circles were being built, for a purpose we can only guess at, by men who knew no letters or numerals. And not much else either.

*

Four thousand years ago Aryan people from the Caucasus, the mountainous region between the Black Sea and the Caspian Sea, drifted south into the Indus valley in India, where the easy-going, smiling Dravidians, who used bullock carts and bronze, knew how to grow cotton and somehow sold it to the Sumerians, hundreds of miles away, lived a contented life in the sunshine. The Aryans imposed a rigid caste system on them, with themselves at the top of the tree and the darker-skinned native inhabitants at the bottom. And started to breed chickens.

"Varna", the Sanskrit word which has been translated into English as "caste", really means "colour". Caste thus originated as a means of racially segregating the conquerors from the conquered, the Aryans from the Dravidians – the Pariahs. It was a system of apartheid, applied because the native people far outnumbered the invaders – and indeed had an older and in some ways better form of civilisation. (The script they used has never been deciphered.) When they arrived the Aryans had been divided, like many other primitive peoples, into three classes, warriors, priests and commoners, but as time passed the Brahmins, the priests, became the highest class. They, unlike many priesthoods, marry and reproduce themselves, but remain exclusive, accepting no interlopers from any other social class. Subsequently, the original four classes (the three Aryan plus the Pariahs) split up into numerous sub-castes, with the Untouchables at the bottom of the pile. Castes may not marry, or even eat with, members of a lower caste, under penalty of becoming an outcast.

*

In China four thousand years ago the silk worm had been industrialised and the first rulers of that huge and complex nation wore layer upon layer of exquisitely embroidered clothing in life and in death. The silk worm cocoons were unreeled by hand, the thread was spun on to bobbins and then woven into cloth by women with nimble fingers. (Silk worms are fastidious little creatures; they dislike noise and bad smells.)

The possibility of an after-life obsessed the Chinese as much as it did the Egyptians. In death their kings and queens were attended by their slaves – who were buried alive – and sometimes were laid to rest in priceless suits made of little pieces of jade wired together with gold – which took craftsmen perhaps ten years to make. The concept of hell existed in China all those years ago; the whip held high to ensure good behaviour. Perhaps to appease the spirits of his ancestors and avoid trouble the Heavenly Emperor, the Father of the Human Race as his subjects called him, sacrificed human beings. But there were other sides to the Chinese: they made beautiful ceramics and exquisite jewellery and played music on zithers with twenty five strings, which they still do. And quite independently of people living thousands of miles away to the west they invented a form of writing.

The Chinese social system had four classes, the cultivated, the cultivators, artisans and merchants. Warriors had little influence. The people who had were the mandarins, the literate men, but unlike Brahmins they were not born to high status but were recruited from all classes of society by written and oral examination. They studied history and religion, music and mathematics, archery and horsemanship. For centuries the mandarins achieved their high status by meticulous knowledge of the past and for this reason were backward-looking and not innovative; little changed in China from the time of its earliest development until about a hundred years ago.

Because the Chinese way had always been to divide a man's land between his sons when he died there have never been great landowners. When repeated division made a patch of land too small to sustain a family it was sold and the owner went to one of the towns where, when he had spent what he had, he and his family became part of a mass of poverty-stricken people. It was from such people that for generation after generation the Chinese government drew the labourers needed for big construction projects such as the Great Wall, canals, and irrigation systems. There was no need for slaves, or to go to war to obtain them.

*

About 3,000 years ago the Aryans decided it was time to move again. Taking over land from the original settlers they developed a Persian empire, which became the greatest that had ever been known. To the east they went far beyond the Caspian Sea, and to the west they conquered the whole of what is now Turkey and half the coast of North Africa. Egypt was theirs, and Palestine and Babylon. The gold Daric became the first coin to pass from hand to hand. From their minds came knowledge about algebra and navigation and from their mouths, poetry: words lightly conveying weighty thoughts. Nearly 2,500 years ago they had hospitals – though what they did in them does not bear thinking about. They made beautiful carpets and metalware and exported these on camels and ships. Persian seamen sailed along the Gulf shores and round the coast of Africa. By this time the wheel and the plough were being used in parts of Europe. In Peru cotton was being grown and a long-haired animal called the alpaca had been domesticated for its wool. In the Far East cowry shells were being passed from hand to hand as currency and in China a thousand different herbal drugs had already been listed. There were sundials in Egypt, and skis in Scandinavia.

So far the account has taken us through three thousand years of slow development in a world in which there was time to spare. An unpolluted world of clear skies and fresh seas and rivers. Nature's world of tooth and claw and creature eating creature but one in which Man had only just begun to superimpose his theories in justification for all manner of unnatural atrocities. Most of the developments took place on a very small part of Earth's surface; for Man the centre of everything lay on the shores of the Middle Sea, the Mediterranean. The other human beings who had migrated in small groups all over the world still lived in a state of savagery in disorganised isolation.

The next thousand years moved much more quickly.

*

The very first scratches on the surface of knowledge had been made on clay tablets in Mesopotamia but it was trade that began to bring races together again who had scattered hundreds of generations before. People travelling on the Silk Route from the Mediterranean through Persia, northern India and on to China exchanged goods and ideas and mixed skills and culture. (It took about eight months to make the journey.)

Language too was being mixed. Pushtu in Afghanistan, Bengali in India, Persian, German, English, French and Spanish all have a common point of origin in south-east Europe, somewhere between the Danube and the Don. About half the people in the world now speak this Indo-European language, including the Russians and the Slavs. The next biggest group is the Sino-Tibetan, which is spoken by the Chinese, the Malays, the Burmese, the Thais and the Vietnamese. The Japanese and Koreans speak variations of a language of their own. The Afro-Asiatic root-language stretches from Turkey through Arabia, the Horn of Africa and across the north of that continent, while people in the remainder of it speak variations of ancient negro tongues.

(English now has a vocabulary of millions of words, though most of the people who speak it know at most 40,000 – exceptionally a few might know about 100,000 – and get by from day to day with one or two hundred. The word "the" is the most used.)

The Etruscans, a war-like race who lived in the uplands of Central Italy, were obsessed with ritualised obsequence to many gods and with the forecasting of future events by priests, who intently studied the liver and guts of dead animals. They did, however, make beautiful pottery, had a form of writing which has not yet been deciphered and a dynasty of kings who, at one time, ruled Rome. They too had a fervent belief in the after-life but unlike other civilisations who buried or embalmed the dead they burnt theirs. Nobody seems to know where they came from or what sort of society they had but they did well enough for six hundred years until the Romans absorbed them. They did not die out completely though: some of their ways became the ways of the Romans, including the fight to the death of gladiators for the entertainment of great crowds of screaming people.

Almost at the same time that the Etruscans had been desperately trying to see into the future another civilisation had begun to evolve in the Eastern Mediterranean. So far there had only been the occasional glimmer of light here and there. Then came the Greeks. It was the Greeks who turned the lamp up high.

*

In early times an aggressive tribe who used bronze metal and worshipped a sky-god of violence called Zeus, and many lesser gods, came south from eastern Europe into what was to become known as Greece, and spread over a sparsely populated farming community. They absorbed some of the ways of the Minoans on the far side of the horizon but in comparison lived very crudely. In their turn they too were invaded by another tribe from the north who brought with them iron weapons and founded a highly disciplined city-state called Sparta. Weak babies were left out on a hillside to die and from the age of seven children were taken from their parents, made to endure hardship and trained to be soldiers.

Further east, other people had founded a city-state called Athens, had colonised offshore islands and built a settlement in Turkey at a place they called Byzantium. Spartans and Athenians, who lived about two hundred kilometres apart, fought each other off and on, the Spartans despising trade and art, the Athenians encouraging both, but together they defeated a Persian invasion and siege of Athens. Nearly 2,500 years ago it was rebuilt and then in an astonishingly short period of time its citizens produced a surge of invention, learning and culture that has no parallel in history.

Greek thoughts were hampered by a lack of knowledge that is beyond our comprehension. They knew nothing about the past and nothing about geography or physics or chemistry. They had no means of accurately measuring weights or the passage of time. And, as has always been the way with men, they were hampered by ideas. They believed, because it eased their consciences, that some people were born to be slaves; their great thinkers were too snobbish to deal with people who worked with their hands; and they were convinced that the city-state was the ultimate form of political control. It is all the more astonishing that they achieved what they did.

During a few decades so much was learnt that not for another fifteen hundred years would thinkers and artists begin to catch up – that is, not until just four hundred years ago. Medicine, mathematics, mechanics; physics, astronomy, geology; poetry, drama and dance; sculpture, architecture and ceramics; and physical competitiveness in sport: in all these things there rose a bouncing fountain that gushed knowledge out of the earth. And from the clear air they plucked philosophy – thinking about thoughts which were to be the core of civilisation in the future. In little more than one generation they produced magnificent architecture and sculpture, the first imaginative literature, the first great poetry and drama.

Much of what they achieved came about because their temples, priests and beliefs were not dominant influences. Most of their gods were in the image of Man; they may have been awesome but they were not fearsome spirits. Mankind's natural disposition to think about truth and morals and beauty, to create and invent and develop, was free to soar in all directions instead of being fenced in by fear of punishment from unseen spirits who acted through a frightening priesthood. A group of clever men talked and argued and became eager to acquire knowledge about nature and human nature. One of them had hundreds of assistants scattered about Greece and Asia who reported facts to him, the first recorded attempt at scientific inquiry. The Athenians were the first modern men.

There were two long shafts to Greek influence over the future: first, the Athenian belief in the importance of the individual, from which we inherited the concept of democracy (the word comes from the Greek "demo", the people, and "krateo", to rule) and, secondly, the power of their thought and creativity. It was they who first discussed those matters of great moment which have confounded men and women since our time began: the origin of the universe, the origin of Man, and the nature of consciousness. And asked the question: what is a person's soul?

Eventually Athens was defeated by Sparta but Alexander the Great, from Macedon in the north, united the nation and through his leadership and genius in the use of military power in little more than a decade created an empire that far surpassed that of the Persians, at its furthest reaching a place in central Asia that was three thousand miles from home. He was even proclaimed Pharoah of Egypt, where he ordered that a city should be built by the sea and named after him. As time passed a great library of manuscripts – not books, but rolls of papyrus – was amassed there. One of his generals, Ptolemy, founded a dynasty, hence it was that the fabulous Cleopatra, queen in Roman times, was Greek and not Egyptian. The Alexandrian library burnt to the ground during her reign, destroying almost all the records of Greek learning, which had been brought there from Athens. Not a single scroll remains.

Alexander's own story is one of violence, treachery and blood, of battles, conquest, glory and dissolution. He died of a fever, after a bout of hard drinking, when he was only 32. His wife Roxane and his sons were murdered and his empire was then divided up by his generals and crumbled away to nothing. However, his conquests had spread the new Greek learning to many places.

Three hundred years after its golden age, when human beings evolved more quickly than they ever have before or since, Greece was over-run by the Romans. (The Minoan civilisation had long since vanished, snuffed out by the shattering explosion of a nearby volcanic island which buried Crete under a shroud of ash and then disappeared under the sea, hissing, in a great cloud of steam.)

*

The Roman system of government was a republic (an elected, not an inheriting, ruler) in which were three groups: a small number of aristocrats with many special privileges, free plebeians (Romans), who had a vote, and slaves – who did not. The early Roman nation had a population of not more than 150,000, most of them dispersed over a thousand square kilometres in rural tribes. In the country areas families had a small-holding on which they grew corn and olives and vines. Nearby there was a fortified village with a temple, houses and shops. Like the population of the city of Rome, the districts were structured into citizens and slaves.

In three hundred years the Romans took control of all the known world, pushing outwards in every direction. They did it, of course, with the sword, organisation and soldiers meaning power over people who had neither. By the time the Empire was at its height there were another 320,000 registered Roman citizens overseas, plus uncounted others who were too lowly to be considered true Romans. At the peak of its strength Rome had thirty legions, each of 6,000 men, many of whom were locally recruited: the population in the homeland could not have supported an army of 180,000. A well trained legion could maintain a rate of advance of thirty kilometres a day, something no troops have achieved for more than a week or two even in this century.

In the early days Rome was ruled by its aristocracy but as time passed and their behaviour caused them to lose the respect of the plebeians they were challenged more and more. Twice the plebeians used the power of a general strike to force concessions, marching out of Rome and threatening to set up a separate state. However, when they had weakened the power of the aristocrats they did no better, demanding more and more slaves in order that they could do less and less. As time passed the slaves numbered almost half the population.

For a very long time the Romans were extraordinarily energetic and inventive, busily organising the territories they captured, founding settlements, trading. They were a bright beam of light illuminating a dull scene in which primitive people lived bestial lives. Looking at the human beings around them, the Franks and the Saxons, the Bulgars and the Britons, they must have felt that they were the aristocrats of the earth, truly a master race. They were intelligent, learned, well-fed and properly clothed, unlike everyone else around them. The houses of important people had marble floors heated from underneath and were decorated with mosaic pictures. And people washed themselves.

When the Romans discovered hot springs they built baths on top of them; and towns around them which, to this day, are the spas of Europe. Where the water gushed up they made shrines to their goddess Minerva and communicated with her by asking the bath scribe to write messages on pieces of lead, which were then folded up and thrown into the water for her to read: "Please put a curse on Atticus for stealing my cloak." Then they would toss in a few coins to buy her attention. (They did not know it but the hot springs they used at Bath, in England, had been a long time rising to the surface. Recent tests have shown that the water which surges up today after being heated by Earth's core fell as rain on the surrounding hills about ten thousand years ago.)

The Roman Empire eventually crumbled but it lasted a long time, over a thousand years, far far longer than any modern empire. The reason for its death lies in the fact that under the smart uniforms and the arrogant brows were fallible human beings. They argued and schemed and fought amongst themselves and came to dote on luxury. (The demand for silk from China was one of the major causes of the drain of gold out of the coffers of Rome in its last days.) And they were diabolically cruel. Most of their prisoners of war, brought in chains like wild beasts from the far outposts of empire, died in the gladiatorial ring for the entertainment of the citizens. But not all. One, Spartacus, led a revolt. When he and his six thousand desperate rebels had been prised out of the crater of Vesuvius, then dormant, which he had turned into a fortress, they were crucifed en masse. The Appian Way leading to Rome was lined not with whispering poplars but with trembling, moaning, dying men.

Towards the end dictators – some of whom declared themselves to be gods – took over from men who had worked with the authority of the Senate, the governing body of elected representatives of the plebeians, but they were unable to stop the increasing lack of control as subject people on the fringes of the empire attacked the garrison legions – in one battle a Roman army of more than 50,000 men was annihilated – and their lines of communication with the homeland.

There, more than half the year had been declared public holidays and a third of the population was being given free bread, paid for by the state. Fifty thousand people at a time would pack the Colosseum in Rome to watch thousands of wild animals or hundreds of people being killed in a single day, and twice that number would throng the streets to watch chariot races. There was a passion for gambling and for versions of Draughts and Backgammon.

The energy of the nation was squandered on unimportant things and inevitably authority began to break down. Then the ever-increasing number of Christians refused to give homage to the emperor. He adopted Christianity as the official religion instead of paganism but it was too late. The empire was dismembered bit by bit by ignorant and savage people who eventually invaded Italy. Fifteen hundred years ago Rome fell.

It left to us the basis of law in many nations, a vast network of roads which are the foundations of many European auto-routes and a language which provides a third of all English words, as well as being the root of several modern tongues. Above all Rome spread its concepts of order and administration and the seeds of Greek thought and culture which they had inherited.

*

Byzantium, founded 2,300 years ago on the site of the settlement first built there by the Greeks, in which language and learning were Greek and law and administration were Roman, held out as a stronghold of culture when Europe went into the dark ages, which were to last for 400 years. But life was not often tranquil; twenty-nine of the eighty-eight Byzantine emperors died violent deaths and one-tenth of the population had to serve in the army in order to defend the homeland. Although they recaptured Italy and took part of Spain the Byzantines were threatened by the many barbarian tribes who had flooded westwards: Huns, the Hsiung-nu tribe who came originally from southern Mongolia and for years had walked towards the setting sun; Goths (who, without justification, gave their name to a splendid style of architecture: because it was new it was considered barbaric); Vandals (who with every justification gave their name to a way of behaviour not uncommon in some modern societies) Avars, Bulgars, Alans and the rest beat upon the gates.

In the north of Europe, wild men mastered the sea and regarded every shore as an open bank door. The Vikings came over the horizon in their long ships, took what they wanted – slaves and women and whatever else they could lay hands on – and usually departed again. They stayed, however, in Iceland and Greenland and on the north coast of France, in Normandy. And they founded the city of Kiev in Russia. They were in Dublin eleven hundred years ago, reached the Mediterranean and the Caspian Seas and a few of them even trod upon the surf-pounded shingle in America. They made some splendid ships and beautiful ornaments but their minds were on other things.

As were those of the Maya, descendants of the Mongoloids who had filtered south from Alaska and taken root in what is now Guatemala, Belize, Honduras and El Salvador. The majority of people lived in huts in the forests but the high point in their lives was to go and stare up at the temples built on the top of giant stone pyramids where priests would kill human beings, usually prisoners of war, to pacify the gods and try to ensure a good harvest or other benefits. Before an important festival men and women were not allowed to have sexual intercourse or eat, and inflicted pain on themselves in the belief that the gods would be pleased. Though there was no contact at all with the rest of the world the Mayas counted in Twenties, had a calendar and studied astronomy.

It was the human obsession with the stars that was the beginning of science: out there in space there were great mysteries; intelligent people observed carefully and then invented ways to record what they saw. As in so many ancient societies it was the priests who were intelligent. Priests had power, and power attracted dominant males. Who became dominant because they were intelligent.

A thousand years ago, for reasons not yet understood, the Mayan society completely ceased to exist.

*

Before the fall of Rome and for two or three hundred years after it there were great migrations of people. Another of Man's inbred characteristics is the wish to know what lies on the other side of the hill, in the belief that it is probably better than what he has got and that it belongs to him as much as it does to whoever happens to be there.

A great westward movement which lasted for generations started in the steppes of Asia. The Huns, at first pushed by the Chinese, slowly crossed Russia and forced the Middle-Asian and then the Eastern Germanic tribes before them. They in their turn migrated into the void left by the Romans. Visigoths went to the Balkans, to Italy, the south of France and Spain. Vandals went there too (hence Andalusia), on to the Rhine and up into the Pyrenees – and even to north Africa. Small numbers of Angles, Saxons, Jutes and Belgae, who had scraped a bare existence on the rich soil of western Europe, made boats and escaped to England, driving most of the ancient Britons, Celts who had originated long long before in what is now northern Greece, into Wales. Other Celtic people, who had come from south-west Germany, went to Brittany and Ireland, and from there to Scotland. But not all these people moved. Some stayed, built, mated and mixed blood and language.

The European tongues were in differently shaped heads. Long faces had evolved in the north, short faces in the south, broad heads in the east. The French have characteristic round heads, which continue on in the people of the Alps, through to the Balkans and along into Asia Minor; a band of genetic likeness sweeping like a thin curved scimitar across the south of the continent.

Christianity was the means by which the learning of the Greeks and Romans was kept alive in Europe when barbaric people arrived from the east – by isolated little communities of monks, almost the only people who could read and write. Even the Emperor Charles the Great, Charlemagne, who built the beautiful octagonal cathedral in Aachen twelve hundred years ago, could not write, however hard he tried to learn. But he could read a little, which is more than most kings and princes could do in those times.

Over a period of forty-six years he master-minded fifty-three military campaigns, most of which were intended to bring Christianity to pagan Europe but some of which were necessary in order to maintain his power. When he died at the age of seventy-five – a mighty age in those days, for a mighty man – he controlled almost the whole of what is now Europe: from the Danube to the Atlantic, from Jutland to northern Spain and northern Italy. It is a tragedy that only one of his sons out-lived him. Not the rake-hell Pepin, whom he had banished to a monastery and who might have been a strong leader, but the gentle muddler Louis the Pious. Quite soon the empire broke up into small kingdoms and principalities, ruled over by ignorant men who, generation after generation, century after century, passed their time in useless and bloody disputes.

By then the last of the great religious beliefs, born in a small village in Arabia, had spread like a forest fire east and west. Again, men had committed themselves to blind faith in the unknown.

*

## CHAPTER FOUR

# RELIGION

Paganism was the first form of spiritual communication. There are two types. In one a living soul is thought to inhabit things such as a tree or the Sun; in the other an animal or thing is venerated because of the power it is thought to have. In both, believers humbly appeal for help by ritually repeating words and actions, and by prostrating their body in supplication. Because the breaking of rules or the infringement of a taboo will result in punishment worshippers live in fear of the spirit, so to appease it they kill a person or an animal as a blood offering, or make a gift of something valuable to them, such as food or money.

Though the first pagan practices were primitive, as time passed they became more complex. Much skill was devoted to making elaborately decorated idols which symbolised the spirits, and much time was devoted by some of the most intelligent people in the community to caring for them. Men who specialised in knowledge of, or attendance on, the idols were assumed to have close contact with the spirits, or to possess delegated powers of their own, and so were given special status and privileges.

In Babylon, Egypt, Greece and Rome there were many gods, some harsh and frightening, some benign and friendly. So it was, and still is, in India.

*

The oldest mass faith in the world, which has a multitude of gods, is Hinduism.

The caste system, which is fundamental to all the varieties of belief embraced by that religion, ties people for life to the social level in which they were born. They accept this situation because they believe they were put there by their Creator as a reward or punishment for their behaviour in a previous existence. Their status in the next will depend on their conduct now, for they constantly shape their future by their words and deeds, but in this lifetime there is no possibility of change. If they transgress in this life they will find themselves in the next in a lower grade of caste, from which it may take them many lifetimes, in a cycle of reincarnation, to get back to the higher status they now have. One of the Hindu prophets, the Mahavira, who lived about 2,500 years ago, believed that even insects could have been, and could again become, human beings. It was therefore important not to eat any live thing, hence his Hindu sect, the Jains, are vegetarian. He also advocated non-violence as a means towards the improvement of Man's condition on Earth.

The Vedas, which sets down a form of ritualised worship – hymns, sayings and gestures – is the earliest Hindu literature. Amongst the Vedic deities are Indra, who gives fertility, Agni, the god of fire, and the Maruts, gods of storm. The Vedas was followed by the Brahmanas, which contains rituals through which it is possible to communicate with the appropriate god who deals with a particular aspect of life. Neither of these holy books can be dated, and nor can the rituals used in them, which had been part of life in India for hundreds of years before they were written down.

In the first Hindu texts worship was intended to persuade the gods to grant the wishes of the believer. In a second phase Hindus turned from ritual acts to thought and meditation; from the external to the internal aspects of worship. 2,500 years ago a third stage was reached with the compilation of the Vedanta, (literally "the end of the Vedas") which contains philosophy as well as magic formulae. To a Hindu the appearance of the world as seen by our senses is an illusion. Only Brahma, the power of ritual devotion, is real. Gods exist, but though superhuman they are no more real than are men and women. Vishnu, benevolent, and Siva, the life-force, are the two principal gods. Siva's female associate, Kali, lusts for blood and represents death. (It was worship of Kali which led to the cult of Thugi, whose followers, until the 19th century, garrotted lonely travellers and buried their bodies in the jungle as an offering to their glittering-eyed goddess.)

Hindus worship the idols displayed in their homes and in temples. Lamps are lit and flowers are presented as offerings to the gods. A semi-magic power is thought to emanate from idols and from sacred things such as cows and Mantras, the ritual texts spoken by Brahmins, Hindu priests. These must be said faultlessly or they will bring a curse rather than a blessing. There are six different orthodox forms of Hindu belief, of which Yoga is one.

Yoga, which is also found in other Eastern faiths, is an attempt to withdraw the mind from bodily sensation by going into a trance, sometimes by adopting unnatural postures, the aim being to free the soul from earthly troubles: only inner contemplation will reveal the truth about life and people's place in it.

As far as can be judged, Judaism came into existence some three hundred years after the beginnings of Hinduism.

*

When in Arabia, before they migrated north to the Middle Sea, the Hebrews had worshipped many pagan gods, of which Jehovah was one. More than three thousand years ago Moses led them out of Egypt and into a desert wilderness. While there he told them that Jehovah had communicated the laws of religion and conduct to him in the Ten Commandments, written on stone tablets which he had found on Mount Sinai. (Four of these Commandments concern worship and the other six set out rules of morality.) Moses taught that Jehovah was the one and only God, and that the Jews had been chosen by Him, rather than any other people in the world, to receive His word and laws.

The Jewish religion is based upon the scriptures of the Old Testament of the Bible, written over a period of hundreds of years by many men, who are believed to have been supernaturally inspired. As well as containing religious and moral guidance the Old Testament is a very detailed and wise account of the beginnings of the Hebrew race. It contains history, such as that of the early kings David and Solomon – recorded more or less at the time – laws of behaviour, myths and the guidance and opinions of prophets, which were probably recorded by their disciples but possibly added to by other writers as the years passed.

Some of the myths in the Old Testament, such as The Flood, originated with the Sumerians: for example, there could be a grain of truth in their account of a great storm which, in the dim past, brought rain for forty days and forty nights to their part of the Middle East, a tale which was later embellished into the fabulous tale of the Ark and the Dove and the animals saved two by two. The mosaic Law, like the Flood, also has its roots in philosophies pondered over in distant Babylon centuries before.

Originally the Jewish religion was centred on blood sacrifice, the killing and offering up of animals, but later it developed into devout rituals based upon their scriptures.The Torah is the moral law of Moses, contained in the first five books of the Old Testament (the Pentateuch) and the Talmud contains Judaic religious and civil law. Jews worship in temples called synagogues, especially on the Sabbath (Friday evening to Saturday evening), which is set aside for devotion and rest. Today, there are orthodox and modernist forms of Judaism, and two traditions: the Central-European and the Spanish, dating from before their expulsion from that country in the 15th Century.

After forty years of nomadic life in the desert the Jews settled in Palestine and built a temple in a town they called Jerusalem, which means "The Home of Peace". During the Roman occupation of Jerusalem their temple was destroyed and they were driven out of Palestine, from where they slowly dispersed, generation after generation, to many parts of the world – the Diaspora.

They believe that one day their Temple of Solomon will descend from heaven on to a site now occupied by a mosque. For thousands of years they have awaited the coming of a Messiah, a supernatural being who exists in heaven, will descend to Earth in judgment of the people on it, destroy the wicked and uplift the Jewish people.

Throughout history the Jews have retained an exceptional degree of racial cohesion despite (perhaps because of) repeated persecution.

The profound wisdom and laws of behaviour set out in the Old Testament have helped to guide the followers of Judaism – and have been of fundamental importance in the teachings of its related religions, Christianity and Islam – through succeeding centuries.

*

Five hundred years or so after the time of Moses, that is to say nearly three thousand years ago, a religion named after Zoroaster (Zarathustra) was founded in Persia. Zoroastrians believe in a god of light, God the Wise One, the Creator, who destroys evil, and that there is a constant conflict between the forces of good and evil in which magic plays a part. The Zoroastrian concepts of Immortality, the Last Judgment and the Holy Spirit, which probably emanated in the first place from Egyptian religions, found their way into Judaism, and thence into Christianity and Islam.

Zoroastrians venerate fire and keep a sacred flame burning in a concealed place in their temples and homes. (Some flames have been kept continuously alight for more than two thousand years.) They expose their dead naked on top of walled Towers of Silence, where carrion birds eat the flesh from the bones.

The Parsee religion in India is a form of Zoroastrianism but there are not many people left in Iran who practice the original faith. Those who do are persecuted by the Moslem majority, as are the Bahais, believers in a much more modern, charitable religion which originated in Iran and most of whose few followers still live there. Bahais advocate the acceptance of the right of other people to their own religious beliefs, and the living together in peace of all human beings without religious conflict.

Some two thousand five hundred years ago people in the East began to worship three great religions, Buddhism, Confucism and Tao, known in China as the Three Teachings.

*

Buddhism was the inspiration of a man called Guatama, who was the Hindu son of an Indian prince. Until he was twenty-nine he lived the pleasureful life into which he had been born but then he left his wife and family and set out, attended by his servant, to find enlightenment. Without success he tried fasting, Yoga and mortification of the flesh but eventually, seven years later, by withdrawing from the normal worries and concerns of life, he reached a condition of detachment which he called 'the roaring silence': Nirvana, a state of emptiness achieved by rigid spiritual and moral self-discipline.

In Buddhism there are four Noble Truths: the fact that we *Suffer*, because we *Crave* what we cannot have but that the suffering will *Cease* through *Self-improvement*.

Guatama, called Buddha by his disciples, did not support or denounce the gods other people believed in but said that they, like the numberless creatures in the world, live in a cycle of rebirth called Karma, forever passing through one stage of existence to another, reincarnated either in human or animal form. He taught, like the Hindus, that the world is an illusion, an hallucination – nothing exists. He urged people to live a better life but did not call upon them to worship a god, saying that we do not know enough to be positive about the existence of a supreme God or to give an opinion about how the Universe came to be created.

His most revolutionary statement was that all men and creatures are equal, a concept which brought many conversions from Hindus who were locked into the caste system.

Over the years the repetition of prayers has come to be thought of as having great value. Like Hinduism, Buddhism uses Mantras, religious texts, as a form of ritualised prayer, but prayers ask for guidance and not necessarily for requests to be granted. Mantras are thought to vibrate power, and are chanted by priests, written on spinning drums, water-wheels or flags, or carved on stones. Each time a wheel turns the prayer is said; the wind moving a flag sends the prayer to the skies; someone passing by activates the power of the Mantra carved on stone. Offerings – flowers or the burning of incense before a Mantra is invoked – are thought to activate its energy.

Dharma is the name for the Buddhist doctrine and Sangha is the order of monks, who live in communities but are not necessarily committed to the priesthood for life. Sexual intercourse, lying, stealing and self-indulgence are forbidden to them.

There are several modern versions of Buddhism, one of which holds out the promise of personal immortality and teaches that doing good for others without hope of reward is worthy.

Buddhism has adherents throughout the Far East, where it exists side by side, and sometimes merging with, other religions. In Korea Buddhist temples have existed since the 4th Century. In the centre of many pagodas is a relic said to be part of the body of Guatama, kept safely in a little golden box . . .

Buddhism is a gentle and compassionate religion which teaches concern for all creatures.

In the high mountains of Tibet bells chime as prayer wheels turn endlessly in the wind, and believers serenely await the return of the Buddha to Earth.

*

Confucius is the Western name for K'ung Fu-tzu, who lived in China 2,500 years ago. He was born an aristocrat but had little money and worked as a public servant for some years. Then he started an academy of wisdom, the basis of its teaching being that uprightness, balance and benevolence should guide human conduct, and that there should be harmony between Man and Nature, each complementing the other. He believed that people can be improved by education, and that clear thinking combined with self-discipline will lead people to the right courses of action.

He accepted as valid the already existing Chinese veneration of dead ancestors, who could somehow guide the living.

To Confucius, men and women could lead a noble life if they aspired to high standards of behaviour, which they could only attain if they lived a well-regulated existence. He urged people to "treat others as you would wish them to treat you", and to practice politeness, justice to social inferiors and deference to superiors. Out of this concept grew the Chinese sense of the importance of etiquette, manners and self-control, and the willingness to accept personal constraints as the price to be paid for public order.

Confucius was more politically aware than the other great religious teachers. One of his sayings, which perhaps sums up his beliefs was: "With whom should I associate but with suffering humanity? The disorder that prevails is what requires my efforts. If right principles ruled throughout the kingdom, there would be no necessity to change its system."

There is no church or doctrine, as such, in Confucism but he wrote the Analects, which are an account of his beliefs.

*

Tao means The Way, and was originally simple guidance for good human conduct. In time this embodied a spiritual meaning and a belief in the presence on Earth of countless good and evil spirits. For Taoists there is no Supreme Being but there is an Ultimate Reality which is invisible, inaudible and beyond comprehension.

A Buddhist sect called Zen, which has its greatest following in Japan, has an affinity with the Tao love of nature. Followers believe that by meditation and self-mastery they will achieve enlightenment and peace of mind. Transcendental ("beyond experience") meditation is a term given to deep contemplation which, fully attained, will take the human spirit away from its earthly burdens. (During meditation the pulse slows down, as does breathing and the rate of change of chemical processes within the body – metabolism. Why, nobody really understands.) Self-mastery requires coordination of the body, achieved through physical health, hence ju-jitsu, wrestling and physical exercise is linked with Buddhism.

The spartan principles of Zen were adopted by the medieval military class in Japan, the Samurai, and inspired their code of conduct called Bushido, faith in which led some Japanese in the 20th Century to commit suicide in battle as a means of achieving instant transition to heaven.

*

Christians believe that a man who lived about two thousand years ago was God in human form.

Joshua, called by the Greeks Jesus, which means "God saves", and later known as Christ, which means "The Annointed", was a Jewish carpenter in a small town in Palestine until, at the age of about thirty, he began to travel from place to place preaching.

A basic theme of his teaching was that people are sinful and unable to achieve life without sin unless they are helped by God, who is Love. He said that God would forgive people their sins if they honestly regretted them, and if they asked Jesus to use his power on their behalf: and that whoever accepted this message as true and was baptised (that is, admitted to the Church of God by being immersed in water, or sprinkled with it, during a religious rite) would receive God's Holy Spirit, which would enable them to lead a better life under divine guidance. He also taught that after death there would be another life in the Kingdom of Heaven – a concept which appealed to those who had nothing to look forward to in this life. (In contrast to Buddhism therefore, which aims to separate the living human spirit from the burden of life, the Christian spirit, or soul, is reborn after death: life has to be endured, but there is a promise of reward in the hereafter.)

The early Christians accepted the Jewish scriptures as their own. Christianity therefore has the same god, Jehovah, the Almighty, the only God, as the Jews, but Jesus broke away from the Judaic veneration of the Sabbath, saying that it was made for Man and not Man for it, and with their belief that they were the chosen race – God was the loving father of all people.

The essence of his guidance for human conduct is contained in what he said to a large crowd of people gathered on a mountainside: love your neighbour and your enemy – harm no-one; give to those who ask of you; live peacefully; if you try to be good you will find that you can be.

Jesus implied, and his followers said, that he was the Messiah, and that all men are brothers and equal. This displeased the Jews, who regarded the claim to be the Messiah as blasphemous and did not agree that all men could be brothers regardless of race or religion, and the Romans, who did not consider any non-Roman to be an equal. He was publicly tried, found guilty by the Jewish crowd and then sentenced by the Roman governor of the province of Judea to be hung on a wooden cross until he was dead, a common form of punishment in Roman times.

Many years after his death four of his followers wrote the Gospels of the New Testament of the Bible, which give accounts of his ministry and teachings. Saint Mark, probably the first of the gospellers, gives numerous examples of how Jesus healed people in a miraculous way. Saint Matthew and Saint Luke dwell on his teachings while Saint John sets out one of the basic doctrines of Christian belief: God so loved the world that He gave his only son so that whoever believed in Him would not die but would live for ever. None of the Gospels describe Christ's physical appearance.

Two hundred years after his death the Christian church came into existence: doctrine and ritual and clergy. The adoption of Christianity as the official religion of Rome a hundred years later spread the faith around the north of the Mediterranean but it was to be another hundred before it began to make an impact in most of Europe and replace the various pagan forms of worship which existed there. By then the years after Christ's birth had become known by the Latin phrase Anno Domini, the Year of Our Lord, which is now the basis for reckoning the passage of time in most of the world.

It was to curb the power of the Popes who led the church that European noblemen created the office and title of Holy Roman Emperor, at first granted to the Byzantine Emperors. When the two quarrelled a deep split developed in the Christian church, out of which was born the Greek Orthodox sect.

In 1517 AD a German monk rebelled against the worldliness of the church and in particular the sale of forgiveness by priests to make money for the church. (Ironically, this was motivated by the then Pope's ardent desire to build the greatest cathedral in the world to the glory of God.) As a result of Luther's protestations, and the later work of the Frenchman Calvin, Christians became deeply divided. The so-called Reformation brought about unending war and distrust between Protestants and the original Christians, the Roman Catholics, and led to the creation of dozens of variations of Christian belief.

*

The Japanese religion, Shinto, dates from the 5th or 6th Century AD. In the beginning, people worshipped nature, but as time passed they combined that concept with the veneration of their ancestors, thus merging paganism with the early Chinese religion. Shinto has a multitude of gods, since anything that gives rise to awe has spiritual significance, but in recent years it has moved towards the concept of one Supreme God. There are thirteen different sects, one of which believes in the power of faith to heal – as do some Christian Protestants.

*

Islam means "surrender to the will of God" and was inspired by Mohammed, also, like Christ, a Semite: an Arab who lived in a small town in what is now Saudi Arabia and whose family were guardians of a pagan relic, probably a small meteorite, in a shrine in Mecca.

In 622 AD he began teaching a faith with simple rules: there is one God; people must pray to Him five times a day; they must fast during Ramadan, the ninth month in the Moslem Year; they must give to the poor; they should visit the holy shrine in Mecca.

Mohammed wrote the Koran, the Islamic holy book on which their beliefs and actions are based. He said he was a prophet, speaking the word of God (Allah, the same Jehovah of the Jews and Christians) but that he, Mohammed, was not divine.

There are religious leaders, Imams, in Islam but there are no idols in mosques, the temples in which they worship – the men segregated from the women.

There are now several versions of the faith – the Druze, Shi'ite, Sunni and so on. To some, Islam is the religion of the sword: death to the unbeliever; to others it is one of peace. Allah is either Jabbar, the enforcer, or Rahman the merciful.

Believers are fatalistic: their future is known to God and cannot be changed.

Two hundred years after Mohammed's death the Sikh religion, a mixture of Hindu and Moslem beliefs, was founded in the Punjab, in India, with its holy place at Amritsar. Sikhs have One God, and believe that all men are equal; and therefore have no caste system.

*

The most modern of religions, at its height long after Mohammed was inspired, enslaved the minds of people in Mexico from the middle of the 14th Century until the early part of the 16th.

Human sacrifice had been an age-old practice in Mexico but the Aztecs, Sun worshippers who believed it would not rise again unless it was richly bribed to do so, killed hundreds or even thousands of people every night, holding them spread-eagled and screaming on a stone slab as their chest was sliced open and their beating heart was torn out, dripping blood, to be raised high and offered ritually to their god. They waged war in order to capture victims for the nightly sacrifice but on special occasions killed the best and most beautiful of their own sons and daughters. As time passed this misdirected devotion began to bring about the downfall of their race but then Spanish invaders arrived, stopped their barbaric practices and destroyed their civilisation.

It is said that on one occasion when a new temple was dedicated 15,000 people were slaughtered. A Spaniard who visited the site in

1519 said he counted 136,000 skulls lying in long racks beside the holy place.

The Aztecs did these things at times when, seven hours ahead of them on the spinning Earth, great thinkers and artists in Europe were asleep in their beds resting from their labours.

*

It is estimated that there are more than 1,000 million Christians in the world, 650 million Moslems, 500 million Hindus and Sikhs, a total of perhaps 1500 million people who practice the four major Eastern Faiths and 18 million Jews: in all, about 3,500 million people who venerate a particular belief out of a world population of about 5,000 million. The rest are pagans, atheists (non-believers), agnostics (people who are unconvinced of the existence of God but who do not deny that there may be one) or children. In addition, in recent years Humanism has found followers who regard it as a substitute for formal religion. They believe in the ability of people to live by a moral code of right and wrong without religion, to do their best for others and to respect their faith, whatever it may be.

There are many many forms of religion. Since the beginning of his time Man has lived in fear of life and in fear of death, has tried to find a better way and has reached out to the heavens for help.

* * *

No matter how arrogant and self-confident people may be in their day-to-day life when, they come face to face with their mortality and true insignificance they are like everyone else: unsure and apprehensive. So it has been from the very beginning, and so it is likely to remain.

In the earliest times of Man's existence this insecurity caused people to seek reassurance from powers greater than their own. At the start this took the form of paganism, the haphazard invention of a great variety of gods, mostly associated with the elements which controlled early Man's existence: rain, sunshine, thunder, lightning, wind. Such gods, and lesser ones, are still worshipped. As time passed and men and women began to think deeply about life they conceived new explanations, new ideas and new ways of expressing their need for spiritual support.

For a few years people's bodies exist and displace a unique volume of air, then they vanish from the scene: given enough time almost completely, but matter is indestructible so it is more a question of a redistribution of atomic particles. While they exist they are a being of supreme importance to themselves, the centre of the Universe. It must be so, because it is only through their own senses that they know they exist: without sight and sound and smell and touch and thought there is no person: no world and nothing beyond it. With sensation the person is alive, vital, but existing only in the body; the Me looking out. That Me is the spirit (the "soul") of the human being, who happens to be male or female, coloured or white, religious or atheist – but is a totally unique living creature.

Since we have a spirit it is not difficult to assume that such a thing can exist unconnected with a body. Accept that, and it is but a small step to believe that a powerful presence can exist in a tree at a point in the forest where the paths cross, in the wind that moves its leaves, or in a sacred totem. Or, better still, that it is nowhere but everywhere.

The belief in supernatural spirits gave rise to such concepts as satanism, voodoo and black magic: if there was a God or gods then there must be leaders of the opposition; if there was a heaven up above then there must be a hell down below for the less deserving; if there was a world on which men trod then there must be an Underworld where unseen forces dwelt. Sorcery, witchcraft and wizardry were all conjured up by the amazing ability of the human brain to devise abstract ideas, as was superstition and the belief in luck, which are hangovers from ancient taboos.

Birth, the future and death have an abiding interest. Primitive men and women believed that in the beginning the gods made men and animals out of clay and then breathed life into them. Babylonians, Egyptians, Hebrews and Greeks all thought that life began in this way, as did Red Indians and Maoris. As *do* African

Bushmen and Eskimos. Michelangelo painted God pointing at Man and giving him life through a flash of lightning. He was nearer the truth, though it did not happen instantly.

As to the future, predicting it has always had a fascination for people. Even today there are those who defer taking action until the omens are propitious – be they the colour of a sheep's guts, the way old bones scatter on the ground or slightly more sophisticated portents. The signs of the Zodiac have existed for thousands of years, conceived by astronomy, born out of astrology: spirits inhabiting starry constellations and, presumably with a celestial computer, keeping tabs on what goes on; the time and date of people's birth inexplicably but forever influencing their character and the events in their life. Zoroastrians believe that the twelve signs of the Zodiac and the seven planets (seven?) rule the fate of the world. Millions of people read their horoscopes every day, ever hopeful. Everywhere, fortune tellers weave a spell. They pore over the lines in a hand, tea leaves tell a tale, the cards fall and the future is there on the table.

Death is the one fact that can be foretold with utter certainty, unpalatable though that is to most people. Some, to sneak around the grim thought, try to conjure up the spirits of their loved ones from The Place On The Other Side, where they exist in indescribable conditions but where it would be nice to go all the same: the planchette skids around on the paper and words magically appear. Sometimes.

Fear attends upon death. The body, once childishly beautiful or passionately attractive or serenely withering is suddenly menacing: inexplicably possesses a power derived from who knows what? It must be disposed of quickly, in some climates more quickly than in others. Depending on the faith of the defunct the carcass is put into a hole in the ground, burnt or left lying around. Burial preserves the body for the after-life; cremation releases the soul, carrying it heavenwards with the smoke; exposure is the least troublesome, providing one lives upwind, since other creatures are presented with the problem.

For centuries cremation was not permitted to Christians; how could the body be resurrected if it no longer existed? In India, even in this century, women threw themselves on to the flames which were consuming their late husband and joined him on the upward journey. Now they each make that journey alone – but in public. In Tibet vultures feed well while the relatives of the dead placidly look on, the grisly scene being regarded as part of the rich tapestry of life.

Life means sexual intercourse, whether we like it or not. Most people do, particularly Hindus, to whom sex is something to be enjoyed to the full. Vishnu, one of their senior gods, thought the man and wife relationship was divine, a more realistic attitude, perhaps, than the Christian, which makes many followers of that faith feel that the act of copulation, unless the desired end is the creation of a new life, is something deplorable and shameful. Amongst other things this leads to the requirement for some priests to be celibate, for which concept there is no foundation in the Bible. Two fundamentally different attitudes about Man's place on Earth are contrasted in the Eastern and Christian religions; attitudes which have dominated people's way of doing things over the centuries. The Eastern ethic is to strive for harmony in oneself and with others, and to live in balance with nature. The Christian's attitude grew from the Bible's injuction, in Genesis, to "be fruitful and multiply, to subdue the earth, and to have dominion over every living thing that moves." Thus, some Christians believe that if they are to obey the word of the Lord there must be no birth control: and that they are pre-eminent over all creatures.

Abstinence is demanded by religions in many things. Hindus must not eat beef and Moslems must not eat pork; and neither must the Jews, whose food should be kosher – prepared in a special way and blessed by a Rabbi. Since the cow is sacred to Hindus it follows quite logically that beef should be forbidden. As to pork, that prohibition probably stems from the fact that to herdsmen of ancient times the beasts of the field were clean whereas beasts which wallowed in mud were not. The drinking of alcohol is forbidden in Hindu and Islamic law, though to some Christians wine is a sacrament turned miraculously into the blood of Christ during the Communion service. Where some must deny themselves, others must proclaim their faith: Sikh men must not shave and must wear a turban; and a bangle on their wrist and a cord tied around their waist – for life. Physical disfigurement is also called for; female circumcision by some priests and male circumcision by others. (In 1984 a very sacred relic, the foreskin of Christ, was reported to have been stolen from a church in Italy.)

The fundamental teachings of Buddha, Jesus and Mohammed have all been changed by their followers. There are Buddhist temples in which Mantras are recited but as Buddha did not commit himself to the concept of God were he to return he might now wonder to whom, or what, the prayers are directed. The roaring silence which he heard, which he believed was a release from earthly concerns and is a physical state which his followers try to achieve, could have been tinnitus, a condition which creates for the sufferer non-existent noise which results in deafness to normal sounds. There are differences in interpretation of Moslem doctrines which have resulted in wide divergences of view and the creation of many Islamic sects. And despite the simplicity of Christ's teachings theologians have made Christianity a complicated religion: the Holy Spirit, the Virgin Birth, the existence of purgatory (a temporary stopping place on the way to heaven where it is hoped that souls will be cleansed of their sins) – such things are difficult to understand, but because some men believe they speak on behalf of God their sayings become church doctrine.

As a result of this confusion Christianity has always been prone to variations of belief, regarded by those who thought themselves to be the only true guardians of the faith as heresies. Frightened of challenges to their power, Christian priests in medieval times were guilty of the most diabolical cruelties. The Spanish Inquisition of the 13th Century brutally tortured people in the name of Christ, and in the 15th testing by torture was practiced: if, in agony, people confessed to a false accusation then that admission was the truth, regardless of their imploring cries of denial when the pain stopped.

Churchmen's interpretation of how Christian principles should be applied led Cromwell's 17th Century Puritans in England to regard all pleasure as sinful. Ale houses were shut! Swearing was made a criminal offence and sports and women's jewellery were banned. On Christmas Day soldiers entered houses in London to confiscate any meat that was cooking. And a law was passed making adultery punishable by death. (Fortunately for those concerned the severity of this punishment was lessened because nothing would convince English juries that the accused were guilty.) Even in modern times some Christians have believed that mortification of the flesh, the infliction of pain upon themselves, would incur the pleasure of God. (A Mayan concept long before it was a Christian one.)

Some deeply-held Christian beliefs are adaptations of earlier religious practices, or have no foundation in fact. For example, nobody knows the year of Christ's birth, still less the date. It seems that the calendar is wrong and that he was born about 8 BC, not 0 AD. Christmas Day, the 25th December, was, for some pagan people, the date of the winter festival when they celebrated the start of increasing daylight. Besides, even now not all Christians celebrate Christmas Day on the 25th December. Similarly, Easter was originally the pagan Spring festival, named after the Norse goddess Eostre. Confession was an Irish invention of the 9th Century, Transubstantiation – the changing of bread and wine into Christ's body and blood during the Communion service – was made Roman Catholic doctrine by a Pope in the 11th. (Sipping the blood of Christ' in communion wine could be an ancient hangover from the primitive practice of drinking the blood of the dead in order to absorb their strength.) The Romans levelled Jerusalem twenty years or so after Christ's crucifixion and later rebuilt it with a new street plan: today, pilgrims who devoutly walk the Via Doloroso, the journey to Golgotha, the Place of the Skull, are not following in Christ's footsteps as they think they are. Nobody seems to be certain where the site of Golgotha is anyway. There are three to choose from . . .

Though Jesus undoubtedly lived, as did Mohammed, Guatama and Confucius, there can be no certainty that he performed miracles, spoke the parables or said the things he is alleged to have said. The most contemporary account of his life is in the letters of Saint Paul, written some twenty years after Jesus was crucified. They say nothing about where he was born, about the miracles or about the parables. As to the Gospels, they were written more than forty years after his death, in times when nearly everyone was illiterate, including Jesus himself. It is probable that the first four books of the New Testament are based on accounts of his ministry which had been passed on by word of mouth. The early Egyptians wrote about virgin birth, the concept of resurrection and the ability of extraordinary people to perform miracles. It is possible that after the death of a man who was profoundly deep-thinking, compassionate, charismatic and quite extraordinary people embellished his story.(When theories such as these were voiced by theological scholars in the 19th Century they were excommunicated by the Roman Catholic church to which they belonged.)

After Luther's Reformation, Protestantism spawned several branches, amongst them Presbyterians, Methodists, Seventh Day Adventists and Jehovah's Witnesses – who acknowledge Him alone and believe that all other forms of Christianity are the work of Satan! Also the Quakers, the Baptists and the Mormons. Yes, even the Mormons, who took unto themselves – and some of them still do – many wives.

Mohammed had ten (possibly as many as thirteen) wives, one of whom, Safiyya, was Jewish, and most of whom were widows; he allowed Moslems four, plus concubines. Women in Islam are second-class citizens and it is doubtful from the writings in the Koran whether they have a place in heaven. Certainly men do, and automatically if they die fighting in a jihad, a holy war. The same bait was held out before Christian Crusaders of the 12th Century when they were urged to liberate Jerusalem from the Moslems, and also to the Hashishiyun, the Assassins, an Islamic sect of the 12th Century who, when they came down to earth after having been made high on the drug and given young maidens to enjoy were told they had visited Paradise, and would return there if they died carrying out the orders of their leader.

Moslems accept Zoroastrians and Christians as followers of faiths recognised by their prophet, and Moses and Jesus as minor prophets, but nevertheless despise all infidels – non-believers in Islam. To Hindus, Untouchables are the lowest of the low, but foreigners are even lower. Christianity regards all other faiths as being false and non-Christians as being beyond redemption: only the Christian God is good enough. Christian soldiers have gone to war against each other convinced that their God is "fighting" on their side, and assured by their priests that it is so.

Because complete faith demands complete obedience and because disobedience is likely to bring retribution, religious belief creates dislike and fear of other religions. It has, therefore, through the ages, created terrible dissension and conflict. Those who have suffered most because of this are, perhaps, the Jews, in early times because Christians blamed Jews who lived hundreds of years before for making the decision to kill Jesus. During the Christian Crusades, when people in Western Europe trudged off to free Jerusalem from the Moslems then occupying it, Jews were slaughtered in the belief that such action would be a favourable start to the enterprise. In the 13th Century Jews were banned from England, and in the 14th many of them died after a hundred thousand or so were expelled from Spain. There have been pogroms in Russia and Eastern Europe on and off for centuries and in the 20th nearly six million European Jews were systematically exterminated by the Germans. Genocide.

Today, Semites fight each other in the Middle East, Jew against Arab. In the Indian sub-continent Hindus fight Moslems and Sikhs – all of whom, essentially, are now of the same race, even if they were not when the Aryans first arrived thousands of years ago. Christians and Moslems kill each other in the Lebanon. Protestant Christians and Roman Catholics fight each other in Ireland and Canada and Belgium. Men and women of faith cannot live in peace together.

What would (or do?) Guatama, Kung Fu-Tzu, Jesus and Mohammed make of it all?

*

## CHAPTER FIVE

# THE MIDDLE YEARS

The man who stood at the gate of the year 987 AD did not know he was there.

If he was a Christian it was not, in fact, the first of January as he thought it was – the calendar which had come into use in the time of the Roman Emperor Julius Caesar was inaccurate and in the meantime several days had been lost: the matter would not be put right until a new calendar was adopted in 1752 AD. If he was a Moslem it was the year 397. The new religion had spread east into Turkey and India and west along the coast of North Africa and into Spain, where it was to stay for nearly 800 years, until 1492. The islands of Sicily, Sardinia and Corsica were Moslem too – and indeed if it had not been for the fact that Charles Martel, grandfather of Charlemagne, had beaten the advancing Moors in France in 732 AD the whole of Europe would almost certainly have become Islamic. If he was Jew it was the year 4747. And if he lived in those parts of the world where time passed and was not measured he did not know a new year had begun. Or care.

This chapter will carry the record forward to New Year's Day 1900 AD, the start of the 20th Century, a time when those who were aware of its significance were full of hope for the future. Man was conquering the world of knowledge and had put barbarity behind him. All was well in this best of all possible worlds; modern men and women were shaping a brave new world. It was an optimistic view for which there is no logical basis in history.

*

By the year 987 AD the entire human population of Earth was probably around 350 million, of whom less than a quarter, that is to say some of the Europeans, had the benefit of Greek and Roman knowledge. Nearly all of them were the descendants of the barbarians who had defeated the Romans – and the ancestors of the people who, over the next thousand years, were to create the world we know. By the beginning of the 20th Century the world's population had increased five times, to around 1,800 million, but the proportion of educated people had risen only slightly.

Everywhere, whether in primitive or advanced societies, the history of the last thousand years has been a shameful one – century after century of brutality and war. But people are not to blame, it is in our nature. We carry within us the seeds of our fathers and mothers from the beginnings of time; the torch in our genes is handed on from one to another as it was by the runners in the first Olympiad in 776 BC.

The record, which is beyond contention, shows the nature of the beast. But there is another side.

*

There are many national histories but there is no true world history. Such a thing is impossible to write because events are recorded from different points of view. Which one is the truth? Also, the writer inevitably brings to his task the bias of his own nationality and culture. An Indian's version will be different to an American's, and a Scotsman's different from an Indian's. The best that can be expected is for someone to do his best to concentrate the essence of the story.

National histories tell us of vanquished rulers or their victories, of incursions and battles, of parochial pestilences and pleasures, but little of what was happening on the other side of the hill; for the very good reason that people did not know. And sometimes even when they knew about events on their own side of the hill nothing was recorded. There is no history to read. Generations lived and died and left nothing behind but their bones.

Only in the 20th Century have communication systems made it possible for a fraction of the world's population to know what is going on while it is happening: but even when they know, they cannot do anything about it. Family and the local community are what matter to most people, now as then: obtaining food, clothing and warmth, and paying for them. Relationships. Birth. Illness. Death.

Most of the records of events which took place between the 10th and the 20th Centuries are inaccurate, biased, falsified or embellished, and anyway are of little real significance. Even the epic sea and land battles between the European nations were minor skirmishes along Homo Sapiens' way, except perhaps those of the Napoleonic Wars of the 18th and 19th Century, which left the British as the dominant power in the world, wealthy and able to begin the great European colonisations of overseas territories. Medieval wars the world over sometimes lasted for generations but the majority of the largely rural populations in the countries involved knew almost nothing about them, and only occasionally was their day-to-day existence affected.

The things that happened during those centuries which fundamentally affected mankind as a whole all started in the minds of European men: a new surge of artistic creativity, exploration of the world, revolution in the mind, negro slavery, imperialism, the birth of industrial science and, perhaps of greater consequence than anything else, the fact that national identity became supremely important. In the sequence of years these things followed one upon the other, starting in the 15th Century; an awakening after centuries of what are known as the Dark Ages when mankind's light barely glimmered.

*

In 987 AD the three principle cultures of Asia, the Indian, the Chinese and the Japanese, had already settled into their divergent ways. India was divided by many warring Hindu kingdoms. Another two hundred years were to pass before Delhi was conquered by Moslems who spread their rule over the whole nation; then other moslems of the Mughal (Mongol) dynasty, founded in 1526, brought new art, ideas and the conversion of many more Indian people to Islam. Less than a hundred years later the first Europeans, the Portuguese, arrived but it was to be another two hundred before, in 1803, Delhi was captured by the British. The effect of these conquests was that India's ever-growing population became mixed in religious belief, fragmented by local rule and, eventually, controlled by a small, well-organised but alien administration. At the height of their power a few thousand Britons controlled millions of Indians. The British, like the Aryans who had arrived long before them, brought their own caste system and remained remote from the native Indians, though, human nature being what it is, they inter-bred, and were to leave behind when they departed a legacy of half-caste people who are neither European nor Indian.

Two hundred years before Jesus walked the shores of Galilee Chi'in Shih Huang Ti governed his nation by means of a closely controlled state civil service. He thus started a tradition of mass acceptance of, and conformity with, direction; decisions were made at the centre, instructions were issued to the provinces and results were then monitored and reported back. It did not always work of course, the most common cause of disruption being war. A thousand years ago, after centuries of internal and border strife and successive dynasties, China was divided between the Sung in the south and the Liao around Peking. In the 13th Century its large population and many walled cities were conquered and divided by Mongols from central Asia but within a hundred years China had been reunited under the Ming emperors. In the 17th Century the Manchus from the north reached Peking and established their rule over the Chinese, forcing them to adopt the Manchu pig-tail form of head dressing but otherwise remaining aloof and forbidding any intermarriage. They stayed for two hundred years. Then during the 19th Century, thinking that China was there for the taking like anywhere else, squabbling Europeans began to establish trading posts on the seaboard but Chinese religions were not divisive – men and women could have different beliefs and yet live amicably together – and the people had much more national cohesion than the inhabitants of India. Though there were, and are, many dialects, the Mandarin language spoken or understood by so many people was a uniting factor. China was not to be had. In the 20th Century the Japanese invaded and obliged China to face the realities of life as it now was: in the surging tides of war old ideas and values were broken and frayed and when the Japanese left in 1945 China began to cast aside its long-established ways. Five years later it turned to Communism.

Most of the first people to reach Japan came from China via Korea but in the northern islands some drifted south from Siberia. Once there, they shut the gates for centuries, creating a way of life largely based on Chinese ideas. Because of the mountainous terrain, communities developed in isolation and it was not until the 5th Century AD that they were forcibly brought together by the chief of one of the tribes. To create unity and awe of his status he emphasised his importance by declaring that he was a direct descendant of the sun-goddess the Japanese worshipped – a myth believed until the middle of the 20th Century. In their own interests his claims were supported by a strong aristocracy, the Samurai knighthood of warrior families who became dominant over the whole country and remained so until a hundred years ago. The divinity of the emperor and the esteem in which obedience and military prowess were held were major factors in shaping the minds of the nation.

In the 10th Century Japan was still a young country. For the next nine hundred years it continued to grow uniquely in its own way, remote from all other influences. Only once were they threatened, by the Mongols of Kublai Khan, and were saved by the Kamikaze – the God Wind – which destroyed the enemy's invasion fleet. (In 1269 Kublai Khan asked the Pope to send one hundred learned men to his court to establish an understanding between East and West. When the Khan's messengers reached Rome there was no Pope because the succession was being angrily disputed. When after two years one was appointed he sent two Dominican Friars, who soon found an excuse to abandon their dangerous journey to China. On such things has the fate of the world depended.)

From the 12th Century until the 19th the Samurai knights laid their swords upon the heads and backs of the people. The Portuguese were briefly there in the 16th Century but not until the mid-19th did the Japanese allow foreigners to enter their islands. In pre-history they did not exist; in the middle years they existed only to themselves, their Shinto, Buddhist and Confucist beliefs the background to a highly-ordered, ritualised, class-structured way of life. At the beginning of the 20th Century they began to notice other people; in the 1950s the world began to notice them, in particular the effects of their intelligence and industry on the economies of other nations.

Europe in 987 was recognisably what it is now, except that four-fifths of Spain was under Arab rule. In the far North there were a scattering of Norsemen but no nations. The English were on their island, as were the Welsh and the Scots, but very few of them, and even fewer Irish next door. France was there, and the German tribes and the Italian city states. Czechoslovakia was known as Bohemia and Moravia. Poland, Hungary and Bulgaria existed but Greece did not.

For hundreds of years what had once been known as Greece was part of the Holy Roman Empire, ruled from Constantinople – which had been Byzantium. Then in the 14th Century Mongol Hordes (the Golden, the Blue and the White) erupted out of Central Asia and surged over southern Russia, Eastern Europe and Persia. Other hordes went to the East; to Tibet, Burma and China. Generations lived and died and the tide turned, the conquerors fell back or were absorbed and their place in the west was taken by the Ottoman Turks, who themselves had fled screaming with terror from Turkestan when Genghis Khan's Mongol armies galloped bareback out of the rising sun. In 1453 the Ottomans defeated the Christians in Constantinople and then progressively took over Turkey, Bulgaria, Serbia and much of Greece, where they were to stay until the 20th Century.

In 987 AD, America, north and south, was a vast, nearly empty land-mass full of undreamed-of treasure. Only the Moche in Peru had a semblance of ordered living; the Maya were on their last legs and elsewhere small tribal groups lived in ignorant savagery on the endless plains of the north or in the southern forests which crawled with venomous life.

It was 988 AD when Slav people who had drifted north-east into other great empty spaces became a new nation called Russia, centred on Kiev. (Which was later to become the capital of the Ukraine. Moscow was to remain a small town for another four hundred years.) To the east the tribe known as the Rus had no boundary. 13,000 kilometres of seemingly endless forest, tundra and lakes, inhabited by small groups of widely seperated people who had many different customs, beliefs and characteristics, went on and on and on until the land ended at the sea of Japan. The population was very sparse and it was to be centuries before the great semi-continent of Russia became the thinly populated place it now is.

In truth there were no barriers anywhere a thousand years ago, except those of prejudice. No frontiers. The world was still one place then but by the time the 20th Century came there were barriers everywhere: in the minds of people and on maps, where demarcation lines had been arbitrarily drawn by politicians; the Earth claimed, apportioned, parcelled-up and labelled.

*

The process started all over the world as a development of leadership by dominant males. Tribal chieftains ruled everywhere and in Europe by the 10th Century the feudal system had been established whereby people were tied for a lifetime of servitude to one particular man. The leader considered himself to be there as of right, and as time went on the led accepted this more and more: challenges to the king came from the face cards close to him and seldom from anyone in the pack.

Leaders were compelled to defend their position, either from real threats or from imagined or fabricated ones. Wars were the natural means by which power was obtained, held or increased. Several victories enabled the winner to proclaim himself a super-chief or monarch, with power over lesser chiefs. Monarchs, being near to God, came to think of themselves as having been born to that eminence by the will of God. Near-gods and their consorts and close supporters required visible signs of the high esteem in which they were held by their followers – fine clothes, jewels and ornaments with which to drape their unwashed bodies. A gold-plated superstructure made small populations top heavy.

Things of significant lasting effect resulted from this. The first was that military prowess was accepted by nearly everyone as being laudable, and military success as the ultimate in achievement. The second was that those with great wealth had time to spare – and vice versa.

Military success does not depend upon heroism but heroism may lead to military success. Even if it does not it is worthy of respect on its own account because it displays a person's ability to overcome the inborn dread of annihilation or pain which is in everyone. A man is strong, in his own eyes and in the esteem of others, if he has glared defiantly at death. So it was that in the 9th Century there grew in Europe – and in Japan in the 12th – the concept of knighthood; the admission to an elite group of those who demonstrated bravery, either in battle or in bloody tournaments. Men fought to gain entry, and men and women admired those who did. Thus violence and killing, no longer essential to man's survival as it had been for thousands of years, came to be glorified, and remains so to this day in most societies.

People had no need to eliminate their fellow men; nature did it plentifully, either chronically, by way of diseases contracted because of total ignorance about infection and hygiene, or acutely, by epidemics. The most frightful of these was the Black Death of the 14th Century, which began in Asia and came west via the Caspian Sea, Turkey, Sicily and the south of France to Paris. In 1348 it reached England and travelled through the land at a speed of a mile a day, killing one third of the population in a most painful and revolting way. In Bristol there were not enough men left alive to bury the dead, and only when the raging fire of contamination had burnt out could that grim task be done by the survivors. Borne by fleas which carry the bug from infected rats, bubonic (from "bubo", a glandular swelling) and pneumonic ("pneumo", of the lungs) plagues came repeatedly to Europe, smiting London again in 1665. They still exist in Asia and Africa today, festering away quietly. But pestilence was considered an act of God in Christian nations, so men were not to blame; and not to be deterred from pursuing their warlike pastimes either.

Where men had money and leisure they began to vie with each other not only in war but in the overt appreciation of beauty – for itself sometimes but also because by glorifying God through art they thought they would do the same for themselves. So it was that in Italy artists, sculptors and architects were given the encouragement and financial support which resulted in the next tremendous spurt of creative activity. Until then, artists had been despised by people of quality because they worked with their hands: now men found that they could rise in the estimation of their peers by reflecting the glories achieved by their patronised painter or sculptor. The Medicis were one such family of enormous wealth – which had come in the first place from the backs of sheep: wool was imported into Tuscany from England. As well as raising some of the most beautiful church spires in the Cotswolds and East Anglia the bleating beasts of Burford and Bury-St-Edmunds contributed to the production of magnificent works of art.

The Renaissance lasted more than two hundred years but was at its peak in the latter part of the 15th Century, during the lifetimes of two men of great genius, Leonardo da Vinci and Michelangelo. da Vinci was the most inventively talented man who has ever lived; an astronomer, mathematician, musician, chemist, anatomist, physicist, engineer, geologist and brilliant painter of pictures. In Florence, Venice, Rome, Padua and Pisa art reached and then far surpassed the standards set by Athens.

Regrettably, this was only a beautiful facade under which the true nature of men remained unchanged. The city-states were constantly at bloody war with one another. In Florence, in 1494, three priests were publicly burnt at the stake for protesting against the despotism of its ruler, surrounded by the magnificent marble-clad buildings, many of them dedicated to the glory of the Christian God, which had so recently and proudly risen. For all that, those confused people left a great legacy of beauty and skill to later generations.

*

Two years before the priests were burnt, Columbus, who believed he too was doing God's will, sailed westwards and, thinking that he had missed China and reached the Indian Ocean, found and named the West Indies. He and his crews sailed in three tiny ships – the Santa Maria weighed just 100 tons and the other two were half the size and were open boats. All had only rudimentary navigation aids. (Magnetic needles had been used by soothsayers in China for hundreds of years – if they pointed the wrong way after they had been spun it was hard luck. Most of the time, of course, they ended up pointing in the direction the soothsayer knew very well they would, though he had not the foggiest idea why. But not until around 1000 AD were they adopted for navigation.) What is more, Columbus and his men thought the Earth was flat. It was a supreme act of faith, or one of astounding ego, that after years of being tossed around on vast and seemingly endless oceans Columbus returned to report his findings. His sponsors would probably have jibbed if they had known just how far he would have to sail, and how long it would be, before they got any return for their money.

His sailors brought back many things from their travels including tobacco and syphilis, a disease which was endemic to the Americas and which was imported from Cuba. It scythed through the people of Europe, killing or maiming millions. Even into the 20th Century the population of some places dwindled because girl children are made barren in their infected mother's womb. Tobacco, however, was to kill far more, in the long run, than syphilis ever did. In exchange for these gifts a generation later Spaniards who called themselves The Sword of the Pope took to the Aztecs in Mexico and the Incas in Peru European diseases which killed off thousands of the people who escaped their blades. They in their turn brought back tomatoes, potatoes, chocolate and turkeys. And much gold and silver.

A few years before Columbus went west a Portuguese captain had sailed around southern Africa towards the east but had been forced to turn back by his crew because they feared they would fall off the ends of the Earth. Fifty years later other Portuguese explorers with a more stubborn captain landed in Japan, taking muskets with them which they sold to people who had not known that such deadly things existed. Until then sharpened steel had sufficed.

It was at about the same time, in 1542, that Copernicus, a Polish astronomer, published a theory that the Earth moved around the sun, which was obviously untrue: Earth must be the centre of the Universe, everybody knew that. Another ninety years were to pass before Galileo, in Italy, was threatened with hell and damnation and imprisoned because he had seen with his own eyes, through the astronomical telescopes he had made, the movements of the Sun and its planets, and said he agreed with Copernicus. The publication of such ideas was officially banned by the Roman Catholic church until 1822, by which time they could no longer refuse to accept the evidence presented. Exploration, of the world and of the mind, was slowly taking people out of the black ignorance in which they lived.

*

The invention of movable lettering, in Germany in 1450, which stemmed from the discovery of a new mixture of metals, was the most important factor ever in the dispersion of information. Printing using carved blocks had first been done in Korea in the 8th Century and the technique was known in Europe in the 13th. In the 14th Century books had been "mass-produced" by being dictated to rows of scribes seated at high tables, but the ability to re-shape text quickly into new pages completely changed society. People learn new thoughts from other people. By the end of the 15th Century dozens of German and Italian towns had printing machines and they were in use in eleven other European countries. In England in 1476 a native language was printed for the first time instead of Latin. It has been estimated that in the first 50 years after the invention of printing ten million books were produced.

Until the advent of printing presses knowledge was possessed by very few people. There was an academy in Athens 387 years Before Christ and one in Baghdad in 800 AD, a university existed in Paris and teaching had begun in Oxford in the 12th Century but in Europe in those days nine out of ten people lived in hamlets on a diet of bacon, beans and black bread, desperately poor, lice-ridden, illiterate and ignorant. By the time Spring came most of them were on the verge of contracting scurvy due to the lack of vegetables. Underclothes and night clothes were not generally worn until the 19th Century and because hardly anyone washed skin diseases were a common thing. Scratching an empty belly was not conducive to thinking. For centuries the local priest had been the only person who could write, except perhaps the landowner, but the slow arrival of news sheets and pamphlets and then books changed all that. Printed paper spurred people to learn to read, and put new thoughts into their heads.

One such was the idea of revolution against the belief in the God-given right of monarchs to rule. After a civil war the English king was beheaded, in 1649, and in 1793 so too was the king of France. Crying "liberty, equality and fraternity", Frenchmen forced their way into the Paris prison, the Bastille, and freed the men shackled there. The fact that they found only seven scraggy captives in the great fortress, one of whom was a raving lunatic, was not the point: their action became a new symbol of the ability of people en masse to enforce change by violence.

The revolutionaries not only wanted to improve the poverty-stricken conditions under which the great majority of people lived, they aimed to free men's minds from what they called the tyranny of the church; from the fears imposed by superstition. They urged people to believe in Reason, not God, and they banned Christianity. They also imposed a ten-day week. However, the French revolution resulted in chaos and in the brutal and bloody slaughter of thousands of innocent people: men broke their chains but found, not for the first time or the last, that mob violence releases forces which cannot be controlled.

The questioning of established feudal traditions which had started in England in the 17th Century was continued by a number of English and French thinkers in the 18th – Erasmus, More, Payne, Voltaire. Their writings had great influence on the minds of the colonists who had followed the English Pilgrim Fathers to North America.

By 1607 when the first British settlement was founded in Virginia the "Indian" population of North America had grown to over one million tribal people spread across the whole continent. Because the distances between them were so vast communities had evolved their own cultures: nearly five hundred different languages or dialects were spoken by men and women who were still at the hunting stage of human development – nomads moving in pursuit of the food they needed for survival. The European newcomers founded more settlements on the Atlantic coastline and then progressively pushed westwards, slaughtering bison on which the Indians depended for their food. (In 1870 two million were being killed each year for their hides. Ten years later there were only two hundred or so left in the whole country.) By 1750 the white population had increased to three million in thirteen colonies and in 1783 the United States won their independence from the British. In 1820 there were ten million Americans; only thirty years later there were 60 million of them and they were fighting each other to decide whether slavery was a permissible human condition.

*

The total domination of fellow human beings by others is a condition which has existed from the earliest stages of our evolution. In ancient times it resulted from capture or conquest in war – the acquiring of labourers who had no rights was a legitimate aim. Everybody did it, even the Greeks: democracy did not apply to the slaves imported to Athens, many of whom came from the 10,000 a day who were sold in the market on the island of Delos. Nor did it to those in Rome, though for them there was a let-out: after the third generation a freed slave became a full citizen. (Because there had been so many, by the 2nd Century AD four out of every five Romans were descended from slaves.) In the 14th Century Florence allowed slaves to be imported. Greek and Russian girls bought in Majorca or Ibiza were used to pay off debts as well as wash the dishes. Until around 1700 AD young Slavs captured by raiding cavalry were sold off in Asian slave markets.

Serfdom in feudal ages was a modified form of slavery in that the man at the top, in his own interests, had some concern for the continued existence of his workers; they slaved for him but he protected them from the depredations of their neighbours. As Europeans became more enlightened under the pressure of Christian teaching serfdom was banned, but it took a long time. The German princes did not abolish it until 1770 and the King of Prussia did not start to do so until 1807. In Russia peasants had been made serfs in the 15th and 16th Centuries and they were not freed until 1861. (In 1815 the Tsar owned 16 million of them.)

The Portuguese were the first to take African negroes into slavery, in 1446. They had found what seemed to be a limitless source of no-cost labour, and other European nations soon began to plunder what they called the Dark Continent, meaning that it was full of black people and was unexplored; no Christian light had shone upon it. In the 17th Century the English, the Dutch and the Portuguese together shipped nearly a million Africans across the Atlantic to the West Indies and the United States – but many died on the way. It has been estimated that when that particular slave trade ended some 9 million black people had died during their transportation to the New World. In America in 1861 the southern States depended on slaves for their commercial existence, the northern ones did not. The North, because of its greater ability to make weapons and maintain its soldiers, won the war and the slaves were freed.

The enforced transportation of human beings who were regarded as a base form of life not far removed from that of animals was to have a long-lasting effect on the future of mankind, since it deposited in the Americas the ancestors of people, who, as the years passed and new, more liberal ideas began to replace the bigoted attitudes which had prevailed, increasingly demanded, and got, statutory political equality. But at the cost of turmoil and a legacy of ill feeling.

*

The building of empires, the conquest of the unknown world, had started with its exploration by the seafaring nations on the eastern Atlantic coast. The Dutch, the French, the Spanish and the Portuguese all sailed towards the setting sun, found empty land, marched ashore, planted a flag and claimed it for their monarch. And so too did the British. Perhaps it was the dash of Viking blood brought over by the Normans in 1066 which, added to the racial mixtures already existing in the England, created a nation which for hundreds of years, from the early 17th Century to the middle of the 20th, dominated the seas.

But to put the matter into perspective, empire-building was not too difficult. The men who sailed blindly over the horizon had enormous personal courage, enterprise, determination, and faith but the entire world population when they started was under 500 million, of which, apart from China and India, most lived in the European homelands; the places they found were almost devoid of human life. (By 1950 the balance had swung completely the other way: there were five times as many human beings on Earth but two-thirds of them lived in countries which do not have a European culture.) Exploration was the natural consequence of curiosity, advances in ship construction and navigation and the desire for commercial gain. Conquest was relatively easy, it was hanging on to what had been claimed that was not. Nations fought a series of colonial wars over disputed ownership because ownership had been proved to be very worthwhile: for decades Spain dominated Europe because of the wealth of treasure its sailors brought back from Central and South America.

The dispersion of Europeans seeking fortune and adventure reached its peak in the last half of the 19th Century, by which time Belgium and Germany, which had not existed as nations when the race for land began, had both claimed territories in Africa. The French were in Indo-China, Africa and the Americas, the Dutch were in the East Indies and South America, the Spanish in north and South America and the Portuguese in South America and India and China. And somewhere under the sunlight as the Earth turned day after day there was a British possession. At its peak a quarter of the people in the world were part of the British Empire.

The Europeans took with them in their small, wind-driven wooden ships the knowledge and culture they had developed over the centuries, and their religion. To those offered these gifts the culture was often superfluous and the religion offensive but the knowledge was priceless: of law, medicine, administration and industrial technology. They brought back goods with which they fed the new way of life that started in Britain a hundred and fifty years ago.

*

The distribution of natural resources, which had resulted from Earth's upheavals during its formation, and the fortuitous migrations of people in early times, became really significant in the 19th Century.

Some nations, such as Brazil, have enormous natural wealth but until recent times the climate and land have made it difficult to get at. Some, such as Canada, the second biggest nation in the world in size of territory, have much greater resources than they have people to exploit them. Very old rocks, in Brazil, Canada, Africa, Western Australia and Scandinavia contain iron, copper and gold but no coal. Younger rocks, in the Alps, the Himalayas, the Rocky Mountains and the Andes, contain metals and have oil deposits at their fringes but there is no coal. The mud-plains, in North, East and Western China, Western Russia and Central and South America, have some oil deposits but no coal or iron. The rest of the world has iron and coal and some oil. Britain had coal and iron in abundance, and a very inventive and buoyant race of people who figured out how to use them.

The industrial revolution began with coal-fired steam engines driving iron machinery. Under tall smoking chimneys, in hot workshops pounded by the noise of engines and the whining of belt-drives, people turned lathes and spun bobbins.

Steam engines were developed out of necessity. As coal miners dug ever deeper into the Earth so it became vital to invent a means of pumping water out of the workings. Engineers applied the technical information discovered by physicists and mathematicians to the making of machines which would produce energy. Trains were carried over steel rails and bridges to link every small town. Clothes, tools and machinery were mass-produced in factories, distributed and sold on the ever-increasing home market and taken overseas in steam-driven, coal-fired British-made metal ships. (With the passage of time the clanking, hissing, four horse-power steam engine of the 19th Century has become the steam turbine of the 20th, developing the power of 28,000!) And with the manufactured goods went the know-how which enabled other advanced nations in the world to build their own railroads and workshops.

Raw cotton was imported to England from the New World, treated with bleaching powder – invented and made in England – processed in mills, made up into garments in factories and then shipped to Asia, where the clothing was sold to Tamils, Bengalis, Punjabis, Malays and Chinese. Rubber was brought from Brazil and, later, Malaya. Cocoa came from the West, tea from the East, gold and diamonds from South Africa and wool from Australia.

In the 17th Century the Cape of Good Hope in South Africa had been a not-too-hospitable half-way house for European ships on the long haul to and from the Far East. In the early 18th, the Dutch and British began to settle there. A hundred years on, the British had taken over Cape Colony from the Dutch and there followed a century of warfare with negroes who had begun a great southward migration out of central Africa.

At the southern extremity of the world Australia and New Zealand were left to their own devices until the 19th Century. In 1820 there were only 6,500 settlers in Australia, mostly convicts; just twenty years later there were 68,000. The first Christian missionaries arrived in New Zealand in 1814; by 1859 the British who followed them had taken over forty million acres of land from the Maoris.

By the beginning of the 20th Century most of Europe and the United States of America had become industrialised and six out of every ten people depended on mines or factories for the money they needed to earn in order to survive. Though by 1900 Russia had started to use the new techniques the great majority of its population were still peasants, whereas in Germany by then only a third of the people were still living off the land.

During the Industrial Revolution the population of London doubled, from one to two millions, and that of Paris increased by a million. Only ten generations earlier, the entire British population had been seven millions. Within three more generations most men and women in Europe had progressed from candle through gas to electric light, from horseback by way of the horse-drawn carriage to the motor car, from the mail coach to the telegram to the telephone, from newspapers to radio to television. But in the early years the majority of the workers who brought about these changes paid for this material progress with sweat, sickness and dire poverty.

Nations grew wealthy from manufacturing processes and trade and so did the organisers, who became the large, class-conscious middle class, but the labouring man, his wife and his children, many of whom also slaved in appalling conditions for half the living day, did not. Industrialisation created turmoil in societies which, from medieval times, had been stable, except for the periodic impact of war. Peasants exchanged a community in which they were known and had a place for a city where they were anonymous and often worthless. Not only did they have to work like beasts or starve, nobody cared if they lived or died.

The man who thought he had found the solution to this problem, and changed the world by saying so, was a German-Jew called

Marx. His theory, published jointly with a man by the name of Engels in the Communist Manifesto in 1848, gave food for thought to the hungry proletariat, the people. Not that they read communist literature but they believed the people who told them they had nothing to lose but their chains. The majority of *them* had not read the Marxist theories either. It was the grandeur of the concept that appealed: from every man according to his ability to every man according to his need.

In Paris, in 1871, the Communards, the working class, took to the streets to fight the unjust system which had developed haphazardly. Nobody had set out to produce such a society. People's natural self-interest had perverted the Christian morality to which they solemnly paid lip-service each Sunday in their churches. Now the upper and middle classes, in France and in other European countries, firm in their belief that God had decreed that they should be born to positions of power and plenty, had a new ethic: to those who have, more shall be given; from those who have nothing, nothing can be taken away. As Prussian soldiers who had encircled the city the year before – and had thus made conditions even more deplorable for the poor of the city – went trudging home, twenty thousand Parisians died in a fierce aftermath to the revolution which, eighty years before, had somehow failed to ensure liberty and equality for all.

Trade Unions had been formed in Germany in the 1850s, in Great Britain in 1871 and in France in 1884, but Marxist theories were to lie dormant for more than thirty years until, in Russia, they found fertile soil in which to grow and flourish.

*

Thinkers, then, were not only inventing machinery. The same phenomenon that had suddenly appeared in Babylon, Athens, Rome and Florence, the surge forward of mankind led by a few individuals, the cross-fertilisation of men's brains by other men's advancing thoughts, happened in London, Paris, Berlin and Vienna.

In the early 19th Century life expectancy was still only 35 years, even in the "advanced" nations of Europe, so in medicine the discovery during the second half of the century of anaesthetics, microbes, antiseptics, the concept of immunology and the application of the rules of hygiene began to make a welcome cut in the death toll due to traumatic shock, wounds and enteric infections. Even so, hardly anyone washed. For fourteen hundred years, ever since the Romans departed, the citizens of Europe did not clean their bodies – still less did anyone else in other parts of the world. As spices were used to kill the smell and flavour of decaying meat, which was eaten as a matter of course, so wafted perfumes drowned the stench of a courtier's lady. The rest of the population just stank. As late as the 1840's "night soil" was still being thrown out of European windows on to the gutters below at well-known times each morning. The mass production of iron piping in England in 1800 began the process of bringing water to the home from a centralised reservoir rather than from nearby wells, streams or rivers. Even so the first public sewer in London was not laid until 1851.

Within a few years sewage systems were being progressively installed in the towns and cities of Europe – not primarily for reasons of hygiene, which was not properly understood, but because the accumulation of smells was highly offensive – but the big breakthrough did not come until 1896, when the Italians began to chlorinate water, by so doing dramatically reducing the number of deaths from cholera, typhoid and dysentery.

In other ways too life was becoming more tolerable. For hundreds of years the poor had been able to see at night only by applying a flame to the end of a rush leaf soaked in oil which burned for an hour or so and gave off a faint glimmer of light. Those who could afford better had tallow candles, and the rich had wax ones (the light being increased by reflecting it off mirrors) and oil lamps. In 1807 street lights in some English towns and cities were lit by coal gas and by 1818 it had been piped into some houses. But the paraffin lamp did not shed light upon the gloom until 1850, and the electric bulb did not appear until 1890. Even so, by 1919 only 6% of houses in the United Kingdom had the benefit of electric light. As for heating, the open hearth had been the centre of the home for hundreds of years, the cooking done on spits or in pots suspended over the flames. The coal heating of rooms did not come until around the 1850s, when iron fireplaces began to be made and fitted into chimney pieces. At about this time too iron baths were made, and porcelain washbasins. Until then people had bathed in a tub in front of the fire, now and then, and washed in a lead sink or a basin. Toilets were privies; holes in the ground or buckets that were emptied when they became too full. The water closet did not arrive until late in the 19th Century. Such advances as these happened only in the towns, and only in those nations which were beginning to benefit from industrialisation. Elsewhere, people in the Northern Hemisphere lived lightless, cold, hungry and uncomfortable lives, while those in the hot places of the world went through life in much the same way, except that they were too hot instead of too cold. The things which today's generation in the advanced nations of the world take for granted, such things as washing machines, air-conditioning, gas and oil-fired central heating, showers and constant hot water did not appear until the middle of the 20th, except very rarely for the privileged few.

In 1859 Darwin shattered the peace of mind of his generation, and succeeding generations, by suggesting that Man had evolved from the apes. In London the insane asylum near the River Thames known as Bedlam (originally called Bethlehem but fore-shortened by the Cockney tongue, and now the Imperial War Museum) was still thrashing and forcibly strait-jacketing its unfortunate foaming occupants when Freud began his study of the human mind and wrote the learned papers which were to become the basis of psychiatry. But when it was opened Bedlam was regarded as an example of modern and enlightened thinking. Until the 18th Century insane people had been looked after in private institutions or locked in an outhouse, often shackled naked on a pile of straw until they died of disease or starved to death: because they had lost their senses they were thought to be no better than beasts, and were treated accordingly. But it is not surprising. Since such things as public executions, dog-fights and bear-baiting were regarded by most people as fun entertainment the treatment of the insane was not exceptional. And neither was Britain. People were still hung in cages outside the cathedral in Munster, or on gibbets at cross roads all over Europe. Or locked in grotesque iron masks or had their tongues and nails dragged out with pincers, sometimes in a hidden place but often in full view of a hooting public. The misfortunes of the unfortunate had long been a cause for merriment and it is only in this century that finer feelings have begun to prevail. In some places. In the mid-1970s in Cambodia Communist fanatics sometimes cut the liver out of their live prisoners, fried it and ate it before their dying eyes.

But all was not gloom. Men and women have always managed to find joy and laughter however hard life was. Simple pleasures pleased simple people and even complicated pastimes have existed for a long time. Polo, a game invented more than a thousand years ago, was played by Saladin with his friends in Cairo and Damascus in the 12th Century, and Chess too, brought back along the Silk Route from China. Playing cards were invented not long after, and variations on how to use them ever since. Magicians in China made things disappear for the amusement of emperors when the Great Wall was being built, and Punch and Judy have made the children laugh for hundreds of years.

*

The importance of the country in which they lived dominated men's minds in the 19th Century. More praiseworthy, it was clear, than monarchy, and less liable to doubts than religion, nationalism, for many, replaced those things as the concept to which people felt they could be most loyal. It was a logical development from the past, from the binding together of people under a leader, from the wars fought and won under that leadership and supported by the voices of religion, from commitment to flags and slogans, but while it unified the tribe who called themselves by a particular name it was a tremendously divisive force for humanity as a whole.

Belgium became a nation in 1830, merging the Dutch-oriented Flemings of the north with the French-speaking Walloons of the south – still an uneasy union. In 1871, after centuries of rivalry between what became their component states, the Italians and the Germans became unified nations. In Germany the Prussians, with their strong militaristic tradition, had the dominant role at a time when it was rapidly and efficiently industrialising.

By the end of the 19th Century black men were living far from Africa and white men far from Europe. Both were going to be the cause of tension and violence in the alien lands to which they had gone. Europe was seething with nationalistic rivalries, which were the products of its history, and with under-currents of proletarian discontent. There were, too, many personal enmities, some of which were due to religious differences, amongst the closely-related crowned heads who ruled the wealthy and important nations. The masses were reproducing with a tremendous spurt, thanks to the reduction in the death rate, and industrialisation had produced the resources and money needed to create citizen armies of a size impossible to imagine before. Men's minds were obsessed, as usual, with furthering their own ends regardless of the consequences.

The portents for the 20th Century were not good.

*

# CHAPTER SIX

# CIVILISATION

The lack of a name has never been a problem.

Long ago men and women began to label themselves as belonging to a family, a group, a class, a religion, a nation. Some also considered themselves to be civilised, by which they probably meant that they were better behaved, more informed about facts, more emotionally sensitive, more refined in their manners and more appreciative of the arts than those who were uncivilised. People possessing the same national label could be evil, ignorant, brutal, vulgar and uncultivated, depending on their class, but as a rule were foreigners.

Most people would agree that a civilised person should not consciously harm others, should be knowledgeable and sensitive and appreciate the arts, and that a truly civilised society would contain a high proportion of citizens who possess these attributes. However, a civilisation is usually judged by its achievements in painting, sculpting, ceramics, architectural design, literature, drama, music and dancing rather than its morality, erudition and manners. Since every society has, in its own way, contributed something to world culture it can be said that mankind is, by nature, creative and artistic.

The oldest form of art is pictorial representation. Perhaps thirty thousand years ago, six times as far back as the Sumerians, a caveman drew the outline of a fish on the sand of a windy seashore with his index finger, then watched a wave swirl over it and obliterate his work, then tried again, squatting on his heels, frowning and intent, adding a dot for the eye . . .

The oldest surviving pictures are cave paintings, some of them done by drawing an outline around the shadow of an animal projected on to a wall by the flames of a crackling fire. But not all – a great variety of animal and human life was depicted; walking, running, leaping, fighting. In Egypt four and a half thousand years ago objects were drawn in ink on papyrus – birds and cats and women and warriors. Three-dimensional art came soon after the cavemen. The first sculptings of human faces we know of were made in Asia twenty thousand years ago and the earliest pottery so far discovered was made in Japan ten thousand years ago.

Religion, at first pagan and later formalised, has been the inspiration for most art. The Earth-mother figure and the boar's head of 30,000 years ago were almost certainly idols. 4,000 years ago Hindu sculptors created stone representations of gods and mortals with which to adorn their temples, many of them entwined in what Western society calls pornographic poses but which, to them, are three-dimensional illustrations of the Karma Sutra, a religious text written in praise of the pleasures of the sexual act and dedicated to the Lord Shiva, a god whose emblem is a phallus. The Greeks and the Romans created stone portraits of gods to venerate in their places of worship.

In Ravenna, in North-East Italy, in the 5th and 6th Centuries, unknown artists created marvellous pictures in stone; mosaics, small pieces of coloured glass and chipped marble cemented to the walls and ceilings of Christian churches, as fresh-looking today as they were fourteen hundred years ago: the unearthly Lamb of God gleaming white on a rich green field surrounded by apostles and emperors haloed in golden glory. It seems that the techniques of producing such visual depth and form were lost for a while after the death of those craftsmen for the works of later painters who decorated churches and holy books are curiously flat, distorted and out of proportion. This was partly because, on purpose, they made important figures bigger in size than lesser people, but also they did not realise that there were rules which governed perspective; the apparent diminishing of size with distance. Nearly a thousand years were to pass before someone discovered the principles.

Medieval stonemasons tried to immortalise Christian saints on the facades of the great cathedrals of Europe which soared up in the 11th, 12th and 13th Centuries. Even the lowly carpet, raised to heights of superb craftsmanship by the people of central Asia and the Middle East (but never perfect: only God can create a perfect thing so the weavers make a deliberate mistake) is often an article used for the glorification of Allah – a Moslem prayer mat. Tapestries too were woven to grace the bare walls of cold European churches as well as the draughty rooms and corridors of castles. In the 20th Century artists are still creating works of beauty in gold and glass and stone and tapestry to grace buildings dedicated to their gods.

A handful of men in Italy during the Renaissance – Donatello, Ghiberti, Michelangelo – made sculptures of astounding beauty but the creation of form out of stone or clay does not seem to have become easier with the passage of time: there are few great names associated with that skill. (Wood and stone were the first materials used by sculptors. A development was to work in clay and then bake it until it was hard – terracotta – or to make a permanent copy in plaster or metal in order to preserve the image. Today, modern chemistry has produced rock-hard quick-setting resins for the sculptor to use.)

It was a man called Brunelleschi who discovered the mathematical rules of perspective – and who designed the huge dome of the magnificent cathedral in Florence which stands a few metres away from the place where the screaming Savonarola and his two disciples fried in the flames. Jan van Eyck, from Flanders, which is now partly in Belgium and partly in France, is credited with being the man who,in the early-1400s, invented oil-based paints. His "Marriage of the Arnolfini" in London's National Gallery is thought to be the first existing painting on which the new medium was used. Before that, coloured pigments were mixed with wet plaster to make a fresco (a picture on a wall or a ceiling) or with egg yolk when painting on boards – canvas came later. ( Egg white for manuscript illustrations.) With oil paints the colours can be mixed and blended on the canvas as the artist works, whereas egg tempera generally dries too quickly. However, it is sometimes still used because of the quality of its glowing colours. In the last forty years acrylic paints, made by modern chemical processes, have been manufactured. They are cheaper than oil paints and dry quickly but do not produce the rich texture of oil colours.

Few designers of buildings have ever received lasting fame even when their creations are recognised as being of supreme merit. At first this was because they were regarded as craftsmen doing a practical job of work, not as creative artists deserving recognition; and because the erection of great medieval buildings lasted the lifetimes of several generations. Paris, Chartres, Cologne, Ulm, Canterbury, Winchester, Lincoln, Seville and many other European cities have cathedrals which are truly magnificent human creations, as is the Hindu temple of Vishnu in Angkor Wat in Kanpuchea (Cambodia), but the names of their architects are generally unknown. Shah Jahan is remembered, who had the exquisite, jewel-like Taj Mahal built near Agra, in India, in memory of his wife Mumtaz, but who designed this masterpiece, which took twenty thousand men eighteen years to make? (A masterpiece was the object made by an apprentice at the end of his trade training for examination by his craft master: if it was good enough he qualified.) The designer of buildings leaves his work as his monument and not, generally, his name. Perhaps, judging from the visual monstrosities which clutter the skyline in modern cities, and the opinions of the unfortunate human beings who have to live in their damp, wind-buffeted, concrete ant-hills, it is just as well.

Pottery started as a matter of utility – people needed utensils for their food – but artifice embellished articles and as time passed became the end and not the adjunct. The use of various clays and the invention of glazes turned very basic objects into works of art: the shape was made, the artist painted or moulded a decoration and then applied chemicals which, when the pottery was heated, became a hard gloss. Thousands of years ago the Eastern races, particularly the Chinese but also the Koreans and the Japanese, developed great skill in making beautiful and delicate ceramics, an art to which the Germans, Italians, French, Dutch and the British, much much later, brought their own characteristics. In between, the Greeks had also applied their special inventiveness to the making of pottery. They took their skills westward when they colonised southern Italy, Sicily and Sardinia and it was from them that the Etruscans developed their distinctive and beautiful pottery. The Romans used multiple brushes fixed to geometry compasses to produce complicated patterns. The lowly potter's wheel gave birth to lustrous and intricately designed articles, and, in time, to miniature sculptured figures.

Labels have been attached to art too, for ease of identification of styles.

There are three principal reasons why distinctive styles evolved. One was the advance of technology, which permitted artists to alter or enhance ways of doing things; the second was that phenomenon of mutual exchange of ideas which has produced periodic surges of human development – painters, especially, compared their work and vied with each other to advance the form of expression then in vogue; and the third was the reflection of the times in which the creators lived: there were eras when people followed existing rules and generations when they rebelled. The words used to denote styles generally refer to painting but may sometimes also be applied to architecture. When decoration is integral to the whole scheme, both merge. Broadly defined the progression of styles through the years is:

Greek Hellenistic: the classical, square form of building with roofs and pediments supported by massive columns. Usually the buildings are adorned with sculpture. This style was re-introduced in Western Europe in the 16th Century as "Palladian" architecture, named after Andrea Palladio.

Roman: being their adaptation of imaginative Greek art to which they added more realism, especially in stone portraiture.

Romanesque, of the 11th Century: principally Byzantine art but also "Norman" architecture: the rounded arch, which flourished in France and England.

Gothic, of the 12th to the 15th Century: characterised by soaring pointed windows and arches.(Calling this beautiful style by the name of a barbarian tribe was a sarcastic reaction to new ideas.)

Renaissance, of the 14th and 15th Centuries: the Italian years of Botticelli, Bellini, Titian and Tintoretto, Raphael and Corregio and, in Germany and England, of Durer and Holbein.

Mannerism, in the latter half of the 16th Century, in which painters such as el Greco, Bruegel and Rubens reacted against the harmony of Renaissance style by mildly distorting the human figure and exaggerating colours.

Baroque, of the 17th and early 18th Centuries when, in architecture especially, particularly in Bavaria and Austria, there flowered a highly decorative style embellished by ornate painting. (Rembrandt, Vermeer and Velasquez, three of the greatest artists who ever lived, worked at this time but their work is not representative of the Baroque style.)

Rococo, also of the early 18th Century, when frothy and romantic paintings were done by Watteau and Fragonard in France. In England Gainsborough and Constable achieved brilliant work in a much more restrained style.

Romanticism, in the first half of the 19th Century, a reaction against previous academic styles in which Gericault and Delacriox in France felt free to fanticise, and Turner in England painted pictures which, in their capturing of the visual appearance of atmosphere, were decades ahead of his time.

In the second half of the 19th Century modern art began with the work of the Impressionists such as Manet, Monet, Renoir and Pissarro. There followed the neo-Impressionists, led by Seurat; Art-Nouveau, Beardsley and Burne-Jones; the post-Impressionists, Cezanne, Gauguin and van-Gogh; the Fauves ("beasts") Matisse and Braque, and the Cubists, of which Picasso was the leading exponent. The break away from conventional representation continued with Expressionism (Munch), Surrealism (Dali) and Abstract art (Miro), in which geometric forms, space and colour make a painting something in its own right, no longer tied to a representation of what the artist sees: "freed from the tyranny of the subject", as someone put it.

The camera had arrived by then and with it the ability to make a more accurate representation of people and places than any artist could. Furthermore, conventional painting had, it seemed, reached the limits of perfection: who could emulate Rembrandt and Turner? In order to create something original artists tried to find a new path. Regrettably, in the process the public has lost sight of them in the inexplicable labyrynth into which they have disappeared. Now it is not possible for ordinary mortals to tell whether there is any merit in what they look at. What special skill does the modern artist possess, other than a highly-developed imagination? people ask themselves. Can the man (or woman) draw? A monkey can throw paint at a canvass – and has been known to do so, given the right incentive. (Picasso was much taken with a chimpanzee painting and bought it to hang amongst his own.)

For ease of identity music is grouped in roughly the same blocks as art, though chronologically it has tended to follow a few decades later. Thus there is Medieval music – simple themes played on rather primitive instruments; Renaissance, when composers wrote for the new Italian stringed instruments; Baroque and Rococo, at first repetitive themes played by the less gifted musicians with the better ones doing the difficult bits but later characterised by so-called chamber music, played by small groups of musicians who stress technical virtuosity; Classical, the era of the great symphonies and concertos.

In the beginning music was not an art in itself, it was a background to dancing and chanting. As time passed it developed in time with the invention of new instruments. The oldest one found, a pipe, was played in the Pyrenees eighteen thousand years ago. The Egyptians had flutes and harps, drums and lyres five thousand years ago. The harp was probably invented by a bowman who made his bow-string taut, twanged it, liked the noise it made and added more. In China more than four thousand years ago they had a five-tone scale. The Spanish guitar was invented by the Moors, which means it may be a thousand years old.

The bassoon and oboe of the 16th Century were the first of the wind instruments; the clarinet appeared in 1778 and the flute in

1794. In early 17th Century Italy, unlikely as it seems, it was possible to draw exquisite melody from the instruments of the violin family by dragging hair from a horse's tail across four strips of tightly twisted cat gut. But not in the wrong hands. (Now, sheep's intestines are used.) The piano of 1709 was a great advance on earlier keyboard instruments. The French horn and the cornet date from about 1825, but trumpets were used two hundred years before by the musical, brutal and licentious King Henry VIII. (Who, some think, composed that well-liked English tune Greensleeves.)

It was the Italians who developed the convention of grid notation used in "Western" music today; hence such words as Fortissimo, Piano, Allegro and Finale. In other parts of the world sounds are not conjured forth out of a book but are an individual's interpretation of, and improvisation on, well-known themes, often using instruments which play quarter tones which sound alien to European ears. Voices too, in Arabia, India and the East, stray from the note, trembling on it or swooping around it: the precision which is judged as the mark of excellence to Western ears is not cultivated or desired. Harmony, the playing of compatible notes within a chord, is unknown, since the concept of chords is unknown.

Much early Western choral music was created as a means of glorifying God in Christian monasteries and churches, while by the 14th Century madrigals, unaccompanied secular pieces for several voices, were being sung in Italy. Then towards the end of the 16th Century some musicians in Florence composed pieces in which dialogue was sung by single voices – the first operas, in which drama was combined with music. In the 17th Century opera spread to France and England, flowering in the 18th with the works of Mozart and in the 19th with those of Verdi, Wagner and Puccini.

Until the 18th Century instruments had been grouped in small numbers, each of them clearly identifiable to the listener; then composers began to add oboes, flutes and horns to the normal string section, thus giving massed instruments a "voice" in their own right. Haydn developed this progression enormously, writing 104 symphonies, while Mozart combined the piano with the orchestra to produce the first concertos of significance, a form of music which in time came to be written for other solo instruments, notably the violin. In the 19th Century Beethoven took choral works, symphonies and concertos to heights never achieved before, and some would say, since, though through Brahms the symphonic form developed to the complexities and power of Sibelius and Mahler. 20th Century composers have added new visions and complexities.

As with the visual arts, modern Western composers strain the ear in the same way that modern artists hurt the eye, and for the same reason: in the European eight-tone scale who can hope to climb the heights reached by Mozart, Beethoven or Sibelius? Shostakovich broke away from convention by composing musical pieces which are simultaneously in more than one key, and by using sounds to make an effect rather than a tune. Schoenberg, Berg, Bartok and others have written music using as a basis the twelve semitones of the octave. Technically it may be clever stuff but it does not make for easy listening and as time has passed the sound of modern music has become more and more the property of musicians and less and less a pleasureful pastime for amateurs. Today, musical effects are achieved by using electronic synthesisers which record sounds, "bend" them into different wavelengths and reproduce them in a changed form. Perhaps that will be the Western music of the future, composed not by someone with a genius for creating melody and harmony but by a technician who understands the psychology of how music produces an emotional effect, and the electronic means of achieving it. Ways of producing conventional notes are changing too: by applying the science of acoustics it has become possible to recreate with absolute accuracy the sound produced by the finest grand piano, using a small instrument which links a keyboard to electronic circuits and loudspeakers. And at one-twentieth of the cost.

Everywhere men and women feel the need for music, though why it should satisfy a human want is difficult to explain. The visual arts can be related to experience, and drama to everyday life, but music acts on the emotions through the brain in an inexplicable way. To some people the duets from La Boheme and Der Rosenkavalier are ecstatic, the majesty of a full orchestra totally transcendental. "Musicals" have modernised opera, popularising a story line through voice and instruments. Most "Pop" music has the same rhythm as the beat of the human heart, to which the listener responds, and gyrates at the same tempo. Ascending scales "lift" the listener, sonorous chords create apprehension, semi-tones and discords twinge the nerves. It is all very strange, but a delight to millions of human beings.

Dancing, like opera, combines drama with music and it too was a very early expression of human emotion: elaborately costumed dancers still perform ancient Hindu rituals which originated thousands of years ago; in the European courts of the 16th and 17th Centuries dancers entertained kings and princes, as they did, and do, in the Arabian, Indian and Eastern worlds. Dancing can display anger and sexuality and create terror as well as pity and pathos.

Watching dancers in a detached way, disregarding what we have come to accept as a normal human activity and seeing it as a form of animal behaviour, it seems an extraordinary performance. Hardly any other species twirls and prances and leaps. Those that do are indulging in a mating ritual, which, perhaps, is how human dance originated; a means by which the male could show his virility and the female her sensuality. Later it became over-laid with embellishments and new concepts. Ballroom dancing is a development of the formal, geometric movements executed with exquisite precision by the upper classes in Europe two hundred years ago. Modern popular dancing is a cousin of the negroid, sexually-arousing, hard beat, pulsing gyrations which attended upon marriage or the inception of new life in primitive societies. Ballet, the strictly choreographed, stylised setting of dance to classical music, was born in the 19th Century of Italian and French parents and grew up in Russia. Its supreme physical precision and unearthly grace has raised dancing to an art form high above the earthy folk pastime it once was – and still is, in most parts of the world – and has taken dancers and their audiences in gilded theatres spinning away out of sight of the simplicity of the original idea.

The performance of drama, as well as the writing of it, is also a very ancient pastime. The Greeks started it with the inter-play of words between a speaker and a chorus. Then a second actor was introduced and then, by Sophocles, in the 4th Century BC, a third. Euripides wrote plays which originated in frightening religious rites. In medieval times mummers and mountebanks acted for the entertainment of their audiences. Then came the established theatre of the West – which, for a long time had a conventional form of acts and scenes – and the set-piece,legend-based mimed performances of the East. Now there is a huge industry of play-acting in America, Europe, India and Japan, relayed by cinema and television to millions of stupefied viewers in most parts of the world. In Space more than fifty circling television satellites beam their programmes over our Earth's surface. Cowboys, cops and Cockneys speak in unlikely tongues; Brideshead is revisited from Brussels to Borneo. People watch and listen in order to escape the moment.

The Old Testament of the Bible was the first book of great significance in the world and remains a powerful force to its Judaic and Christian readers. About 700 BC the epic poems the Iliad and the Odyssey were written by the Greek Homer. (Perhaps. Accounts vary as to when he was born and in which of seven different places, but generally these epic tales are thought to have been written by him.) The Greeks thought that poetry was "the voice of a man who had a god to prompt him." Prose literature started as a means of recording history, the first great writer being Herodotus, another Greek who lived from 485 to 425 BC, but from the time that alphabets were invented records began to be kept, on papyrus or parchment (the dried skin of a sheep) or stone. Then in China, two hundred years before Christ lived, paper came into use. When the Chinese attacked Samarkand in 751 AD paper-makers were taken prisoner, from whom the Moslem occupants learned the skills. From there, paper was passed from hand to hand around the Arab world and into Spain, where the Christians took it from the Moors. Where men had a blank sheet of paper some of them felt compelled to write upon it. One of those who did with lasting effect was Dante Alighieri of Florence, in the 13th Century. His Divine Comedy is an elaborate poem written in rhymed Italian verse, but he also wrote in Latin. The 14th Century brought Chaucer in England but not until the 16th was the world to be given the genius of Shakespeare in England, Rabelais in France and Cervantes in Spain. He it was who wrote the first great novel, fiction presenting an interpretation of real life. Imagination had been around for a very long time, flights of fancy, but the conceiving of totally new and unique people and situations out of the recesses of a writer's brain added a new dimension to literature.

In fiction much of what appears on paper is born out of the subconscious, quite involuntarily, before it surfaces in the conscious, formative mind. The novel is a mirror of the author's personality; a work of non-fiction is a presentation of sifted evidence. In recent times writers, like artists and musicians, have found it increasingly difficult to present a coherent picture; the light from the mirror blinds the observer's eye from seeing the shape. For all that in the United Kingdom alone more than four thousand novels are published each year – and that is but a tenth of the total number of books printed. There is a human compulsion to write, and to read.

Novels can be written from a total God-like over-view or as if the writer has become the "I" narrating a story. They may also be narrated by an observer who tells the reader what happened, or they may, less frequently, take the form of letters exchanged between two or more people. There should be an exposition which establishes a situation, a setting in which the characters live, a conflict between some of them and a climax which brings about the resolution of the conflict. Somerset Maugham, who should have known, listed the qualities of a good novel: a widely interesting and enduring theme told coherently with a beginning, a middle and an end; episodes which develop the theme; and believable characters who act as you would expect them to. Above all, the book should be entertaining. If it is not, if it is a labour to read, then it fails. D.H. Lawrence called the novel the bright book of life because it can do more to make a man "tremble" than poetry, philosophy, science or anything else that is written.

Essentially the writing tradition has been a European one, though in the 20th Century there have been exponents in the English-speaking world and a few in distant continents. The English produced great writers in Austen and Fielding, of the 18th Century, and in the Brontes, Dickens, Thackeray and Trollope of the 19th; the French in Balzac, Flaubert and Stendhal and the Russians in Pushkin, Dostoevsky, Tolstoy, Chekhov and Gogol, all in the 19th Century. The Americans had Melville in the 19th and Faulkner, Steinbeck and Hemingway in the 20th. It was the alphabets available to these people which gave them the means to become great; the very act of trying to write in Mandarin, with its eight thousand different characters, or in the convoluted script of Arabic, must prove a considerable obstacle to the pursuit of a train of thought. Perhaps when computer word-processors are developed which automatically convert the spoken word into script Arabic and Chinese authors will suddenly speak volumes.

*

One of the most astonishing things about the artistic process is that so few people have actually contributed to it. Someone has estimated that since Man evolved 75,000 million human beings have lived and died, yet there have only been a few hundred greatly talented artists, composers and writers, of whom only a very small proportion have been women. Why? Why so few altogether, and why such a small number of women?

The answers must surely be found in the right half of the brain, extraordinarily enriched in some people and more so in men than women because of the biology of birth – the addition of that extra testosterone to the male foetus.

It seems as if those who possess very special powers of creativity are born with an unusually highly-developed group of brain cells, a special coordination of the senses. For example, a great painter sees colours with a vividness and truth not seen by other people, sees form and depth with sharper clarity and has the ability to connect his drawing hand to what his eye sees directly, as if the two were joined mechanically, whereas ordinary mortals do not see things in the same way and have great difficulty in making that connection – or cannot do it at all.

Music is mathematically based: notation is, if you like, addition and subtraction, multiplication and division, development and diminution. Harmonics are numbers divided by whole numbers, discords are the numbers split by fractions. Add to that a perception of the senses – a feeling for the passions and poetry of life – and the mathematician becomes, through music, an artist. Musicians are sometimes astoundingly precocious: Mozart entertained the public at the age of six; in the middle of the 20th Century a French girl, Ginette Neveu, played the Mendelsohn Violin Concerto at a concert when she was seven. But they would not have done so if their talents had not been recognised and encouraged. Thousands of potentially brilliant artists must have lived and died without even beginning to know that they had the inherent ability to develop greatness simply because they never had the opportunity to utilise their skill. (Just as there must have been many world-beating sportsmen and women who never ran faster than anyone else or jumped higher.)

But talent in a special sphere does not mean that the gifted person is one for all seasons. An artist may be dull at mathematics, a sculptor tone deaf, a scientist oblivious to the finest craftsmanship.

There is one other thing. For a reason which is, no doubt, associated with the exceptional development of special sections of the brain and an awareness of its rarity, great artists are very conscious of their talents and feel compelled to utilise them to the full, regardless of the consequences to them or to anyone else. Until the day they die many of them feel they must not squander their gifts. Some, it seems, believe that even beyond death they will be able to continue their work.

Beethoven, who was totally deaf for much of his composing life, during which time he wrote sublime music, said as he was dying "I shall hear in heaven."

His fists were clenched at the time. Perhaps it was an order, which would be quite in character, and not a statement of belief.

*

## CHAPTER SEVEN

# WAR

In any conflict an obstacle must be destroyed in order to achieve success. The obstacle will usually be a physical one or it may only be the opposer's determination to continue to obstruct but when the confrontation has ended one side will no longer be able to present an obstacle – be it a sword-arm, a fortress, an army or significant mental resistance – to the other's intentions.

In the beginning, wars were contests between small tribal groups in which the threat was obvious and real and so was the need for group solidarity. When groups became nations the threat was less personal, and sometimes fabricated by the leader for reasons of his own, such as personal aggrandisement. At their most complex, wars have been on a global scale between millions of people who found themselves committed to fight because of their nationality, because of their willingness to believe what they were told by their leaders and because of social pressures: they were persuaded that their lives or ideals were in peril and were intimidated by the thought that their fellow citizens would despise them if they did not support the nation, even though as individuals their wellbeing was almost certainly more threatened by war than it was by the continuation of peace; as to the threat, it only became real when people put on uniform.

Naval warfare began in furtherance of trade and conquest. Conquest could be motivated by the urge to extend power but was usually motivated by trade: at its simplest the exchange of goods which were in abundance on one side for things that were rare on the other: for example, in times past, spices grown in hot parts of the world for metal products forged in the cold; in modern times the sale of manufactured goods in exchange for oil vital to the life of a nation.

Navies had four functions: to make the seas safe for the passage of their own nation's trading ships; to pillage foreign coasts; to establish a foothold for land forces and/or immigration; generally to dominate the oceans in order to allow the continuation or expansion of trade. Thus the Phoenicians, the Greeks and the Romans fought sea battles in the Mediterranean in order to ensure their continued supremacy in the Middle Sea; the western European nations – the English, the Dutch, the Spanish and the French – fought for power over the others during the years of exploration and empire building. In the 19th Century the British in particular created an enormous navy in order to safeguard and further their global expansion. Today, the advanced nations, East and West, make move and counter-move in order to ensure their interests in a world where all nations have to be interdependent in order to support their complicated societies or growing populations.

Ships and weaponry advanced in size and power with the progress of invention: from the men-propelled, triple-tiered galleys of Rome to the four-decker sailing ships of the line of the 19th Century to the steam-driven Ironclads and battleships of the 20th; from the sling-propelled projectiles of the Middle Ages to the gunpowder-driven iron balls of the 16th Century to the rocket-propelled missiles of the 20th. However, naval warfare has seldom been a deciding factor in conflicts between nations. The destruction of fleets has sometimes curbed a nation's expansion into overseas territories but usually land forces have decided the outcome. The Spanish Armada was destroyed by the winds of nature and not by men; Trafalgar put paid to Napoleon's megalomaniacal dreams of world conquest but it was Waterloo which ended his domination of Europe; Jutland, the ironclad British/German clash of the Great War, was inconclusive, and in the Second World War only the destruction of most of the Japanese fleet in the Pacific during one engagement could be said to have started to turn the tide in the war between America and the Oriental conquistadores.

Similarly, air warfare, new in this century, has not, of itself, greatly influenced events. Before the Second World War politicians, soldiers and people quailed at the thought of whole cities being destroyed from the air, and airmen were sure that ships, men and armoured vehicles would be so vulnerable to assault from above that sea and land warfare would cease to be the dominant factors they had been. But between 1939 and 1945 these theories proved to be wrong: cities were gutted but their citizens continued to resist; ships were sunk but fleets got through; soldiers were pounded but enough of them survived. Today, fleets are vulnerable to air attack unless protected by other aircraft or by anti-aïrcraft missiles and guns – as was recently demonstrated in the Falklands War of 1982 – and with the development of ever more sophisticated air-delivered warheads which can saturate soldiers and armoured vehicles with lethal fire land forces can be badly scarred from the air. Also the value of air power has become increasingly important because it is one means of delivering atomic weapons of mass destruction. Nevertheless, direct physical confrontation between males on land has been, and remains, at the heart of warfare.

Factors which have affected armed conflict since time began are glory, acquisition, weaponry, protection, organisation and support.

Glory is pride, in personal or group achievement, and renown, as judged by those whose good opinion is valued. In all armies glory has been, and is, rewarded – by praise, promotion, or the conferring of medals. Such awards nourish pride and when an army is in the ascendant help to create high morale; when it is not, they are meaningless tokens, except perhaps to the individual. There is no glory in defeat.

Acquisitiveness is motivated by pride, greed or need – for food, resources, dominance. With the passage of time these needs have tended to fade in that order, until today confrontation is caused primarily by opposing ideologies, political or religious. (Though disputed control over the energy resources vital to the continued existence of a sophisticated society would still be a valid reason for resorting to the use of force.) The greed of the leader for personal power or acclaim has often been the motivation for war but where a nation has a democratically elected government such excesses are more likely to be held in check. Sometimes personal political survival may depend on national pride, and may compel the leader to resort to war.

The long contest between protection and projectile has always been the underlying cause of changes in weaponry. Bronze, made by mixing copper and tin, was a step forward from stone, and iron from that. Brass (copper and zinc) was used to make cannons a few hundred years ago. Steel, which is iron hardened by carbon atoms, was made by mistake as a by-product of the manufacture of iron for centuries, but mass-production methods were not available until 1856. Gunpowder, a mixture of Sulphur, Carbon and Nitrate, is said to have been invented by the Chinese long before it was first used by the English against the French at the battle of Crecy in 1342. "Greek Fire", a crude-oil (or naptha) and Sulphur mixture, was used by them and by the Romans, the Byzantines and the Crusaders, and was a forerunner of modern napalm, which is an oil-based flammable agent dropped by aircraft. The manufacture of Nitro-glycerine-based explosives was pioneered by a Swede named Nobel – who later originated the annual prizegiving for, amongst other things, the furtherance of world peace, perhaps because of conscience. Tri-Nitro Toluene is one of many detonating chemical compositions which have accounted for the lives of millions of people. In the 1914-1918 war chemical weapons were used: mustard gas which burnt the skin and lungs, Phosgene which choked a man to death. During the 1939-1945 war man progressed, and developed nerve gases which paralyse, but chemical attack was not used by either side for fear of retaliation. Since then bacteriological warfare has become a possibility; the viruses or bacteria which cause such things as anthrax or bubonic plague have been bottled for delivery. (It is said that Russian scientists are trying to blend cobra venom with bacteria to produce a new genetic strain of killer chemical.) But nuclear fission, which brought us the atomic bomb, is in a class of its own when it comes to breeding death. Nobody will need to use bacteriological warfare when nuclear weapons can do the job much more effectively.

Spears and swords were used for five and a half thousand years at least, and bows and arrows for longer than that. The cross-bow, wound up mechanically so as to put considerable tension on the bow string before it was released, projected a bolt 150 yards in the 12th Century but the long bow, of Welsh origin, could send an arrow fifty yards further a hundred years later – and through a plank of wood three inches thick. The match-lock hand-held gun was a triumph of modern technology in 1500 AD but was surpassed by the flint-lock two hundred years on. (The latter was set off by a spark, the former by a flame.) Leonardo da Vinci is credited with having conceived the idea of the hand gun, the pistol, but it did not come to much until a Mr Colt in the United States, in 1835, made one with a revolving chamber which rotated one bullet after another in front of the firing pin. Starting in 1851 Herr Krupp, of Essen, did a lot for the gun: round stones were no longer slowly projected out of dust-bin-like iron buckets; instead, exploding high-velocity "shells" were fired out of steel barrels which had grooves cut on the inside of the tube to impart a spin to the projectile and keep it stable in flight. The distance at which a man could engage his enemy increased from fifty yards with a short bow through 2,000 yards with a heavy cannon in the 16th Century to 25,000 yards with heavy artillery in the 20th. Inter-continental rocket-propelled missiles can now deliver the arrow-point thousands of miles away from the trigger finger with an accuracy of about thirty metres.

The first protection was a leather jacket but by the 11th Century chain-mail, made of interlocked iron rings, was a standard requirement for any self-respecting knight; it covered him from head to foot and if his tenants could afford it he had some made for his horse as well. It took three years hard labour by all the men in a village to earn enough surplus money, after they had meagrely provided for their family, to equip the lord of the manor so that he could go off on a Crusade to the Holy Land. Two or three hundred years later his descendant wore plate armour that was so heavy that if he fell off his horse he lay like a boulder, unable to raise more than a forearm to weakly summon assistance. By then it required a year's labour by twenty-five thousand men to raise the money needed to forge the gold-inlaid armour of a king. Body armour is now made of laminated nylon which can stop a high-velocity bullet at point-blank range. There is no body armour, however, which can prevent a man in close proximity to high-powered explosives, such as those that are put into terrorist bombs, from being blown to shreds and tatters. The ultimate in mobile protection for the vulnerable flesh of a soldier is the armoured vehicle, a British invention first used in the battle of Cambrai in France in 1916.

Earth ramparts were the first fortifications. The ancient Britons raised them and today Offa's Dyke, made in the 8th Century to keep the original natives from coming back out of Wales into England, can still be traced along much of its length from the coast in North Wales down to the River Severn. The Romans built ramparts too. It must have been one of the least welcome tasks for a legionaire on foreign service to supervise the work of the stunted, skinny, dirty, impressed labourers who were made to slave for years on end constructing, with brittle iron spades and rickety wicker baskets, fortifications built up from thousands of tons of soil. (But more welcome than belonging to the Legion which marched with pride and strength into Scotland and completely vanished. No trace of it has ever been found but where on Earth can it have got to?)

When stones were to hand they were raised one on top of another. Chester was walled by the Romans, and so was Silchester, one now a thriving town in the north of England, the other a crumbling, overgrown ruin in the south. The Romans also bisected the north of England with a wall to ensure that the barbaric way of life of the Scots was kept at a distance. The Crusaders learnt a lot from the Saracens (the name they gave to all the Middle Easterners they encountered) and raised the art of fortification to new heights. Le Crac des Chevaliers, the Castle of the Knights, in what is now Syria, could garrison more than four thousand soldiers and a thousand horses. It was never breached but was given up by the Knights Hospitaller – soldier monks of the Order of Saint John of Jerusalem – because they were tricked by the Turks – originally Chinese people from a tribe called the T'u Kue who had migrated west in the 11th Century. Strongpoints in Europe dominated the area for miles around and for centuries were the bases from which the feudal lord, and his sons after him, conducted their local skirmishes.

The Great Wall of China is the biggest-ever monument to the concept of raising a physical barrier to an enemy. Its construction was started on the orders of the emperor who founded the Ch'in dynasty more than two hundred years Before Christ and continued in the Ming Dynasty (1368-1644). The wall goes on and on for 2,700 kilometres, is around nine metres thick at its base and between nine and twelve metres high. As well as being a barrier, its top was a roadway along which soldiers could patrol, or march to reinforce places which were being attacked by barbarians from Mongolia and Central Asia. But gunpowder put an end to the eminence of stone fortification during the warfare of the Middle Ages: cannons blasted holes through walls. (The Great Wall of China is the only man-made object that can be seen on Earth from a spaceship.)

As armies grew in size it became necessary to create organisations which could control them; in other words, to delegate command and control from the top down to lower levels. The Roman legion consisted of ten cohorts, each of six centuries (commanded by a Centurion, as you would expect, but strangely enough having less than a hundred men in them): in total between four and five thousand soldiers, so well-trained that cohorts could leap-frog through one another in the heat of battle and so keep fresh troops in hand-to-hand contact with the enemy. The Khan's Mongols were in "toumans" of ten thousand, which were divided into ten battalions of a thousand, each of which had ten troops of ten men – not so well trained as the Romans but making up in numbers and ferocity for what they lacked in military knowledge. (In today's British infantry battalion, which has four companies of four platoons, there are about 800 men.) In the Holy Land, during the hundred years when crusading Europeans established a kingdom there, the Knights Hospitaller were commanded by their Master, under whom was the Preceptor – his deputy – , the Constable, who was the fighting leader, the Drapier, who was responsible for equipment, the Master Esquire, in charge of the horses, and the

Turcopolier, who commanded the locally-enlisted levies. Each troop was led by a knight, who had a number of sergeants in charge of the men-at- arms. At the right hand of the Master, and of each Castellan in command of the many Hospitaller castles such as Le Crac des Chevaliers, was a Treasurer, who held the purse strings. Things have not changed much: today an infantry battalion has a commanding officer, a second-in-command, Company commanders, a Quartermaster, a Mechanical Transport Officer, a Regimental Sergeant Major, subalterns, sergeants and a paymaster.

Arms, armour and organisation are the body of any army, Fire and Movement the two elements which bring it to life. Put another way, soldiers aim to strike at the enemy with their weapons and kill him – or at least make him keep his head down until they get close enough to do so. At the end of the day there has to be face-to-face contact between individuals, and at the end of the battle the land formerly held by one side must be possessed by the other. Occupation and control of the nation should be the outcome of the campaign, only achieved by destruction of the enemy army (or its will to fight) and the transfer of power from the defeated leaders to the occupying force.

In the earliest battles a group of warriors engaged their enemies while another group moved to outflank them and attack from a less-well-defended point. When the saddle came into use in France in 100 AD – Gaul, as it then was – men were able to stay on horseback while using their weapons: cavalry had arrived, could move faster than foot soldiers and spurred the development of new tactics and weapons. In the Middle Ages horsemen were masters of the battlefield and often decided the outcome of the contest, riding down and scattering the infantry – though it did not work at Agincourt, where, in 1415, a few hundred English bowmen slaughtered thousands of French knights as they rode forward into a narrowing funnel formed by forests on each side and foundered ten deep under plunging hooves and arrows.

By the beginning of the 19th Century cavalry were very vulnerable to the rapid fire which could be directed at them. They did not do much at Waterloo or in the Crimea, where bravery could not deflect bullets, and they met their end in the American Civil War when the Gattling guns spat streams of lead which mowed down men and their mounts. (That conflict was the first truly modern war, when weaponry took over the battlefield from men.) At the beginning of the 20th Century cavalry could not face massed weapons firing bullets which travelled thousands of feet per second: on the Western Front horsed regiments waited for years for the big break-through which never came. Then the tank took over as the mobile weapon carrier, which also provides its occupants with body armour. But the basic principle of fire and movement has remained unchanged.

At the lowest level a section of infantry fires at the enemy while another section moves closer; it then "puts down fire" while the first moves, and so on until the attackers are close enough to go in with the bayonet. *En masse*, the enemy is saturated with artillery and aerial bombardment while the battalions move in for the kill. Today, the theory is that nuclear weapons would be exploded where the enemy has concentrated, thus neutralising his firepower and permitting movement and manoeuvre around him on the battlefield.

Providing support for the soldier – feeding and clothing him, patching up his wounds, replacing his broken equipment and providing him with enough ammunition and transport – has always been a problem. Alexander the Great got it right two thousand three hundred years ago but as recently as 1854, in the Crimea, the British got it scandalously wrong, even though Marlborough had shown them how to do it a hundred and fifty years earlier. However, requirements vary considerably, depending on the nature of the soldier. The Khan's cavalry could subsist on the milk of the mares they rode; every horseman had eighteen mounts. Now, the stoic Eastern races, unused to much and expecting even less when they go to war, can get by for a long time on a small bag of rice and a stolen chicken or two, whereas the enlisted man from the West begins to fret if his rations get monotonous.

With the increasing complexity of warfare the difficulties have become greater. The tens of thousands who set off on the Crusades in the 11th Century, the barbarian hordes who swarmed out of central Asia in the 12th and 13th, the Tartars who fought the Mongols and Russians in the 14th Century, the Spaniards who evicted the Moors from Spain in the 15th, the Turks who took on all their neighbours in the 16th Century, the European Christians who devoutly tried to kill each other in the 17th all picked the land clean as they went, murdering the population if they tried to prevent them. But that is no longer enough: today, on the computer-controlled battlefield swarming with petroleum drinking vehicles which lurch and roar under a sky full of aircraft, shells and missiles, the effort needed to maintain combat is enormous. The rate at which equipment is destroyed and munitions used in present-day warfare is such that the resources allocated to the support of a force must be a considerable proportion of the whole package: for every two or three men firing a missile, emptying rifle magazines or kicking and cursing a broken tank track there must be one at hand to give them another or mend it. The cost of it all is gigantic, and increasing far more quickly than nations can make the money they think they need to spend on armaments.

*

Man's history is a long catalogue of wars. In many parts of the world a state of war has, for decades and even generations, been the normal background to life, and peace an interval between conflicts. At every moment someone, somewhere has been killing other human beings.

A great many of the battles fought before the 19th Century had no significant effect on events in the long run, thus proving the old cliché that war is futile. But it was not always so. In days gone by technology could overwhelm the minds of primitive people: Cortez demolished the Aztecs with four hundred iron-clad men and a few small cannons; Pissaro beat a million Incas with a company of musketeers and a horse or two. Today, even the most primitive African or American is armed with highly sophisticated weapons – which to the world powers who have supplied them are obsolete and superseded. War is being fought on two levels: in the mind by the "advanced nations", who are designing ever more complicated and costly killing aids, which cannot be used for fear of the consquences, and on the ground by bands of badly trained but well indoctrinated illiterates. Technology does not overwhelm their minds but often the skill to keep it functioning is far beyond them.

Academies for the training of army officers were founded in Britain in 1802, in France in 1808 and in Prussia in 1810. More often than not their students were taught how to fight the next war with the last one's weapons and tactics, but nevertheless these three wealthy, proud and industrially strong nations started to produce educated professional soldiers. The Prussians took it more seriously than the others. In 1870 half a million of them invaded France, encircled Belfort, Strasbourg, Sedan and Paris and reached the Channel ports. The atrocities committed against each other by citizens of two of the most civilised nations in the world formed enduring hatreds which were to have incalculable consequences for the whole world in the first half of the 20th Century.

*

## CHAPTER EIGHT

# CARNAGE

If you buy maps of Belgium and France printed for the British Commonwealth War Graves Commission you can easily trace the Western Front from Ypres to St. Quentin. Nearly all of the hundreds of mauve dots on the maps mark the location of a Great War British cemetery. The others contain the graves of soldiers of the second British Expeditionary Force which went back to France twenty-one years later.

The cemeteries of the Great War, so beautifully laid out, are sited where the battalion Medical Aid Posts used to be. There the wounded were brought. Some died and they, and the bodies carried back from the trenches, were buried there. Eventually the whole ghastly mess was tidied up, walled and graced by a tall stone cross with a steel sword inverted on its face.

Some of the cemeteries are small, no bigger than a rose garden, and contain the bodies of a few friends ("pals", they were called then) who enlisted with a smile, trained together and died a grim death together. Others are gigantic: at Tyne Cot thirty thousand men lie on the slope; they came from the United Kingdom and from Australia, Canada, China, India and New Zealand – and many other places. If you take the road West from Arras you will pass a German cemetery. In it are the bodies of more than fifty thousand young men who died for their fatherland; and there you can find a stone monument on which is carved the words, "I had a comrade: no better ever was."

If you go on south from St. Quentin you will be able to follow French front-line cemeteries all the way to the Swiss border. On the way you will pass Verdun, where Man made hell on Earth; more than half a million Frenchmen and Germans died beside the road from Luxembourg to Paris.

From Paschendael, north-east of Ypres, all the way to Switzerland there are thousands and thousands of bodies, or bits of them, under turf or concrete. They have no grave. Some of the headstones in British cemeteries bear the inscription: "A soldier of the Great War", and no other mark. On some of the graves whose occupant is known there is an additional small marble plaque put there by a mother or wife or sweetheart on which is carved a message for the rain to wash: "To Peter, with Love" – or it may be John or Bill or Jack. In other places there were, for many, many years, until time took away the loved ones, tattered, wind-blown black ribbons on which were the faded names Pierre, Hans, Wilhelm or Ivan. Unending butchery it was, nothing less. Like cattle to the abattoir they went. Why?

Soon after the turn of the century the Russians – who by then were a great European power with an army of three and a half million men and control over Finland, the Baltic States, the Caucasus, the Ukraine and half of Poland (including Warsaw) – were ignominiously defeated on their Far Eastern frontier by the Japanese, who had suddenly and quickly changed their introverted way of life. They had bought warships from Britain and had their sailors trained by the Royal Navy and they used their knowledge to sink Russian ships, also built in Britain. On the mainland they assaulted and beat Russian soldiers. The Russians were humiliated and Asians, astounded, were delighted to find that the white man who had swarmed all over the world was not invincible.

In 1905, just after the war ended, the Russian Black Sea fleet mutinied – some of the sailors threw their officers into the ship's boilers – and in St Petersburg there was serious rioting: nearly a thousand unarmed people were killed by soldiers as 200,000 workers marched to the Winter Palace to present a petition for improved conditions. There was unrest in many cities and amongst intellectuals deep concern and much division of opinion about the need for reform. Rimsky-Korsakov was sacked from his post in the St Petersburg Conservatoire of Music for siding with his students and Rachmaninov decided to leave it, and Russia, never to return.

The French-speaking Tsar (it was a sign of superior breeding to speak French in St. Petersburg) though under great pressure to do something dithered and did very little. Perhaps he, the Little Father of his nation as the peasants called him, the man who under Russian law was "an autocratic and unlimited ruler", was more interested in gossip about his cousin the Emperor of Germany, who was the nephew of the British king. (Queen Victoria's descendants were scattered throughout the dynasties of Europe.) As for the Tsar's advisers, though recommending some concessions to the people they were more concerned about what was going on in the Balkans, where that melting-pot of races was bubbling with hatreds and jealousies. Meanwhile the ragged Russian proletariat muttered, stamped their feet, blew on their cold hands and waited.

In the first decade of the 20th Century the southern Slavs (Serbs, Croats, Slovenes and Bosnians), who regarded the Tsar as their protector, were carved up between the Turks and the Austro-Hungarian Empire, which ruled them partly from Vienna and partly from Budapest. In 1911, Serbs, Bulgars and Greeks combined to defeat the Turks, and Serbia, long disliked and distrusted in Vienna, emerged from the confusion as the strongest of the Balkan states. Fearing the setting-up of an independent south (yugo) Slav state the Austro-Hungarians threatened to invade Serbia. At this point the consequences began to dawn on some people.

If they did the Russians would support Serbia. Should the Russians attack Austria, Germany would retaliate. The Russians had an alliance with France, who would therefore be obliged to go to war with Germany. France, through the Entente Cordiale of 1904, was allied with Britain, who would be honour-bound to join in. For a time it seemed as if the Austrians would invade Serbia, but at the last moment they drew back from war. Clearly the tangle of alliances, which had been intended to keep a balance of power in Europe, with no single nation able to dominate the rest, had created a highly dangerous situation.

It is deplorable but not in the least surprising that the lessons which could have been learnt from the events of 1911 were totally ignored. Russian statesmen solemnly discussed the threat posed by the aged Hapsburg Emperor, which was better than thinking about the insuperable difficulties of trying to improve the appalling conditions under which most of their population lived. Frenchmen excitedly talked of avenging the Prussian defeat of 1870. The Germans, to intimidate the British and assert themselves overseas, arrogantly continued to build up an unnecessarily large navy, while the British pompously vowed to retain their place as the world's greatest maritime power. There were thirteen million men under arms on the continent of Europe. The bonfire had been built and soaked in paraffin and only needed the hot touch of a match.

On the 28th of June 1914 a nineteen year old Serbian youth shot the heir to the throne of the Austro-Hungarian empire dead and Europe went up in flames.

*

In August 1914 a Russian army which had advanced into East Prussia was decimated at Tannenberg but further south their soldiers inflicted heavy casualties on the Austrians. Because of the vast distances on the Eastern Front neither side could man a continuous trench line, an expedient which was forced on the armies of those days by the effect of machine guns and artillery on exposed infantry, so for two years, large forces manoeuvred around each other: like overweight wrestlers they wheeled and locked and broke away, trying to achieve a decisive result, but by the end of 1916 the Russian army was war weary. At home a particularly harsh winter had led to food shortages: this time when a quarter of a million workers went on strike and rioting started the soldiers refused to fire on the crowds. In March 1917 the Tsar was forced to abdicate and a liberal government was formed. A month later the Bolshevik leader Lenin returned from exile in Switzerland. (Bolsheviks were so named because they had been the majority party at a congress in 1903: there was nothing symbolic of revolution in the title then, though there is now.)

In the West, it was another story. By the end of 1914 modern weaponry had obliged frail human flesh to take refuge in holes in the ground. Not even Neanderthal people had existed like that but for four very long years millions of men who had lived at the peak of civilised development slept, ate and were smashed to bloody pieces in earth burrows. The new weapons which were masters of the battlefield, and temporarily put an end to the age-old concept of fire and movement, worked on the principle of using energy generated by the firing of one bullet to feed the next one into the barrel: a rapid-fire, high-velocity, flat "torch beam" of lead was thus projected from the muzzle and because the gun was pivoted could be swept from side to side, scything down the ranks of infantry who periodically and suicidally appeared in view. It is astounding that they did it time after time, and quite inexplicable to later generations, who tend to sneer at the stupidity of it all. Stupid it was, unbelievably so, but also incredibly heroic. Young men with their whole lives before them threw them away as if they were throwing dry leaves on a bonfire. Why? people wonder.

All history is a sequence: new pictures flash up on the screen, new sounds are heard and attitudes follow one upon another. It is important to understand the times as they were and not judge them by present-day ways of thinking.

In 1914 the people of Europe were locked into a rigid class system which closely resembled that of the Hindu's: centuries of feudalism and bondage followed by monarchy and obedience and then decades of industrialisation and near-slavery had conditioned most people to accept their status in life just as unquestioningly. Also, deep down there was the competitiveness which lies in every male; the wish to prove, to himself and to others, his strength and value. On top of that there was society's acceptance of war as a means of settling disputes, and its adulation of military success. Superimposed on everything was fervid nationalism, which was encouraged by princes, politicians and priests because it reinforced their own position in the state.

The result throughout Europe, on every side of the conflict, was that social groups played their parts in a pre-determined way. The leaders, some able, some not, were mostly drawn from the upper class. (Some, like Haig, the British Commander-in-Chief, thought that they communed with God and were doing His work.) Lower down the scale industrialists and administrators of the middle class sustained the war effort, and benefited financially from the work required of them to do it. But it was their sons who so gallantly led their men into action – the cannon fodder from the lower classes who joined in the carnage because they were intensely patriotic, because they believed their country was in peril and because everyone else was doing the same thing. All classes sacrificed themselves willingly on the battlefields. There were, it seems, very few anywhere, east or west of the Vistula or the Rhine, who did not think that they were acting from the best of motives. Those who did and spoke out were despised, or, if they had experienced the horrors of that war themselves, were said to be shell-shocked.

The battles raged for years while the invention of mechanical things leapt forward faster than it ever had before. Motor vehicles, powered by the internal combustion engine, which had been a rare sight in the first decade of the 20th Century, were soon to be seen in their thousands, transporting generals in staff cars, factory workers in buses and dying men in ambulances. In 1915 soldiers in the trenches looked up in wonder at the sight of aviators chasing each other round the sky in rickety biplanes or triplanes trying to get close enough to shoot one another with a pistol; but very soon someone invented a way to ensure that bullets fired from a machine gun went between the blades of the propellor as it rotated: 'planes were ripped out of the sky and fluttered, blazing, to earth. By 1916 petrol engines had been clad in armour and the first "tanks" lumbered on to the battle-field, but too late to break through the fortress lines in any strength. Throughout the war submarines became bigger and bigger and more and more were made until the Unterseeboot became a serious menace to British ships in the Atlantic. As for guns and their ammunition, the developments were fantastic.

At Verdun in 1916 the German Crown Prince attacked the forts which guarded the route to Paris. Fourteen hundred guns had been brought there, with two and a half million rounds of ammunition, in the belief that by striking at a key point the French would feel compelled to defend it at all costs; their soldiers would be drawn into a great artillery killing ground and in time their army, bled white, would surrender. The German appraisal was right up to a point – the French did defend the place at all costs and Verdun became a slaughterhouse – but they did not surrender. With the slogan "They shall not Pass" drummed into their ears French divisions trudged up the one and only road to Verdun night after night and vanished into the frightful morass: and on the other side of the hill the Germans did the same. In less than five months in an area sixteen kilometres by twelve nearly a million men were killed or wounded. (Petain was the French commander and lieutenant colonel de Gaulle was one of his officers.)

Further north, in an attempt to relieve the pressure on the French Army, the British launched an attack in the area of the River Somme on the First of July 1916 and in that one day recorded 57,470 casualties. It was a beautiful summer morning when the young men climbed out of their trenches, walked forward and crashed to the ground dead or dying as larks sang in the sky above them – despite the fact the shells from fifteen hundred guns were screeching through the air. In the autumn of 1917 at Paschendael the scene was very different; for many months wounded men drowned in a man-made marsh of slimy mud, and at Caporetto, in three weeks, the Italians, on the side of the Allies, lost nearly 300,000 men during an onslaught by German and Austro-Hungarian soldiers. By then the Americans had joined in the conflict. Though at first they contributed very little their presence was a weighty factor, carrying as it did the promise that eventually, when they had fully mobilised, two million men would join the first contingent. In 1918 the Germans made a last convulsive effort to defeat the Allied forces but were counter-attacked and started to withdraw.

Though the German army was not broken some soldier's councils had been formed, and at home communist workers had started to agitate and strike. The nation which had created the biggest army and had more of its soldiers killed than any other had had enough. In November the guns, at last, were silent. And so too were at least thirteen million people who had been alive in 1914.

At the height of the conflict 64 million men had been at war. The British Empire had nearly ten million under arms, of whom 947,023 died. The French put fewer men into uniform but more were killed: 1,375,000, one-tenth of their male population. 115,660 Americans died in an argument that was not of their making and Russia suffered a total of nearly seven million casualties, killed and wounded, but it was the Germans who mourned the most: hundreds of thousands of their soldiers were maimed for life and a million eight hundred thousand of them never came home at all.

One who did was Corporal Adolf Hitler, an Austrian who had been a battalion "runner" (he delivered messages from his battalion headquarters), had been at the Somme, at Ypres and at the battle of Arras, had been wounded twice and twice awarded the Iron Cross for bravery. To most German men these were strong commendations.

*

In 1918 the Spanish 'flu ravaged Europe. An estimated eighteen million people died of it: illness could still strike harder than war. There were no antibiotics and many of the stricken died of pneumonia – a peaceful death, so it is said.

In 1918 a new kingdom called Yugoslavia came into existence. The Serbians had got what they wanted but the consequences of the war for the rest of Europe were catastrophic: a whole generation of young men had been eliminated – what they could have contributed to the world from the wealth of their education and talents is quite incalculable – but the gravest lasting effect was that from then on the two great resourceful land masses and populations, the Russian and the American, would unchallengeably become the strongest nations in the world and inevitably divide it into communist and capitalist, East and West. Europeans, who were generally at neither extremity of politics, would no longer be the leaders in the march of time.

In Russia the war had made the lives of the people worse than ever. Millions of skilled factory and agricultural workers had been drafted into the army without regard to the consequences: industrial output declined and there were serious food shortages. The German blockade of the Baltic, and the closure of the Black Sea exit to the Mediterranean by the Turks, had cut Russian trade outlets and prevented them from importing vital raw materials. Two million disgruntled soldiers had deserted and found their way home. As Lenin put it, they had voted with their feet. There was no effective political direction and the nation was in chaos.

Such a situation could not continue. In February 1917 a Soviet – a people's council – was set up in Petrograd, formerly St Petersburg, and very quickly 600 other Russian towns and cities formed their own. In the countryside peasants took over the large estates and started to burn down the landowners' houses. "All power to the Soviets" replaced Liberty, Equality, Fraternity as the rallying cry of the 20th Century revolutionaries as they surged here and there not knowing quite what they wanted or which of their leaders they were following. In October 1917 Lenin decided for them, and in 1918 started to negotiate peace with the Germans, who were determined to impose harsh penalties. With their army disintegrating and the Germans advancing against no opposition the Russians were obliged to accept the loss of a quarter of their territory, including the great food factory of the Ukraine.

The next three or four years were ones of enormous turmoil. The Red Army, born out of the rebellious elements of the old Imperial army, fought the White Army, the remnants of it who were anti-Bolshevik, and French, English and American forces who had landed at Odessa, Murmansk and Vladivostok in an attempt to snuff out the rebellion and bring Russia back into the war. When that ended they became disinterested and went home: and left behind them a deep distrust of those nations in the minds of the men who were to rule the new heaven-on-earth.

It was not until 1922 that the central government established control over the whole vast territory of Mother Russia and soon after they did the population discovered that nothing had changed: under different labels the old traditional Tsarist system of centrally-directed autocratic rule enforced by secret police was retained, controlled instead by the Central Committee of the Communist Party, which was taken over by Stalin three years after Lenin's death.

Stalin was an Asiatic from Georgia, not a European. Inscrutable, ruthless, self-centred and ambitious, and in his later years quite mad, he progressively eliminated his rivals and tightened his grip on the nation. The idealism which had inspired the proletarian revolution expired in the death camps of the Gulag archipelago, where millions of Russians who dared to voice its principles were sent to atone with hard labour for their sins. It is not known exactly how many – though it may be a closely-guarded secret in the Kremlin archives – but an estimated twenty million of them lie in the frozen ground of Siberia.

Idealism was trying to work in Europe too. France proposed a scheme for the creation of a new state which would be a buffer between it and Germany, but agreed not to pursue the plan if French security could be guaranteed by the League of Nations, an organisation proposed by the American President which would work to prevent the recurrence of international conflicts. Countries which had signed the peace treaty became the founder members, thus excluding Germany. (Ironically, America itself did not become a member due to the refusal of the United States Senate to confirm the terms of the treaty.) Germany became a member in 1926 and Russia in 1934, but by that time the League had shown itself to be ineffective. It had no peace-keeping force of its own and economic sanctions, when they were applied, proved to be no deterrent to what was being done by nations in defiance of the League's rules. (It lived on until 1946, providing employment to a fortunate body of international civil servants and convincingly demonstrating that some organisations can be totally self-generating, needing no external stimuli to justify their continued existence.)

In the fifty years before the Great War, while European empires were being established, international trade flourished and the United Kingdom, because of its lead in the industrial revolution, its maritime supremacy and its world-wide interests, became the world's banker. During the war Britain had lent enormous sums of money to its allies but had also borrowed (half as much) from the United States. With nations shattered by the conflict and trade disrupted Britain proposed that all war debts should be cancelled but the Americans would not agree. Not only had the great powers of Europe been bled white on the battlefield, they had been financially gutted as well, as a result of which the hub of world trade and banking shifted across the Atlantic to the only nation which was still economically strong. But that situation was not to last. In 1929 the American stock-market collapsed and a deeper worldwide financial crisis developed, to some extent because the unpaid national debts were interlocked.

America's troubles were partly caused by the fact that immigration from Europe had almost ceased due to the manpower losses nations had suffered: for a few years after the war poor people were able to stay where they were and find work whereas for decades before it many had been obliged to leave their homelands or starve. (The Irish were an example; the famine of the late 1840s, which was due to a blighted potato crop, forced a million and a half of them to travel across the Atlantic in appalling conditions to find a new and better life.) Between 1860 and 1910 the population of the United States doubled but after 1918, when they badly needed more people to expand industrial production, few came. Also the European requirement for food dropped – there were fewer mouths to feed and no money with which to buy it – as a result of which American growers over-produced. Sadly,the signs were ignored. America was booming, people said. It must be, just look at the stock market: never before had there been so many financial transactions. Then a sudden crisis of confidence led to panic on Wall Street. Stocks and shares valued at $30billion were sold and the whole system collapsed. Thousands of firms went bankrupt and twelve million men lost their jobs.

Because the dollar had replaced sterling as the base unit of currency European money values plunged and tens of millions of unemployed workers joined the limbless ex-servicemen who begged on street corners. In Germany their plight added to the bitterness people felt about the outcome of the war. The scapegoats blamed for the situation were, as so often before in history, the Jews. (A scapegoat was, in Biblical terms, a tethered goat on to which, once a year, the Jewish High-priest symbolically laid the sins of the people before it was allowed to escape, and carry their transgressions away from them into the wilderness.) As the Nazi Party, led by the charismatic corporal, began to take over the country some fortunate Jews managed to escape, but not many.

Hitler exploited, to an extent never achieved by anyone else, the human wish to worship. Using total control of the mass media he fed the Germans with virulent propaganda which inspired hatred of the Jews, who were alleged to control all the key centres of finance and to be internationally linked, of Communists, who were blamed for the defeat of the nation, and of all non-Aryan people, who were branded as sub-standard human beings. (Jews and gypsies were sub-human, and very soon were physically branded like stock animals.) Having produced a large measure of unity by focussing people's resentment on selected targets Hitler then created the symbols through which national pride could be directed to him alone: slogans, banners, bands, badges and uniforms. As the armed forces were enlarged officers were required to take a personal oath of loyalty to The Leader. The armaments industry was rapidly expanded, financed by wealthy anti-communist Germans, and unemployment decreased. Krupp built a castle while at brilliantly stage-managed mass rallies, filmed and shown to overwhelmed, suddenly proud people all over the Reich, the newly conceived Master-race roared its message to the world as the little manic Austrian strutted, screamed and preened himself. It was astonishing; and even, to some people outside Germany, laughable.

It was in Italy that Benito Mussolini had shown Hitler how to do it. Accusing the Roman Catholic church of opposing a new liberal government and emphasising the bad economic situation, political corruption, and the need for Italy to have an empire into which it could expand – it had been left behind in the European rush for overseas territories – he, in 1922, at the age of thirty-nine, had formed an administration. His Party was called the Fasci, after the bundle of rods which was the Roman symbol for justice. In the 1930s Fascism became synonymous with racialist, totalitarian militarism controlled by Hitler and Mussolini, but though the French started to re-arm and hastened to complete the chain of fortresses they were building along their eastern border the League of Nations did nothing, despite the fact that, theoretically, it had the authority to prevent German re-armament.

In 1932 President Roosevelt instituted a programme of recovery and by the late-'30s the United States was again its buoyant self. In the intervening years some aspects of American life which were reprehensible had, because they were entertaining, become the basis for many of the dramas produced by the expanding film industry. As Hitler and the SS – the strong-arm of the Nazi faith – put on a real-life show of a similar kind people all over the world, but particularly in America and Europe, sought escape from their problems by watching hoodlums shooting policemen and cowboys slaughtering Red Indians. Violence had always been part of the battle for existence in the self-styled home of the brave but thanks to the cinema now became an admirable part of folk lore. Men, women and children gazed pop-eyed at a multitude of instant, bloodless, painless and meaning-less deaths while popcorn or silver-paper crackled and tongues lapped icecream. For whole generations of people in many parts of the world Hollywood's money-making make-believe portrayal of life became a misleading and confusing vision of how things really were: the world could be simply divided into the good, the bad and the beautiful, violence was fun, money counted, love was sexless, bliss was everlasting, kids were cute and there was always a happy ending.

*

The Spanish civil war which started in 1936 became a focus for political ideals which, in Europe, were polarising Left and Right, though its basic cause was parochial: should there be a monarch, who represented tradition, the Church and the army, or could the antiquated, poverty-stricken way of life of the people be improved by a more democratic system? The Nationalists under General Franco were supported by the Right-wing Falange party and by Hitler and Mussolini, and the Republicans, identified with the proletarian struggle, were reinforced by an International Brigade of forty thousand socialists from fifty different countries and assisted by Russia. More than half a million Spaniards died in yet another example of a needless bloody conflict fiercely, bravely and stubbornly contested by both sides. It was a rehearsal for the far more devastating confrontation that began soon after the Spaniards collapsed exhausted on to the rubble of their cities, leaving the nation under Franco's dictatorship.

During the 1930s an industrialised and militant Japanese nation increased its domination of the Far East and by 1939 had occupied Korea, Manchuria, Taiwan and most of China: once again, as in Roman and medieval times, organisation and soldiers brought power over far larger numbers of people who had neither. (In 1938 the Japanese had even fought another short but bloody war with the Russians.) The French in Indo-China, the Dutch in Indonesia, the Portugese in Macao and the British in Hong Kong, Singapore, Malaya and Burma were concerned, but at home it was Germany that was the focus of real anxiety.

Years of mass adulation had convinced Hitler, and the German people, that he was unstoppable. World conquest, it seemed, was suddenly within the grasp of one man, one nation. It was intoxicating. Expanding into more "liebensraum", living space, considered rightfully theirs, feeling infallible, the German army first took over Austria and then Czechoslovakia.

Poland was next on the list but what about the Russians? They had their problems but the territory taken away from them by the Germans in 1918 had been restored by the Allies in 1919, they had expanded east and south and now controlled one-sixth of the world's land surface. And their manpower potential was vast. To prevent any threat arising from them Hitler, despite his long and brutal anti-Bolshevik crusade, signed a non-aggression pact with Stalin. Mindful of the slaughter of the Great War, and dreading that it could all happen again, the British nevertheless guaranteed to assist the Poles should they be invaded. As in 1914, Britain and France were allies. The peoples of Europe were once more arrayed against one another.

Poland became a nation in the 10th Century but in the 13th was invaded by Tartars in the east and threatened by the Teutonic Knights in the west. (They, like the Templars and the Hospitallers, were one of the military orders founded during the Crusades: Christian monks who took up the sword and became soldiers. Though the power of the Teutonic Knights was reduced in the 15th Century their militaristic, spartan attitudes continued to exert great influence on Prussian thought for generation after generation.) Re-united in the 14th Century Poland expanded, and became one of the most powerful states in Europe: in 1610 Polish troops even occupied Moscow and in 1683 they defeated the Turks besieging Vienna. Then Russia began to retaliate, to be joined in the late 18th Century by the Prussians and the Austrians. For one hundred and twenty five years Poland ceased to exist, carved up between those three states, until in 1918 the American President pledged the Allies to re-create the nation. It took another five years before the contentious issue of its boundaries was resolved and even then the result was unsatisfactory: Poland's only outlet to the sea was to be through a thin corridor of land that separated East Prussia from the rest of Germany – and was inhabited by Germans.

Carried forward on a spate of megalomania, contemptuous of the British and French forces, using the liberation of Germans who lived in the Polish corridor as an excuse, Hitler invaded Poland on the First of September 1939, and on the 3rd Britain and France declared war.

In the West, the United States shied away from being drawn into another European argument. In 1823 President Monroe had proclaimed that America would no longer permit any European power to colonise the Western Hemisphere. Implicit in this doctrine was the message "You stay out of our business and we'll stay out of yours", and for years this attitude had been the basis of American foreign policy. Reluctantly they had been brought into the Great War by prolonged German harassment of Atlantic shipping but the post-war wrangles and the years of depression had reinforced the feeling in many Americans that they should steer well clear of European quarrels. Isolationism was the political label given to this point of view.

In the east, Russia was not prepared for war with anyone. The Marxist dream had foundered on the rocks of human nature: people, unbelievable though it was, would not work as willingly for the community as they would for personal reward. The collectivisation of farms, begun in 1928 soon after Stalin was in full control, had been a total disaster: Muscovite theories did not work in Omsk and Samarkand; clerks in offices did not know how to grow wheat or breed pigs. The peasants killed and ate their pigs and cattle rather than lose personal ownership of them; half the livestock in the nation perished. Kulaks who wanted to own the land denied to them for centuries and opposed collectivisation were deported en masse to Siberia, and millions of those left behind starved. In consequence there were severe food shortages in the towns. Then in 1933, to teach people to be obedient, Stalin had carefully engineered a famine which killed more Ukranians than the Great War had done. During the middle 1930s any senior officers of the armed forces considered to be a threat to him had been shot, and thousands of the officer corps had been despatched to Siberia to join the one-time leaders of the Party and the multitudes of ordinary people who were already there.

Because the agriculture programme was in chaos money was not available to expand industry. But the potential was there:a huge pool of obedient manpower available to generate industrial production and put on uniform, and a vast territory packed, as in America, with natural resources. Hitler's easy conquest of Poland was watched with mixed feelings, which turned to relief as the Wehrmacht and the Luftwaffe faced west and set upon the French, the Belgians, the Dutch and the British Expeditionary Force. It was a breathing space which Stalin, ever distrustful of everyone, used to good effect.

In five weeks, starting in May 1940, the Germans defeated the Allied armies. Striking hard and fast with tanks and divebombing aircraft they outflanked the French Maginot Line and smashed their way to the sea. The British were fortunate to be able to withdraw 330,000 soldiers across the English Channel but the French reeled and capitulated. Marshal Petain, branded a traitor, became the leader of the nation: perhaps the long, dark shadows of Verdun had never left him and he could not bear to see more loss of life. Seeing the triumph of Fascism, Mussolini decided to join in the war.

In December 1941 the Japanese struck the American fleet in Hawaii, at dawn on a Sunday morning out of a clear blue sky. Earlier in the year they had invaded French Indo-China; now, in 1942, in less than six months, they took a whole chain of Pacific islands and Malaya, Singapore (with 75,000 British and Commonwealth prisoners-of-war), the Philippines, the Dutch East Indies, New Guinea, Burma. Reaching the hills of Assam they looked down into India. The days of imperial rule were numbered.

In Berlin Der Fuhrer had not been idle. In April 1941 his army (he was the commander-in-chief) had stormed through the Balkans and two months later it reached out for Russia. In another Blitzkrieg nearly two thousand Russian aircraft were destroyed in two days. By September the Germans were besieging Leningrad – Petrograd, that had been St Petersburg – and in December were in the suburbs of Moscow. But for Hitler, as it had been for Napoleon, that was the beginning of the end. Throughout the winter months the Russians fought back ferociously, at times in temperatures of minus 30 degrees. During 1942, while the Allies were fighting peripheral battles in the Mediterranean and the Pacific, the German army pushed forward in the south but as winter came again the Russians counter-attacked: at the end of January 1943 a hundred thousand Germans surrendered at Stalingrad and in July, at Kursk, where thousands of armoured vehicles incinerated and smashed each other in the biggest tank battle in history, the guts of the German army were torn out of its body. In twelve months it had sustained one and a quarter million casualties. The heart continued to beat but from then on it was only a matter of time.

In June 1944, after a successful campaign which had forced Italy out of the war, an enormous Allied army assaulted what the Germans called Fortress Europa, clawed its way ashore, liberated Paris and Brussels and pushed relentlessly towards the Rhine. By the Spring of 1945 the beleaguered Germans were fighting desperately on two fronts but they deserved, and got, no sympathy. Not only had the Wehrmacht fought a bestial war – especially against the Russians, whom they regarded as no better than animals – the SS were to leave the German nation with a legacy which will forever dishonour its people who lived at that time: the worst act of appalling, cold-blooded, pitiless brutality in all history; the creation of death camps in which millions of frightened human beings, including little children, were despicably abused before starving to death or being made to shuffle, naked, trembling and moaning, into gas chambers. On 30th April 1945, while bombs and shells and ash rained out of the sky, the demented Hitler committed suicide. As the smoke from his burning body mingled with a great black cloud hanging over the ruins of Berlin the Reich which was to have lasted a thousand years writhed convulsively. A week later it expired.

In 1940 the British, inspiringly led by Churchill, had stood alone against Hitler but as in the Great War the Empire gave its moral support and servicemen. From every part of the world troops fought with the Allied forces while the civilian population in England were pounded by German bombers and, later, rockets. For the British there were two decisive battles; in the air in 1940 above the green fields of Kent, where the Luftwaffe wings were shot out of the sky, and, until 1943, when the tide turned, in the grey Atlantic, where U-boats sank thousands of tons of shipping on which the island depended for its life. (Although the Battle of Britain was a turning point the Royal Air Force lost far more men in bombers than in fighters: more than 60,000 aircrew died in the bombing raids on Germany and occupied Europe.)

In the Far East the Japanese had also been fighting a bitter rearguard action against the Chinese, the Americans, the British and the Australians and New Zealanders. Doggedly the Americans fought them off one island after another, inflicting heavy casualties, and at sea, at the battle of Leyte Gulf, sinking most of the Japanese fleet. For seventy-two days they bombarded Iwo Jima before making an amphibious assault: only 212 Japanese surrendered out of a force of more than 20,000. It seemed as if the war would go on forever. Then on 6th August 1945 an atomic bomb was exploded over Hiroshima, to be followed three days later by another above Nagasaki. The Japanese capitulated.

*

The Second World War cost an estimated $12 billion, to say nothing of more than thirty million dead, including seventeen million civilians, of whom fifteen million were Russians. In all they suffered thirty-six million casualties, and Germany more than ten million.

Like the figures in Chapter One these are so great that the mind cannot interpret their value, but as an indicator the war dead and wounded together amounted to the combined populations of the Netherlands, Scandinavia, Switzerland, Austria and Belgium. The amount of destruction and the waste of resources, time and talent was beyond belief. Surely, people said, shaking their heads in sorrow, mankind had learned its lesson.

*

# CHAPTER NINE

# POLITICS

The events which followed the end of the Second World War were of tremendous importance in shaping the world we now live in. More than ever before, decisions made in distant places were to have an effect on people far away; though they might exist as they had in times past, concerned primarily with their own lives and with parochial matters, in the background there was to be, and there remains, the shadow of global conflict; the mushroom cloud beyond the horizon.

It was, of course, naive to think that mankind would learn its lesson from the catastrophe of the war. To ordinary people who celebrated the end of it all by getting drunk and dancing around in Times Square, Red Square, Trafalgar Square or the Place de la Concorde the signing of pieces of paper which formally put an end to the fighting might have seemed of enormous significance, but in fact they were not. In the first place nothing begins or ends at a precise time: all events are a consequence of what has gone before, a complex overlapping of many factors. Secondly, for every person who danced there were many who mourned; who would take with them to their own graves hatred of those who had deprived them, and would pass it on to younger generations. Thirdly, the seeds of the next confrontation were sown even before the war ended by the leaders of the Allied powers. The decisions they took, born out of their national histories and personal attitudes, were to lead to the Cold War of the 1950s, to the progressive polarisation of East and West, to military combat in Eastern Asia and to conflict by proxy, whereby communist and capitalist nations support others with economic or military aid, or both, in order to extend their own influence.

During the war, propaganda had been used by the Western Allies to reverse the attitudes which had previously been encouraged: communists were no longer the enemies who threatened freedom and the capitalist way of life, they were the brave defenders of democracy fighting against the Nazi hordes. A lot of people believed their own propaganda, including, it seems, President Roosevelt, who was instrumental in permitting the Soviet Union, by formal agreement, to exercise control over the nations of Eastern Europe which it would overrun in pursuit of the retreating German army. In so doing, Russia was allowed to exert influence far further to the West than it had ever done before, and to no longer be predominantly an Asiatic power: the whole structure of world politics was changed.

In 1943 Roosevelt, Stalin and Churchill agreed that some Polish territory would be transferred to Russia by moving the Russian and the pre-war German border Westwards; that Germany would be divided into zones to be administered by each of the four great powers – America, Russia, Britain and France – and that Berlin, which would lie in the Soviet-controlled area, would similarly be divided. Then, in 1944, Churchill and Stalin decided that the Balkans should be split into Russian and British spheres of influence: the Slav nations, Bulgaria, Hungary and Romania, were to be regarded as being of special interest to Russia, while Greece and Yugoslavia were not. Lastly, in 1945, all three leaders decided that, pending a final decision about where Poland's western frontier should be, Germany, east of the Oder and Neisse rivers, would be administered by Poland, which, in reality, meant Russia. Also, Russia was to administer the north of Korea, though the Americans were to have the south.

The overwhelming result of these decisions was that by the middle of 1945 the Soviet Union had effectively pushed its western boundary forward to a line only a hundred kilometres from the Danish frontier and the same distance from the Rhine in the centre of the western zone of Germany. They gained control over an enormous area of Europe and a steel wall descended in front of a hundred million people who until then had lived in sovereign nations. To consolidate their position the inner-German border was immediately sealed, communist governments were soon established in those nations, and to ensure that they could keep a strong grip on them the Soviet Union retained an army of three and a half million men. In contrast, the democracies hastily demobilised their forces, ever mindful of the fact that their servicemen have a meaningful vote.

Though the world leaders had taken decisions about the control of Europe in the post-war years they had also given thought to the need to preserve peace in the future. In 1945, in San Francisco, representatives of forty-six nations signed the charter of a new world forum which would replace the discredited League of Nations. Unfortunately they created it in such a way that it, like the peace, was flawed from the very beginning.

The constitution of the United Nations Organisation was based on the supposition that the wartime unity of the four great powers would continue. It crumpled almost immediately. Each of the members of the Security Council, the main task of which is to secure world peace, were given the right to veto – that is, to block – proposals put before it, the theory being that none of them would ever undermine their unity of purpose by using it. It was not to be: in the first ten years of the Councils' existence the Soviet Union vetoed seventy-seven proposals, so completely nullifying the effectiveness of the new organisation.

The reasons for the aggressive Russian attitude towards the West are clear. First, they had twice in thirty years had a terrible hammering, and had no intention of letting the Germans become a strong nation capable of doing it again: the partition of Germany was – and still is, to them – a means of ensuring this. Secondly, there had already been signs that in the West the expedient but sham wartime unity of purpose was being replaced by the pre-war fear of, and antipathy to, communism: on the 8th May 1945, the day the war ended in Europe, the United States stopped giving aid to Russia, and even recalled a convoy then on its way to Murmansk; furthermore, Stalin had been told nothing about the development of the atomic bomb or the decision to use it. Lastly, and most important of all, the Soviet Union has always declared that its long-term aim is to spread communism throughout the world by any means possible, including the use of armed force: this doctrine was recorded in the first programme of the Central Committee of the Communist Party in 1923 and has been repeatedly proclaimed ever since.

The war, fortuitously, with Allied financial and material assistance, had transformed Russia from a disorganised, largely-peasant nation into a highly industrialised power with gigantic potential standing astride much of Europe and casting its shadow over the rest. It was inevitable that America, a democracy politically dedicated to minimum state interference in the economics of supplying demands generated by hard-earned money, and which at its roots is Christian, should clash head-on, if not with the Russian people, with the Soviet system. Isolationists in America, however loudly they shouted, could no longer be heard. Whether they liked it or not the United States was henceforward committed to being a world power.

It was quick to respond to the new situation. When in 1947 Britain announced that it had no money and could no longer continue to prop up the Greeks, the Americans undertook to support free people everywhere who resisted attempted subjugation by armed minorities or by outside pressures. At the root of their concern was the loyalty felt by communists everywhere to the founding-fathers of their ideology: Russia, at that time, led all Marxists. There was a real possibility of a communist take-over in Greece, and in France and Italy too, which was bound to mean that those nations would become puppets of the Soviets. In time democratic freedom might be snuffed out in the whole of Europe. Soon the Marshal Plan was announced, whereby, to raise the standard of living in devastated Europe and avert the threat of a slide to communism, the United States would give material aid and money, which they did with bountiful generosity. Strange to contemplate in these days, the original plan included Russia and the Eastern Bloc nations, but the offer of help was rejected by them.

In 1948 the Soviet Union permitted their zone of Germany to become the German Democratic Republic – and in the same year stopped all road and rail access to West Berlin, which lies 160 kilometres behind the inner-German border: two million people were to be starved into Communism. For eleven months American and British aircraft brought the supplies needed by the besieged Berliners, flying in 13,215 tons of supplies in a single day at the peak of the operation and using 1,383 aircraft to do so. In the face of such determination the blockade was lifted. Meanwhile in Jugoslavia Tito broke away from the central direction of Moscow. Surprisingly, Russia did not take retaliatory action, and by so doing accepted that a new situation existed: for the first time there was an independent communist regime in the world.

In 1949 the West German Federal Republic was created, and, faced with the realities of the physical and mental barriers so swiftly erected by the Russians, so was the North Atlantic Treaty Organisation. In 1954 a Russian application to join NATO was rejected; it was feared that they would block all progress in NATO as they had done in the United Nations Organisation. In 1955 the Russians, jittery about an American pledge to keep troops in Europe for as long as was necessary, retaliated by grouping together the armed forces of the Eastern Bloc – which had been allowed to come into existence in order to enforce communism on the subject nations – under the terms of what was called the Warsaw Pact. As a counter-move, because the East Germans had become part of the Warsaw Pact, the West Germans were invited to re-arm and join NATO.

Step by step, move by move, the two sides acted politically to preserve a European balance of power, the principle that had twice led to havoc, and militarily to create parity. The Russians modernised their air force and their armoured divisions, began to plan a big navy and started to make nuclear and chemical weapons. The West equipped itself for totally mechanised warfare fought in a nuclear environment, while overhead the big birds of the American Strategic Air Command, loaded with atomic bombs, maintained a 365-day vigil. Without them the Russians could have walked across lightly-defended Europe at any time: with such a threat held over them the Russians were even more determined to catch up. The arms race was on.

In the period between 1945 and 1952 more than two million East Germans had crossed the border to the West in order to escape from the repressive regime under which they lived, a damning indictment of the Communist system. When, in March 1953, Stalin died it seemed as if there might be a brightening of the gloom but it was not to be. In June, tens of thousands of people marched through the streets of East Berlin in protest against the raising of industrial "norms" – the amount of production expected from each worker – by the East German government: Russian tanks backed up the para-military police who fired bullets into the crowd, and in the following days imprisoned thousands. In Poland, in 1956, workers mistakenly thought that they could strike for better wages; during rioting forty-four of them were shot down. A few months later, while the West was pre-occupied with problems in the Middle East, the people of Hungary revolted. The mass, anti-Soviet, rising was crushed by Russian tanks, despite Article One of the Warsaw Pact which pledges its members to refrain from the use of force and to settle international disputes by peaceful means. More than twenty thousand Hungarians were killed, their leader was permanently disposed of and 200,000 of them fled into Austria – from which, in 1955, all occupation troops had been withdrawn on the understanding that it would remain neutral. At the height of the battle the Hungarians had desperately appealed to the West for help, but had been ignored.

In 1960 China and Albania broke away from Moscow's leadership, underlining the fact that Russia was no longer the leader of worldwide communist ideology, and injecting another factor into world politics. In 1961, feeling the uncertainties created by this situation, aware of the internal tensions in the Eastern Bloc countries, with East Berlin acting as a floodgate out of which thousands of East Germans poured to begin new lives in the West (in just five days of August another eight thousand people had decided they could bear no more of it and had risked their lives to get away) and with the economy of East Germany in danger of complete collapse, the Soviets built a concrete wall along the East Berlin border – and, as the months passed, a mined and fortified barrier along the entire demarcation line between East and West Germany.

Not to keep their opponents out but to keep their own people in.

*

This complex series of moves and counter-moves had all been done in the name of people who belonged to many nations, and in the name of politics, the social systems by which they are governed.

Politics is defined in one dictionary as the art or science of government. Art is a practical skill guided by principles, and science is knowledge gained by critically-tested experiment so, clearly, politics is neither an art nor a science. It means the many different theoretical ways in which men believe society can best be organised.

By the 1930s various categories of political activity had evolved. At one end of the spectrum, on the extreme Left, was Communism, the complete control of a nation (its resources, its means of production and distribution, and the release of information) by the government, which shades into Socialism – the means of production and distribution under the control of the community through nationally-owned organisations.

At the Centre is Liberalism (moderate social reform) and to the Right is the belief in free enterprise and minimum state interference (Capitalism) which is known by various national labels – Republican, Christian-Democrat, Conservative, etc. To the far right are Fascists, who are violently anti-communist, extremely nationalistic, racially bigoted and totalitarian (that is, they do not permit other political parties or Trade Unions to exist.)

In simple terms these political groupings could be classified as Revolutionary, Populist, Moderate, Reactionary and Racist.

Generally, the freer a society is the more involved are its politics. Elements of all groupings are likely to exist, with believers adhering to variations of the basic concept. (Politics, like religion, is open to much modification by people who think, on reflection, that they have a better solution than the one they have just heard.) In all Communist countries such selfishness is not tolerated and only one point of view is permitted, This does not, of course, stop people from thinking.

Communism is different from other political systems which may be challenged and replaced by normal democratic processes. It is an atheistic ideology which, for great numbers of the human race, has taken the place of religion. Whereas various shades of political belief can live together within a democratic system, total state domination can accept no challenges from within: a state which has become God cannot live with other, lesser, gods; other political parties cannot be endured. For this reason, and because they do not feel secure enough to do so, the Soviet Union and other Communist governments have never permitted elections in which candidates can stand in opposition to the State Party.

In the undeveloped parts of the world political theories are unknown, except by the small educated element of the population, who gain power from their knowledge. There, because distances are great and communication is difficult, age-old tribal systems based on local leadership, customs, credulity and obedience control people's lives. But, often without knowing it, the population are affected by the titanic clash of ideologies which has mushroomed since 1945. As has the number of nations. At the last count there were 174 of them in the world.

The creation of several new nations after 1800 AD, followed by the enormous increase in the 20th Century, was an unfortunate development for mankind. Every nation has an identity which demands allegiance from its citizens and narrows their point of view to matters of self-interest. Every nation has a top structure which is self-perpetuating: political leaders, administrators, military officers, businessmen and, usually, a priesthood. Most of the human beings in these categories feel compelled to defend the continued existence of the nation which provides them with a better life than its lesser citizens.

The more nations there are the greater is the probability of conflict, especially as many national boundaries arbitrarily cut across tribal, cultural and religious groupings. (For example, the Maasai tribe live half in Kenya and half in Tanzania.) Except for islands, by far the majority of nations exist only as a line drawn on a map: very few have visible frontiers, except at some of the places where roads and railways cross the political border.

The creation of so many new nations* after the Second World War came about because of the dismemberment of the European empires, which itself was caused by the effects of the war on the attitudes of the governed and the governing: the turmoil of world conflict had kicked over the beehives and the swarms would not settle until they found a place of their own. Until the age of imperialism the places to which European powers went had been inhabited by scattered tribes; by the middle of the 20th Century the tribes had been drawn together into nations. Then the thirty years from 1945 saw a progressive withdrawal of colonial governments and their replacement by local ones, despite the fact that often the original tribes maintained their historical antipathies. Frequently, the process of withdrawal was accompanied by armed conflict: the imperial rulers were reluctant to leave and/or local factions fought for the future control of the new nation. Gradually, a world grouping emerged which in time came to be referred to as the Third World, the capitalist West being one and the Communist Eastern Bloc being the other.

Because of their history many of these new nations were inclined to side with the East rather than with the ex-imperial West but some retained their old ties – the ex-French colonies, for instance, and those who joined the British Commonwealth, the new name given to the British Empire – and some played both sides at once and got help from capitalists and communists.

The Third World was to become a weighty force in international politics, first because of the power of their block vote in the United Nations, secondly because they own some of the world's most

*For more information about nations and the UNO see Appendix One

valuable resources, and thirdly because they are nearly all very poor: the theory of communism appeals to those who have nothing, and many desperately poor nations turned towards Moscow. To counter the spread of Marxism, America and Europe began to give money and material aid to most of the underdeveloped countries. And both East and West sold or gave armaments, to preserve the balance of power in different areas of the world; not least France, which was to become one of the biggest exporters of war munitions to countries of the Third World.

After the war the French, feeling shamed by the collapse of their army in 1940 and by the collaboration of Petain's government with the Nazis, had reclaimed their overseas empire, only to find that they could do nothing right. A disastrous conflict in Indo-China culminated, in 1954, in their withdrawal from the Far East. In the same year they began a bloody, bitter and seemingly endless war in Algeria, and in 1956 pressure from President Eisenhower and Secretary-General Khrushchev forced them, and the British, to abandon their joint military operation, conducted in collaboration with the Israelis, to re-open the Suez Canal, an international waterway arbitrarily nationalised and then blocked by the Egyptians. In 1958 the French people turned pleadingly to the man who, to them, symbolised the nation's one-time greatness, General de Gaulle, leader of the remnants of the French forces who had fought with the Allies during the war.

With difficulty, he extricated them from Algeria and by applauding their history, culture and post-war economic successes gave them back their self respect. French élan was, however, bought at the cost of extreme nationalism, which ungratefully under-valued the debt they owed to the United States, and isolationism, which in many ways began to estrange them from the rest of Europe. (In 1966 the General, as an ultimate gesture of independence, was to withdrew French forces from the integrated military structure of NATO – though retaining representation on its political controlling council. Even so, 50,000 French soldiers still remain stationed in the French Zone of West Germany.)

*

Economically, East and West had also polarised in opposition to each other. The formation in 1949 of an Eastern European Council for Mutual Economic Assistance (Comecon) had helped to achieve a lot in the Satellite countries during the 1950s – for example, a third more people working in industry, twice as much steel made – but much of the increased production was taken away by Russia. The Soviets had a huge army to pay for and their economy was under strain: fifty years of indoctrination had failed to eradicate human greed and selfishness; agricultural production was less than it had been before the war (and six times less than in the USA); centralised controls could not react quickly enough to market demand; there was much unemployment – but no financial assistance for those out of work because giving it would admit that the system was fallible. The Russians had set themselves the target of achieving parity with the USA, in production per head of population, by 1970, but it was an impossible task, requiring an increase of four times their existing output. And they had to face the fundamental contradiction of communism: that if it succeeds in raising the standard of living the need for the communist type of solution to people's problems diminishes . . .

In the early 1960s one Russian in every 350 owned a car, compared to one in eight Britons; one in thirty had a television, compared to one in four. Ideology or not, people regard material improvements as a measure of personal success, and personal success matters to a human being. Caught on a forked dilemma the hard-faced men of the Politburo were obliged to prove that the system worked by making more consumer goods (washing machines, refrigerators and so on) available, though they grudged doing so because it diverted production capacity away from armaments. Despite this in 1957 they launched the first spacecraft, and two years later one of their rockets reached the moon. Then in 1961 Yuri Gagarin became the first of the species Homo Sapiens to circle his planet and look down on its continents.

In the 1960s the Bloc nations of Eastern Europe at last began to see some return for their hard labour and their standard of living improved. But twenty years after the end of the war there were still ruined buildings everywhere, in contrast with the West, where the scars of war had been effaced and the affluent society was bringing the fruits of the earth to a very small proportion of its inhabitants on a scale never before given to any fortunate men and women. In 1946 Churchill had spoken of a European family and a "United States of Europe", as a first step towards which it would be necessary to form a Council of Europe. In 1949 the French, the Dutch and the Belgians did, and in 1951 the West Germans joined them in the European Coal and Steel Community which, in 1957, became the European Common Market. At first the United Kingdom had declined to be a member of the Community for fear of losing national sovereignty, and from a wish to build on existing economic ties with the Commonwealth, but when it became clear that the vision of a closely-integrated Commonwealth was not going to materialise Britain applied to join. In 1962 General de Gaulle vetoed the proposal on the grounds that Britain's special relationship with the USA might result in the Common Market coming under American influence. Perhaps a more important factor was that if Britain became a member of the Community France would no longer be able to dominate it. Nevertheless, in 1975 Britain too became a member.

By reducing the difficulties of selling goods in each other's nations the European Economic Community created vast opportunities for trade. The specialities of each became their strengths: Danish farm produce, German electrical goods, French cars, Italian machinery and so on – all these flowed unchecked by import taxes through customs posts, increasing competition, forcing prices down, creating more demand, increasing trade, increasing wealth. People began to expect an ever-greater improvement in their standard of living, an unending growth in their share of the world's good things. Trade Unions, which had improved the lot of the working classes and had fought valiantly for the removal of unfair and inequitable practices, lost sight of the inviting goal of productivity and abused the referee instead. Demanding more and more for their own members they forgot that prosperity depends on the combined effort of all workers. As time passed Western output began to drop and, inevitably, so did the growth in the standard of living.

Not so in Japan, where toil is regarded as a worthwhile endeavour and therefore earns its just reward. With a population about twice the size of each of the big Western-European powers, with ingenuity, dexterity and total dedication, they flooded the markets of the free world with low-priced, good-value products which began to pose a major threat to other nation's economies. Governments protested but the Japanese smiled, bowed and went on making more and more at less and less cost.

*

Today, in 1986, after forty years of so-called peace, a quarter of the world's nations and four million troops are at war: in Central America, the Persian Gulf, Africa and the Far East. Since the two atomic bombs were dropped on Japan in 1945 the long sequence of conflicts that have flared and died or smoulder on have cost many millions of lives; so many that it is difficult to make an estimate.

The confrontation between the two superpowers and the withdrawal of European nations from their overseas territories are the two political themes behind most of the events which have occurred in the years since the Second World War. Because they involved several nations and were on a large scale the wars in Korea and Vietnam were the most important, though they did not end the most lives: the Partitioning of India and the 'Restructuring' of Cambodia claim the top awards for demonstrating Man's capacity for killing other people simply because they have a different label.

The British did their best, which sometimes was not very good, to leave things tidy as they pulled out of the places which had caused Victorian and Edwardian hearts in the homeland to swell with distant pride. But other nations did no better, and sometimes a lot worse. The Belgians departed in unseemly haste from the Congo, leaving a tangled mess which erupted in tribal war, and the French interminably from Algeria. It took them seven and a half years and the two sides a total of nearly half a million dead before they were able to cut themselves off from the colony which had become the abode of a million French settlers but was the home of nine million Algerians. The Dutch came home from the East Indies after a difficult and sometimes bloody withdrawal. The West Indies, by now inhabited by the descendants of negro slaves who had been forcibly brought there long before, slowly cast off their colonial ties. Those were some of the places from which the Imperial powers departed. There were others. It would be very difficult to name many that are any better off as a result but it is not difficult to list those which are worse off. They constitute a source of smouldering friction which flares and dies down and flares again, and keeps the world in a state of war, somewhere, at all times.

Palestine remains the trouble-spot it has been for thousands of years. India was a place the British left in too great a hurry, war-weary and faint-hearted and pushed away by excited people who were eager to grab the reins and perks of power. Cyprus, a jewel of a place, is split like a badly cut emerald. Lebanon, a fringe of country on the blue shores of the Mediterranean, overlooked by the hills in which lie the ruins of Baalbeck, one of the world's oldest towns, has been ripped by civil war for more than a decade. Ireland, partitioned in 1922, torn by religious antipathy and historical differences, has been fighting its own mini civil war for nearly two decades.

Iran, under its fanatical high-priest of one of the Islamic sects, the Ayatollah, backed by Syria and Libya, is fighting another year of bloody trench warfare against Iraq, most of whose citizens belong to another Moslem sect and are supported by Saudi Arabia and Jordan. Getting on for three million refugees have crossed the border into Pakistan since the Russians invaded Afghanistan in 1979, and in an attempt to bring the rebels to heel Russia has used chemical weapons and aerial bombardment on people who live in abject poverty. In Kampuchea, which was Cambodia, national forces are scrapping with Russian-backed Vietnamese invaders, while the smiling tyrant Pol Pot takes cover behind the burial mounds he made. Next door, in Laos, 50,000 people have died since peace came to Vietnam in 1975. Further north the Chinese periodically accuse the Vietnamese of harassment and the two sides exchange artillery fire. In India Hindus, from time to time, slaughter Moslems and Sikhs. Africa, from North to South, is wracked by warfare: in the north, Libyan forces are fighting in Chad, a former French colony; the puny war between Somalia and Ethiopia, which started in 1977, is still going on; in the south-west, Angola and Namibia are sore spots from which inflammation spreads into South Africa, where apartheid divides Black from White, physically and mentally. There, some behave as if God is an Afrikaaner. Central America is being militarised as part of the power bloc struggle: Soviet Russia aiding Nicaragua while the United States turns Honduras into a line of defence against creeping communism – the domino theory again: the land of the Maya is steaming with the sweat of conflict. Even gentle Sri Lanka is a combat zone in which more than four thousand people have died in the last four years, and damp England cannot find an answer to the Irish problem.*

In most places where these wars are going on the Super- powers, and the lesser ones, have eagerly sold weapons to the warriors on two grounds: that their side might win and help their own ideological battle – and that anyway if they didn't somebody else would. The most cynical military people regard the minor battlefields as a testing ground for new weaponry. Politicians argue that the money they obtain for the weapons will help their own economy in the long fight against capitalism or communism. Some regard the arms industry as essential to the maintenance of employment and therefore the good-will of voters in the next election. If there is one. Democracy is the exception, not the rule. Tyranny is the most common form of government.

*

*For information about the causes of tension in the world see Appendix Two.

# CHAPTER TEN

# PROGRESS

The Victorians, British or otherwise, were right in thinking that the advent of the 20th Century was important, for indeed it was. It was the Y junction of evolution. If they went one way, with open minds and tolerance, mankind had a promising future; if they went the other, in bigotry and selfishness, there was no future. Behind them lay creation, the ancient world, the middle years and enough acquired knowledge to point the way, if they could but read the signs; in front was Volume Two, unopened.

Scientists had begun to take off the wrappings but the information inside was still a closed book. Then in Europe the Great War accelerated new ways of thinking, outpaced attitudes about people's status in social classes and left behind the comfortable life-style of thousands who had depended upon millions: in the United Kingdom in 1914 domestic service was the second biggest employer after industry: one third of all households had living-in servants. After 1918 things changed.

Officers and men who had shared the foul privations of the trenches, had seen the best qualities and the worst in all classes, had been obliged to get to know each other very well as human beings where before they had seldom brushed shoulders, no longer regarded themselves as people separated by a great gulf of birthright. Far fewer at the top, British, French, German or Italian, wished to go on treating their social inferiors as human inferiors and those at the other end of the scale were no longer inclined to let them. Quietly – enough blood had been shed – the Somme, Verdun and Caporetto brought about a greater social revolution than the guillotine had done in Paris. And so, no doubt, would the battle of Tannenberg, given time. But Lenin was in a hurry.

In the 1920s Modern Man was in the air, in more ways than one. Flight was only one way in which he could move about. He had a new toy on four wheels which, as the years passed, was to consume his time and money and material resources beyond measure. Intellectually, at the top end of the scale a few bright stars began to shoot away, leaving others earthbound, while in the middle a narrow education, firmly grounded in mythology and dead languages, took many who learned very little of practical value even further away from those who knew next to nothing.

By the 1930s the very atmosphere had been invaded and the world was a smaller place. Bouncing radio waves off a part of Earth's mantle of air which is electrified by the Sun's rays – the Ionosphere – voices crossed continents. Physicists in America started to piece together very large and complicated objects called digital computers and invented the cyclotron, which accelerated the movement of sub-atomic particles. In England they were looking deeper and deeper into atoms and beginning to realise that there are many things that the eye does not see, while in 1939 two Germans achieved what was called nuclear fission.

When the 1940s came men were obliged to push on even faster. Aircraft had to overtake bigger ones carrying bigger bomb loads and shoot them out of the sky before they could drop their explosives. When conventional aircraft could not break through the barriers imposed by existing technology German scientists developed the ballistic rocket. And it was top priority during the war to discover a treatment for malaria, not because millions of people in the world have always suffered and died from it but in order that soldiers visiting places where mosquitos ravaged men could stay healthy long enough to kill other visitors.

When in the 1950s Modern Man slowed down for a breather he found that he had somehow lumbered himself with a frightening invention which suddenly made it possible for men to rid the world of Man. What on Earth was to be done? Forty years on the question is unanswered but meanwhile there are now fifty-five thousand carefully guarded nuclear warheads available should they ever be needed. The advent of missiles and fast jet-propelled aircraft enlarged the number of options open for the delivery of such weapons, themselves improved by the production of the hydrogen bomb. Things called plastics, made by putting clusters of carbon atoms obtained from petroleum under great pressure and temperature so as to string them together, began to be used for all manner of things; now, it is difficult to understand how people managed without them. In 1956 a Swiss made a microscope which could magnify two and three quarter million times. Things would never look the same again.

In the 1960s it was said that people had never had it so good. Some people. Those in the Western democracies. The rest remained much as they had always been, though the communist nations were beginning to catch up and even some of the underdeveloped ones could see a gradual improvement in their prospects. In the West the oral contraceptive for women, the Pill, came into general use and changed sexual attitudes.

In the 1970s the Arabs shook the world by sending the price of petrol sky-high because they were piqued by losing another war with the Jews and because it had dawned on them that when their oil ran out they would revert to being the inhabitants of a not very useful part of the world. Having begun to enjoy having more money than anyone else, that idea did not appeal. (Human nature being what it is, much of the money had been kept in princely bank accounts, and did not seep down to the populace but as time passed and they accumulated so much gold that even they could not spend it all they began to heed the Prophet's instructions, and, benevolently, gave to the poor. Even so, today gold-plated sub-machine guns feature in the budgets of wary sheiks.) The effect of the oil crisis was to shake the economies of the industrial nations and strip much of the Third World's thin flesh back to the bone: not able to afford to buy cooking oil the enlarging populations cut down more forests for firewood, and with no petrol to burn in vehicles the new administrative structures which had creaked into existence stopped dead in their ruts. Once again famine lurked over the horizon.

In the 1970s people travelled as they had never done before and peaceful places became packaged-holiday bedlams full of miners, car makers and mechanics from the affluent West. The '70s also saw the end of America's confrontation with its conscience over the ethics of their war in South-East Asia, and brought Irishmen into confrontation because religious bigotry stifles conscience. It also began to dawn on many people that progress, in the sense of an automatic, never-ending increasing possession of material goods, is not one of the inalienable facts of life even though progress, to many people, is measured by the invention of new machines – the electronic and mechanical things which shape modern life.*

However, fascinating though they are, and a measurable indication of the incredible intelligence of Mankind, they do not, in themselves, change our nature or the way in which the great majority of us live. It is the care of the mind and the body, and the availability of food supplies, that affect the human race most.

*

During the Great War studies began into the workings of the human mind; British and American psychiatrists had a large "captive" population of men and women in the Armed Forces who could be catalogued, tested and observed. The effects of brain surgery on wounded men could also be monitored, giving some indication of what the different parts of the coiled tubing in the cranium do. Between the wars, care for the mentally ill took on a new meaning; people tried to cure them rather than just confine them, and the Americans in particular began to compile data by analysing the behaviour of lunatic people. During the Second World War even greater numbers of men and women could be tested and analysed, by which time there was a better foundation on which to work. In the last forty years there has been much interchange of information internationally, out of which modern psychiatry and psychology have evolved.

*A short account of these inventions, from the motor car to the computer, is at Appendix Three.

The treatment of mental illness has been helped by the invention of drugs which block or reduce the activity of those parts of the brain which cause instability: drugs which interpose a chemical screen in the path of the lightning flashes of electrical activity which generate involuntary impulses, hallucinations and fears in the human mind. There are fewer raving lunatics about than there were but in the stressful developed world there are far more people who feel ill at ease. It has been said that depression destroys more adults than any other disease. Some societies consume tranquillisers by the ton. Mental illness is more controllable than it was but the root causes have not yet been attacked.

Schizophrenia, which literally means split mind, is the name given to the sickness of those who at times behave as if they were two totally different people. It is the most serious and prevalent mental illness; it brings about the disintegration of personality and affects about forty million people in the world. Research shows that schizoids may be ill because their corpus calossum lacks the chemicals needed to transfer information correctly; that sometimes the impulses from one side of their brain are isolated from the modifying effects of the other side's thought processes. That the name given years ago because of behaviour is the reality: that the mind is literally split. Work is being done to try to identify the chemicals responsible and it should then be possible to administer them to make up the deficiency.

Psychologists can now test individuals and determine their basic personality traits, and having done that can match them to specific work requirements. For example, psychometric tests can be used to screen out people who should not be employed on special types of dangerous activity: such as, for example, bomb disposal men, astronauts and sub-mariners. With a high degree of accuracy the tests can identify those characteristics which would make them unsuitable – nervousness under stress, impulsiveness, vertigo, claustrophobia . . . Such tests could, and in time no doubt will, be applied to a much bigger range of activities – such as politics, where a person's character can bring about international disasters.

Increasing concern about human behaviour led scientists to study the way in which human beings live together. Sociology involves social groupings, race relations, religion, sexuality, the family, education, politics, economics, science; in fact, all the many facets of life. Like psychology, sociology is still a very imprecise science because of the complexities of human nature. Sociologists are as much concerned with deciding how to get and assess information as they are in using what they have, but in time it may be possible to establish the basic reasons for human behaviour and, knowing them, to forecast events and avert mistakes.

In Europe, long before scientists began to study society, people with the power to do so had tried to improve the living conditions of the poor. At first, Christian beliefs required them to help their fellow human beings; after the French Revolution, charity and common sense told them that if they did nothing a highly dangerous situation could develop. For centuries the needy had been able to get help from the Church, which gave alms, from craftsmen's Guilds, which pre-dated Trade Unions and made charity benefits available to their members, and from their family which, more than it does today, felt responsible for the old and sick but it was in Britain that the first attempts were made to organise a system of national assistance for those who scratched around for the crumbs lying under the table.

In England, as long ago as 1601, the Elizabethan Poor Law Act instituted a system of relief. Though generous in concept those who refused to work were harshly punished. As time passed it was decided that the cost of caring for the poor should be defrayed to some extent by selling the products made in their Work Houses but despite that between 1786 and 1818 the burden on the rates quadrupled, leading to much discontent amongst rate-payers. A Royal Commission decided that the poor were getting better treatment than the lowest-paid workers and in 1834 the law was amended; in future only the bare minimum needed to support life would be provided, and strict discipline would be enforced on the unfortunate inmates of Workhouses. The prospect of being confined in such places came to be dreaded by poor people: wives were separated from husbands and parents from children, and for many once they were incarcerated there was little prospect of ever leaving, except in a plain wooden box destined for a pauper's grave.

For all that, something was being done, which was more than could be said for other parts of the world where, as had always been the case, the poor sank down until they went under and perished. Then in Europe in the late 19th Century governments started to provide shelter, financial assistance and medical care for the destitute. By the beginning of the 20th Century political parties were vying with each other in their promises to the far bigger slice of the population who had been given the vote: the liberalisation of attitudes, in part due to the influence of socialist ideas on the lower classes and the resulting pressure from them to have a say in what was going on, had resulted in more representative democracy. First, men without property were allowed to vote, whereas before only house owners could, then women were.

After the Second World War Britain became a Welfare State, in which the citizen is cared for by the nation pre-natal to post-mortem. Over the last forty years the rising cost of this concept (due in part to progressively more expensive medical technology and drugs and in part to increased popular expectations) has brought about the need for those who can to contribute to the services they get, but the poverty-stricken pay nothing.

In the 1950s and '60s more and more nations legalised social conscience and now all developed societies, capitalist and communist alike, have welfare schemes intended to ensure that no-one is homeless or starves, or dies for want of medical attention.

This situation does not apply in most Third World countries because they have neither the money nor the administrative resources to cope with a situation where almost all the population would qualify, by European and North American standards, for state aid.

*

Medicine has advanced a long way since, 3,000 years ago, Egyptians bored holes in the top of a madwoman's skull to let out the demons fighting inside, but for most of Mankind's history people have had to put up with whatever ailments they contracted. The Chinese operated to repair hernias, remove kidney stones and cut away piles and cancers 2,500 years ago, but from then until the middle of the 20th Century European surgeons doing the same things knew very little more than the Chinese did. Only in the last thirty years has knowledge advanced greatly.

The smallpox vaccine was discovered in 1789 and the disease was totally eradicated 190 years later. The last recorded case was in 1979; like the dinosaurs, it has gone. Antiseptics and anaesthetics started to be used in the second half of the 19th Century but then there was a long pause in major medical discoveries until, in the 1920s, insulin was manufactured for the treatment of diabetes. The way in which vitamins assist in the maintenance of health was understood at about the same time, and soon after came inoculation for the prevention of diphtheria, whooping cough, tuberculosis and infantile paralysis. But it was not until the late-1930s that ways were found of curing diseases after they had been caught, and another decade or so before theory could be put into general practice.

Penicillin was not produced in quantity until the 1940s, which was when quinine was first made synthetically and used to fight malaria; and when inoculation against tetanus and typhoid was widely practiced in the Armed Forces. Antibiotics did not arrive until the '50s; an ever-increasing range of drugs which kill those bacteria which cause illness in the human body. Unfortunately some bacteria develop resistance to antibiotics, so new ones must be developed.

With new techniques for suppressing the body's rejection of foreign cells, heart and lung transplants can be done – but only with limited success. Micro-surgery, using high-powered optical enlargement, which enables the surgeon to see in detail where before he blindly slashed, enables limbs to be sewn on again if they have been severed. Lasers, highly concentrated light beams, can excise some tumours, seal off blood vessels and remove birthmarks.

Since the 1960s many computerised electronic systems have been developed to diagnose symptoms and assist curing processes. There are body-scanners to seek out tumours, electro-cardiograms to measure heart performance, encephalograms to check how the brain is functioning, dialysis to do what the kidneys should do – and ultra-sonic or shock waves to smash kidney stones without cutting the patient open! Life-support machines can keep a body functioning indefinitely. Old people's ailments can be cured so that their lives are much prolonged: indeed one of the great problems for the future, in some parts of the world, is going to be the increase in the number of geriatrics; elderly, infirm people who are unable to look after themselves.

Children are being born by artificially putting into a woman's egg male sperm, from her husband or a donor. Tiny embryonic babies are being cultured under glass in a laboratory for up to nine days and then implanted in a woman's womb, in due course resulting in normal birth. Deep-frozen sperm has been kept and used successfully years after it came from a donor. Deep-frozen embryos have been unfrozen, implanted and have become normal animals – not human beings, yet. Zebras have been born out of the wombs of mares, and goats and sheep have been crossed in a test tube and then carried and born by ewes. The manipulation of genes has already achieved the "cloning" of simple species, the reproduction of an *identical* creature. Inevitably, before long, the same thing will be done with human cells . . .

Only a hundred years ago leeches were kept in jars in every self-respecting doctor's surgery, ready to be applied to suck out blood, bad blood being regarded as the cause of many ailments. That same doctor would have been incredibly ignorant about sexual matters – though not about his instincts, which are unchanged – and even Charles Darwin was not aware that children are conceived when a single sperm enters a female egg. Most of those doctors thought that only "loose" women had any sensual feelings. In the 1930s Solomon Islanders believed that children were "given" to them by their ancestors, and until the 1960s some aboriginals thought that a woman became pregnant when she sat close to a hot fire. For many primitive people, totally ignorant about the simplest biological function, the only purpose of the sexual act was, and is, to give pleasure.

The arrival of the Pill in the 1960s brought about the same attitude in many advanced societies, where promiscuous sexual activity became all the rage. Total intimacy was now expected by the male in exchange for an evening's companionship, gratifying up to a point but also demeaning for the female, still a bed for the seed of men but now an infertile one – and as such frequently, if unconsciously, regarded with contempt by the male. On the other hand, casual sex is, for some, the only way in which they can obtain a fleeting feeling of affection. The advent of sexually transmitted diseases such as Herpes and Advanced Immune Deficiency Syndrome are now, however, resulting in less promiscuity. The latter disease is believed to have originated in Africa, spread into the Americas and then into Europe. It is incurable and is transmitted by blood-to-blood contact. Though it can be contracted by blood transfusions, or the use of infected hypodermic needles shared by drug users, the following statistics, relating to known cases in the United Kingdom, are self-revealing:

| | |
|---|---|
| Total cases | 599 |
| Total male cases | 582 |
| (of which 533 were homosexual or bisexual) | |
| Total female cases | 17 |

*

Famine, like the poor, is always with us, historically more often in the wheat-growing areas of the world than in the rice-growing areas. Provided the supply of water is properly regulated by irrigation rice is a reliable crop. Thousands of years ago rice was grown in river mudbanks, especially along the Yang-tze, where, because topsoil was deposited as silt on the river banks, it could be cultivated again and again without any need to add fertiliser. Later, the early Chinese emperors exercised discipline over their people by rationing the release of rainwater naturally trapped in lakes, often through man-made canals, down to the rice-growing fields. No compliance, no water. Today, rice feeds 60% of the world's population. It does not need crop rotation and can produce two or three yields a year, provided the fields are well fertilised. Due to the scarcity of cattle in rice-growing areas, human excreta is a very necessary element in the production of rice.

Wheat, on the other hand, needs crop rotation, (the cultivation of a series of different annual crops – say, wheat, roots, barley, grass – over a period of three or four years so as not to exhaust essential minerals in the soil) and is dependent on adequate rainfall. Modern farming methods – the development of high-yield strains (two hundred grains of corn grow where one grew before; ewes produce twins instead of single lambs) and the use of chemical fertilisers and pesticides and enormously powerful harvesters – can greatly increase agricultural production but having the technology and being able to apply its benefits in the right place are two different things. The infrastructure of a nation (its administrative efficiency, transport network, availability of labour and standard of technology) and lack of money may raise problems, and so too may nature's unpredictability.

Droughts or torrential storms can nullify the best laid plans: we have no understanding of precisely why weather changes, let alone how to intervene in the process. Recently sand from the Sahara fell from clear skies across southern England, carried by wind currents at about 15,000 feet above Earth for hundreds of kilometres. Nobody knew it was coming or could have stopped its descent if they did. Man is still as susceptible to the elements as ever.

As we are to so many things.

When Einstein was asked what his reaction was to the explosion of the first atomic bomb he replied: "Everything has changed, except human nature."

*

## CHAPTER ELEVEN

# PREJUDICE, POPULATION PILLAGE & POLLUTION

Prejudice began when an ape man fought over a bone or a woman; when a woman turned and snarled at an ape man because she had a headache, or at another woman because she had cuffed her child; when, like two dogs, people's hackles went up because they felt threatened, or because they did not understand one another. Or, quite simply, because they did not like the look of each other. Strangeness breeds prejudice. And so does condemnation of someone out of the mouth of another person: we eagerly believe whatever we hear – unless it goes against our prejudices.

There are racial, religious, family and historical prejudices but there are no hereditary ones.

We changed our colour and physical characteristics because we spread to the many different climatic regions of Earth and adapted to the conditions . But in the process, because small groups were separated by great distances, they developed different beliefs, different cultures, different clothes and different mannerisms – became different races. These things make us strangers to each other, and strangeness causes dislike, wariness and even fear. So whenever strangers meet it takes time to accept the new and to break through the barriers which snap down across the mind. For many people this is too much to ask: their inheritance and their past experience has created an unbridgeable gap of prejudice.

Such gaps occur where races meet, where they have migrated, and where their cultures are very alien to each other. Racial boundaries exist, for example, where Arab meets negro in Africa.

The gap also exists where races have migrated and overwhelmed others – the Americans and the Red Indian, the descendants of

Spanish and Portugese settlers and the native South Americans, the Australians and the Aboriginals, the New Zealanders and the Maoris – or where migrations, forced or voluntary, led to a dominated element of the population: slave negroes in the United States, negroes in the white Union of South Africa and, in recent times, Algerians in France, Indonesians in The Netherlands, West Indian negroes and Indo-Asians in England, and Turks in West Germany. The Algerians and Indonesians are ex-colonials and so are the coloured minorities in England but many of them, like the Turks in West Germany, were invited in the 1950s and '60s to come and do the lowly work. (Those who have been born and bred there are doing well. In a school in Dortmund more than 30% of the pupils are Turkish. They achieve better results in comparison with their numbers than the German children: from illiterate Anatolian peasants to high-achievers in a modern environment in three gererations, one reason being the personal and parental urge to succeed.)

The cultures of Asia are alien to one another – Indian and Chinese and Eastern Soviet and Japanese – and so too is that of the European with all others. That creates a special problem because the European (which includes those in North America and Western Russia) leads the rest of the world in scientific progress, and in what Europeans define, and the educated world increasingly accepts, as civilisation.

Religious differences are the most intractable to overcome because spiritual beliefs should be strong enough to carry believers beyond this life into what they think will be the next, be it resurrection of the body, reincarnation or whatever. How can other people's beliefs be accepted without denying or doubting one's own? In that spiritual strength is the source of great prejudice, made worse by the fact that where people are harassed for their beliefs they usually cling more strongly to them, and are prepared to suffer and even die for them.

"Family" prejudices stem from the close proximity of antagonistic tribes who will not forget historical conflicts: Ukranians and Russians; Poles and Russians; Greeks and Turks; Basques and

Spaniards . . . The history of war makes long-standing prejudices, unto the seventh generation and beyond: the French and the British, the French and the German, the Russian and the German. The list goes on and on, and so do the dislikes.

But prejudices are not inbred. If they were they would be carried in our genes, the hereditary package we all have in our bodies, but genes do not carry memory. Continuity of type and some "programmed" instructions, yes, but memory, no.

A human being is a community of thousands of millions of cells which work to support each other. A cell is an infinitesimal speck of several clusters of Carbon-linked atoms surrounded by water (which makes up 70% of the human body) and contained in a membrane, a very thin "skin" which allows chemicals to pass in and out but keeps the cell separate from others. Each cell is a small "industrial unit" full of unceasing chemical activity linked to the specific purpose of the cell – where it is in the body and what it does. Normally no alien cell can be part of your body, or part of any other living thing's body: only the cell with the right key can function.

At the centre of every cell, in every living thing, is a nucleus of groups of atoms (D Nucleic Acids – DNA) upon which depends the thing's unique identity – yours or the dog's or the daffodil's. DNA contains the genes, the combinations of atoms which determine precisely how the body of the living thing is constructed: its shape, size, texture, colour, and so on. Genes are small groups of atoms strung, in "side-chains", along a backbone of atoms. There are only four different combinations of atoms in the side-chains which make up genes, and therefore life: the language of genetics has only four "letters". A cluster of genes makes up a chromosome, of which there are twenty-three matched pairs in every human cell – except our sex cells.

The nucleus also contains "R" nucleic acids (RNA) which carry instructions from the first group to different clusters of atoms (proteins) floating about in the water. In all proteins, whether they are in animals, plants, bacteria or viruses, there are only twenty different sets of linked atoms, called amino acids.

*All* living things use the same four-letter language to carry genetic information and the same twenty sets of atoms to construct their proteins. It is an astounding but apparently little-known fact that *all life on Earth is all of a kind*. Every living thing recreates itself out of the same basic groups of atoms as every other living thing. All living things are related. There is only one creation.*

Another factor in inheritance, apart from genes, is "natural selection", the term given by Darwin to explain why species adapt to their environment.

If a particular attribute can enable a creature to survive, the genes responsible for it somehow become dominant, and those that are now superfluous become recessive – that is, they weaken and are less likely to continue into future generations: the dominant ones tend to push out the recessive ones when cells split. The species changes, though it takes many generations for this to happen.

The proof of the selective process can be seen in the controlled breeding of those species which Man has managed to domesticate. (In all, there are only sixteen!) Dogs show the effects most clearly but domesticated beasts have also been changed by Man.

Like the human races some dogs adapted to their environment through successive generations; grew long shaggy coats to keep out the weather, or long legs to run fast with if they had to pursue their food over long distances; grew big, to take on large animals, or small and nimble to evade them. In Europe and North America in the last hundred years or more many variations of these basic types have been bred until there are now some very odd-looking things indeed: creatures which nature itself would never permit to live, such as dogs which have had their noses bred out until they hardly exist, in consequence of which they cannot breathe properly and pant and snuffle.

The ability to control breeding comes from the selection and mating, progressively, generation after generation, of those dogs and bitches which have the characteristics which the breeder wants

*For more information about genetics and how human intelligence is linked to inheritance see Appendix Four.

to develop. Pups which do not have the desired features are either destroyed or not bred from. Because the gestation period of the bitch is short results can be achieved within a comparatively short time.

Hundreds of years ago the Lapps in Scandinavia started to herd reindeer. Because they wanted the animals to be more easily controlled they castrated the wilder ones and bred from the docile ones. After many generations the nature of the beasts changed, so that now they can be herded like cattle and are quite unlike their North American cousins the caribou, which remain wild and shy of human beings. Quite unconsciously the Lapps, who rely almost exclusively on reindeer for their livelihoods, used natural selection to produce a new strain of animal.

A lot has been achieved since 1910 when Morgan in the USA first identified gene clusters on a chromosome, but we are still only at the beginnings of discovery; only about 10% of the genes in a chromosome have been mapped but amongst those which have are those which cause colour blindness, manic depressive psychosis and haemophilia, the inability to clot blood and stop bleeding. The group which has been most studied is that which makes haemoglobin, the oxygen-carrying pigment in blood. The fact that it alone has 70,000 clusters of chemical combinations shows the magnitude of the task of compiling a comprehensive list of what each gene does, but when that is achieved it may be possible to find out how it does it, and then regulate its activity.

For example, cancer is caused by the body's normal creation of new cells getting out of control. If it could be discovered why dividing cells are not acting normally then it might be possible to bring them back under control. At present cancer treatment is based on killing off the erring cells by radiation or chemical treatments, but healthy cells may be damaged at the same time and there may be unwanted side-effects.

There are two special points which come out of these paragraphs on heredity: first, genes do not control behaviour. A human cell contains a random half of the hereditary components of two separate human beings which have been blended into a new one, in which are the genetic instructions which make it uniquely what it is in terms of appearance and attributes. But though genes influence enzymes, which regulate behaviour by their chemical action in the body, they do not implant in a human being particular attitudes, as they do red hair or brown eyes. Therefore prejudice is acquired and is not inbred.

Secondly, characteristics can be changed by natural selection. The rapidity of change depends on the gestation period – the time between conception and birth – and how long it is before the new generation becomes sexually mature and starts breeding. In Homo Sapiens genetic change takes a very long time in comparison to the speed at which the species is developing in knowledge and killing power: our brains have outpaced our behaviour. We do not know how to control the animal instincts which still dominate our actions.

*

By this time tomorrow there will be an additional quarter of a million people alive on Earth.

When the Normans invaded England in 1066 there were about two million people living there, a figure that is quite accurately known because of the census they did soon after they arrived. Five hundred years later, when Will Shakespeare was a toddler, there were seven million men and women in what he was to call his "sceptred isle", and perhaps 450 million in the whole world. Four hundred years on, in 1966, in spite of all the rotting corpses lying in the ground as evidence of Man's increasing cleverness in the skills of self-destruction, there were more than 50 million Britons, and on Earth 3,000 million mouths. Now, in 1986, there are more than 5,000 million. It took more than thirty thousand years of development to reach that number but it will have doubled again in just another fifty or sixty. No species has ever reproduced itself at such a rate.

The problem is due to "exponential growth", words used to describe what happens when something not only becomes greater in numbers but does so at an increasing rate. If two living creatures enclosed within a circular wall breed and double their number in a week, and successive generations go on doing the same, it will not matter at first because there will be plenty of room for everyone. The time will come though, no matter how long it takes, for the compound to become half-full; then, in just one more week, the number will double and there will be standing-room only. What will happen during the next week? Quite suddenly what was an acceptable situation becomes a terrifying one.

The world's population is increasing in that sort of way, though the rate of growth is not evenly spread amongst all nations. North America and the Soviet Union, (with a density of eleven people per square kilometre, compared to over 300 in Japan) are more or less in equilibrium between births and deaths but can afford to expand their numbers because of the size of the land they occupy and the resources available to them. Indeed the USSR, which is by far the largest nation in the world (more than twice the size of the United States), and is in most ways self-supporting, has incentives to do so: greater numbers utilising existing resources to increase production; more people available to defend the regime against its enemies. Europe's population is also stable but there are a great many people in a relatively small space (ninety-seven per sq km, or even more) and there is no room for expansion. (The birth rate in Western Europe has declined by almost half in the last thirty-five years. In 1950 the population amounted to 8.8% of the world's numbers but by the First of January 2000 AD it will be only 4.5%, and by 2025 only 2.3%.) It is in South America, Africa, the Middle East and Southern Asia that population growth is enormous – and it is there that children will be born into deplorable ignorance and poverty. Because there is no money available to expand schooling the ignorance will continue, and because numbers will increase faster than the conditions of life can be improved the poverty can only get worse.

A century and a half from now there will be standing-room only on the world's land surface – a lot of which is not fit to live on. Furthermore, if all the new people were to have somewhere to live 2,500 cities would have to be under construction at the same time, with a new one being completed every three and a half hours! However, such lunatic, though factually correct, estimates take no account of the depletion of the world's resources. There will not be enough materials left to create those cities: iron to make steel girders, copper for electric wiring, aluminium for pots and pans, plastics for plumbing.

To give a few examples: at forecast rates of usage – even allowing for population growth and the increasing demand for materials – there is enough iron left to last another 88 years, enough aluminium for 30 years, enough copper for 16 years, but enough tin for only 10. Even if unknown deposits are discovered to boost reserves *five times* all gold will have been mined in 25 years, petroleum and natural gas will have been burnt off in 45 years and the last of the world's coal will have vanished up the chimney in another 125 years. We are using up irreplaceable assets at an ever-increasing rate. As much was manufactured by the world's industries between 1977 and 1984 as was produced in the whole of history up to 1945.

*

Population controls can be applied by governments using compulsion, persuasion or inducement.* The increase in numbers can also be controlled by nature.

When rabbits in Australia bred to such an extent that there was no food to eat and no room to live a mutant (that is, genetically changed) strain of disease evolved which wiped them out by the million. Myxamatosis spread to many parts of the world and until the animals developed their own resistance threatened to totally eradicate the species. Even now, worldwide, the disease kills off a proportion of the remaining rabbit population.

There was nothing astonishing about this mutation: it was the natural antidote to an intolerable situation, ensuring the return to a balance between numbers and environment, and there is no reason to expect that in a similar human situation another mutant strain

*Some notes on population controls are at Appendix Five.

would not develop to re-create a tolerable balance. It could even happen without the pressures of over-population.

The 1918 influenza was a strain which normally lives only in pigs, but it ravaged human beings. (In 1976 it was thought that the same virus had killed a soldier in the United States and it was decided to vaccinate the whole population: after six months enough vaccine had been made to protect only a small proportion of Americans. Fortunately, it was not the same strain.)

Until the 20th Century nature's methods – war, famine and disease – had limited the increase of population. (If there had been no such controls the number of human beings would now weigh more than the whole universe.) War, however, wasteful and stupid though it is, has not held back the growth of numbers significantly: all the men and women slaughtered between 1914 and 1918 had been replaced by new births in Europe within twenty years and because by 1945 the world population was so much bigger, and had a large proportion of young breeding people, even the vast numbers killed in the Second World War were replaced in five years.

Today, death rates in primitive agricultural societies reach catastrophic peaks during famine, with perhaps half the population dying. When lack of food is not the primary killer in the most unfortunate parts of the world appalling living conditions and ignorance about hygiene results in 45% of infants dying before they reach the age of 5. If they get past that first great hurdle few will live longer than 50 years because of poor nutrition and medical care, and on average they will die by the time they are 35. But that is at the low point of the spectrum – places in Africa, South America and South-East Asia. (In India men can expect to live until they are 47, and women until they are 45. The place with the lowest expectation of life is Guinea, where the people, with a life expectancy of 27 years, are worse off than Neanderthal Man was.) At the other end, in the highly "civilised" societies, where food is abundant and the newest medical techniques and drugs are available, life expectancy is now about 68 years for the male and 74 for the female – and will probably continue to rise. (The fact that women in India live for a shorter time than men is due to the fact that their society demands that they do far more physical work than does the Western society.)

Medical science has totally changed the future because its benefits have reached more and more parts of the world in the last few decades. Societies which are not as badly off as the least fortunate have been able to reduce infant mortality and prolong life but they have done this without the mass knowledge, will and means to reduce breeding. In time they will find themselves in the same situation as those who live with famine as a fearsome and not infrequent visitor.

It has been said that increases in food production will compensate for the increase in numbers and that the problem will therefore be contained. Certainly farming methods have improved immensely during the 20th Century but a lot of the increased production so far has gone into the mouths of those who already have too much. For all their generosity to other nations over the last forty years it has been estimated that the American people carry, in total, two million tons of excess weight on their bodies!

They are, of course, not alone in over-indulgence. The British have the highest mortality from heart disease anywhere in the world because they consume far too much animal fat. One Swiss eats as much as forty people in Upper Volta. Many Europeans die from liver failure due to over-eating and over-drinking. But even if all these lucky souls were to reduce their intake for their own good there is the problem of how to transfer their surpluses to where they are needed. In Europe the Common Market produces large surpluses of dairy products and fruit, some of which are sold to Russia and the other Comecon nations at give-away prices. The rest are destroyed. They do not reach the people in Africa and South America who are starving because those people have no money to buy the goods or pay for their transportation. (If they could get the food the populations of those countries would not necessarily increase because, according to the United Nations Children's Fund, once the death rate in poverty-stricken countries is lowered the birth rate comes down: people do not feel compelled to breed in order to ensure that one out of their five or six children lives.)

*

We have, then, a population detonation, a voracious, unthinking and uncaring burning-up of irreplaceable natural resources and a grossly inequitable distribution of food. And as if that were not enough there is the problem of conserving the environment. Due to population pressures and ignorance a lot of the assets we have are being progressively and quickly eroded or polluted.

The printing presses of the world need millions of tons of wood pulp every year to meet the inquiring human mind's demand for a daily paper. In the more affluent nations the increase in population creates a need for more and more wooden furniture. Billions of people in the Third World have no choice but to destroy their own means of survival: forests are being cleared to provide more growing space for crops and to produce fuel for cooking and heating, a process that has gone on since our species began but not on this damaging scale. In another fifteen years half the temperate region forests will have gone and in another eighty there will be no tropical rain forests left at all, with probably catastrophic effects on the world's climate and crop-growing patterns.(The Sun's heat creates great upward air surges over the forests, which suck in moisture-laden air from the oceans and raise it high into the sky where it disperses in gigantic cloud movements.) The rain forests also provide the plants from which nearly half our drugs are manufactured.

Because much of the cleared land is not being re-planted soil is being blown away: every year new deserts three times the size of Israel are being created. In the Sudan the desert has advanced 100 kilometres in the last fifteen years. In America 4,000 square kilometres of agricultural land disappear under roads, reservoirs and concrete buildings every year; lazy or quick-Buck farming methods have resulted in thousands of acres of land losing their top-soil. In another twenty years or so one third of all existing cropland will vanish. Already the United States has lost a quarter of its growing potential and the loss of fertile fields in the world as a whole is estimated to be 65,000 square kilometres every year. One third of the surface of Earth is in danger of turning into desert; the people who live in those areas now – about 470 million of them, nearly one-tenth of the world's population – are under-nourished or actually starving. New islands are growing in the Bay of Bengal due to the accumulation of silt carried down by India's great rivers from land far away that has been denuded of vegetation.

Hundreds of species of animal and plant life die away each year. This is not new, it has always happened through the years as life on Earth evolved,and will go on happening naturally as environments change. But the loss of some types of plant life could be catastrophic because we must be able to grow new strains if we are to ensure the continuation of our food supply. For example, only four varieties of seed are used in the great wheat-growing areas of the United States and Canada. If they are to remain immune from infection those types must be genetically changed every so often. If there are no other strains left from which to breed new ones the time could come when much of the Western world's food is wiped out by bacteria or fungi.

Throughout the world, but particularly in the developed nations, the burning of coal, oil and gas has been filling the air with Carbon Dioxide and slowly creating a filter high in the sky which prevents Infra Red rays from the Sun from being reflected back into space. The effect of this is to heat the atmosphere and raise our air temperature. Scientists have estimated that in thirty or forty years it will increase by two degrees, enough to melt part of the ice caps, raise sea levels, swamp vast areas of low-lying land and further change the world's weather patterns.

There are other ways too in which the world is being progressively polluted: sewage pouring into the rivers and seas is killing marine life; chemically-laden smoke from factory chimneys is creating "acid rain" which falls from the sky to wither crops and forests hundreds of miles away; car exhausts are producing toxic chemicals which kill off trees. In Norway there are more than 2,000 lakes which have no fish living in them because of what industry is doing to the atmosphere in Britain and Western Europe. In Germany, America and Canada forests are dying because of the fumes which pour out of cars and lorries which pound the roads day and night.

Garbage, much of it valuable material which should be re-cycled, not dumped, is an enormous problem. New York produces 22,000 tons of it every day. People sailing on the seas drop glass and plastic containers overboard in shattering quantities – with more than 70,000 merchant ships afloat nearly a million glass and plastic containers are being thrown into the sea every day, with disastrous effects on wild life, let alone the fouling of coastlines.

Wars have left the oceans and vast tracts of land dangerously contaminated with explosives and chemicals. Seventy- and forty-year old unexploded shells are turned over by the plough nearly every day in France and Belgium, Germany, Poland and Russia. Unexploded Second World War aircraft bombs are discovered regularly wherever the air armadas dropped their loads. Parts of Vietnam are huge, uncharted, lethal minefields. At sea the corroded remains of chemical and explosive weapons, dumped there after the world wars, are dredged up or washed ashore, and periodically dead fish float to the surface, killed by phosphorous seeping out of piles of ammunition brushed under the carpet of the sea: out of sight but not to be forgotten.

In 1983 the 6th United Nations Trade and Development Conference was held in Yugoslavia to discuss, amongst other things, how to ease the lot of 125 under-developed countries: seventy-seven nations were represented. The only decision they made was to continue to send food to Kampuchea for another year. Also in 1983 the leaders of the world's nations, great and small, met in Mexico to discuss the population detonation, food supply, material resources and conservation. There had been great hopes that many worth-while plans and projects would result from their discussions. They made no decisions at all. In 1984 an "economic summit" was held in London at which Western leaders tried to resolve some of their problems, such as inflation, unemployment and the massive debts owed by Poland, Mexico and most of the South American countries, debts which threaten to topple the whole capitalist system. They made no decisions either. They, it seems, like the others before them, thought it was all too difficult.

And in 1986 we had Chernobyl. Apart from the localised effects and the air-borne pollution that contaminated people, animals and plants in many parts of the world one direct consequence is that nearly all the reindeer in Lappland, more than half a million of them, will have to be killed because they live off mosses which have absorbed, and hold on to, lethal quantities of radioactivity. The reindeer eat the moss and the radioactivity enters their bodies, making their meat inedible and their pelts, which were used for all manner of things, unsafe. Even people who have lived isolated lives, minding their own business, cannot now escape the consequences of what other people do hundreds of miles away. Nor can any of us.

*

## CHAPTER TWELVE

# FLASHPOINT

People are apprehensive about human nature. They feel that it is not to be trusted. They fear, deep down, that an untamed brute lurks under the thin cloth of civilised behaviour which a proportion of the human race has worn for a very short time. Men's instincts have not changed and even the gentle sex have a capacity for causing insidious mental cruelty which is as damaging in its way as the more obvious male aggression. Human nature is not a night at the opera, it is rage and destruction in the glare from burning buildings, it is the shrill voice of cold contempt.

Even so, with the passage of time people have become more caring and compassionate. Only four or five generations ago crowds in London would gather in their thousands to watch a man being hung, dismembered and disembowelled; today in Britain the death penalty has been abolished as being uncivilised and inhuman. But even now in some parts of the Islamic world a man's hand may be publicly struck off for stealing, and in Africa witch doctors burn "evil" people. In China during the Cultural Revolution of the 1960s and '70s pianists' fingers were broken because they played the music of Mozart and Chopin. And only forty years ago in one of the world's most civilised countries the leaders of the abortive plot to kill Hitler were hung up on meat hooks thrust in between their shoulder blades. Nobody can predict what people will do.

If it were possible to do so a scientist wanting to study mankind would take a microscopically thin wafer of human tissue from the body of the United States to represent the whole of the genus Homo Sapiens. In it he would find specimens of every race on Earth, and mixtures of many.

The United States is the fourth largest nation in the world, after Russia, Canada and China,and has the fourth largest population, after China, India and Russia. Until 1803 most of its people were white, Anglo-Saxon Protestants and during the years between 1830 and 1860 nine out of every ten of the immigrants arriving in America had British or German blood. Then between 1860 and 1921, when strict quotas were imposed, 30 million more people went to the great land of opportunity, most of whom were Polish, Russian, Slavic, Irish or Italian – and believers in the Roman Catholic faith. Some Chinese and Japanese settled on the West coast. Today, only 45% of Americans are descended from the original settlers and there are around 50 million Roman Catholics in the nation, slightly less than a quarter of its population of 240 million.

In the early years of American evolution it was very necessary to instil in the people who came there from so many different places a feeling of national identity. The Flag, the Anthem, the Hand-on-Heart were, and still are, overt means of bringing together people of many faiths, traditions and cultures. However, though this has succeeded to the extent that the great majority of Americans are proudly patriotic there are many vocal and influential minority groups who retain their ethnic basis and seldom marry outside it – Jewish, Italian, Spanish, Black. The American population is not an integrated mixture of people and races, and its central core of wealth and power remains what it was when George Washington became the first President: White, Anglo-Saxon and Protestant.

The offspring of the black slaves imported in the 18th and 19th Centuries now number 11% of the total population; there are about twenty-five million of them. They, on average, live seven years less than their white neighbours and take home around 70% of what a white man earns for doing the same job. One third of them live below the recognised poverty line. However, between 1960 and 1970, thanks to government response to the Civil Rights movement, their share of the better jobs in the nation increased by 72%, and has gone on increasing. Today, the mayors of six of the principal cities of the United States are black, including the capital, Washington, Los Angeles and even Chicago, not long ago one of the greatest centres of racial stress.

Of the original inhabitants of the land, there are eight million descendants, so despite the culling of the Red Indians, which ended only about a hundred years ago, they have bred well. However, they are financially worse off than than anyone else in the nation, die, on average, twenty years before the rest of their fellow Americans and are prone to alcoholism. Nearly half of them live in poverty on reservations, in very poor conditions. There are also around ten million Americans of mixed native/Spanish descent, who originated in Puerto Rico, Mexico or California. Like the Indians they have a below-average standard of living and a high crime rate.

There are six million Jews in America, one third of all the Jews in the world. Three quarters of them are "white collar" workers (as distinct from "blue-collar" labouring people), and 95% of the time they marry other Jews. Intelligent and energetic, and spurred on perhaps by the determination to prove themselves in the face of prejudice, they produce a disproportionately high number of clever thinkers, musicians, writers, artists and businessmen. They prove that a closed group passing on its genetic inheritance in a good living environment produces talented human beings. The 20th Century world owes much of its scientific knowledge and medical progress to Jewish people, and its entertainment to Jewish creativity: musicianship, the cinema, the musical, drama and humour are especially theirs.

North America evolved out of a turbulent past. War with Britain in 1812, when Americans invaded Canada and the British burnt Washington (the city, not the man.) War with Mexico in 1846 after the US annexed Texas, and at the end of which Mexico was obliged to sell California and New Mexico to America for fifteen million dollars. A bloody and punishing four years of mutual massacre in 1861. War with Spain in 1898 – one result of which was that the United States acquired the Philippines for twenty million dollars. (At least a quarter of a million Filipinos were killed during the American suppression of insurgency in that nation.) And the everlasting war of attrition as Christians moved westwards, finding homesteads, founding cities and bringing God to the savages, if they could find any left alive. All these conflicts took place while the nation was growing and spreading in size and numbers.

When the first pioneers arrived alone in a wilderness they chose a likely spot, unharnessed the horses, unloaded the wagon, built a shack and started to dig the soil. Where towns began to grow beside a river (except where wells were easily dug all human habitation, until the invention of hydraulic pumps in the 19th Century and their general use in the 20th, was near running water) those in charge laid out a rectangular street plan based on the square mile and divided up into blocks. When trains arrived along the newly laid railroads they brought materials to make new blocks, and the people to live in them. As the migration moved ever westwards the goods and food people needed were transported from the expanding centres of industry and agriculture in the east. Then in the 1920s the face of America began to change: the motor car pushed its bull-nose along dirt tracks that were progressively "metalled", and a ribbon of dwellings, garages, factories and shops mushroomed along the new highways. On the United States' nine million square kilometres of land they have etched a tracery of six million kilometres of roads, and around them towns have merged into cities and cities into each other. Three out of every four Americans live in urban areas. On the East and on the West coast there are huge interconnected human settlements in which live thirty million people. Twelve thousand people work in the Sears Tower in Chicago, which rises 1,454 feet into the sky. Upwards and closer they go, surrounded by great open spaces.

By 1940 there were thirty-two million vehicles in the USA; now there are getting on for 120 million! To Americans oil is the fuel of life itself. The number of people employed in the transportation industry alone equals the total populations of Sweden and Norway. Americans are forever on the move, still, mostly, Westwards. One fifth of them move house every year; forty million people looking for the good life and, mostly, finding it. The mobility of labour, the willingness of people to move in order to increase their purchasing power, helps the economy, since new enterprises are not still-born for the lack of workers. New is nice and change is good in its own right. They are forever tearing down the new to build something even newer – and better.

Politically, the USA has developed on the basis of the American Dream of opportunity for all and freedom of choice. For the fittest the sky is the limit. The policy is to encourage competition, and for this reason many of the services which are nationally controlled in other countries, such as telephones, railways and airlines, are in private ownership. Most day-to-day administration is conducted at state level, with the federal government coordinating only those matters which are important to the nation as a whole, such as foreign policy, defence and jurisdiction. Because in the early days people nearly always made good there has been a tendency to expect the sick, the lame and the halt to get on as best they can: if they do not do well then it must be their own fault. In the 1960s state assistance to the unemployed was as low as $600 per annum for a family of four – starvation income – rising in some places to around $2,000, but this situation has improved over the years.

In all societies there are people who have more than others. In Britain the top 1% of the population own about a fifth of the nation's marketable wealth, the top 10% own 56% of it and the top 50% have 96% of it; it is bad news to be on the bottom half of the nation's inheritors and earners. In America things are not quite as bad; 10% of the population possesses more than a quarter of the nation's entire wealth. Most of those who do are WASPS. Nevertheless, nearly all Americans enjoy the highest standard of living of any people anywhere; their annual income per head is more than twice that of the average in developed countries and *twenty times* that of people in the undeveloped ones. The relatively low earning power of the Blacks and other less privileged Americans still leaves them far better off than most people in other parts of the world.

With only 6% of the world's population Americans consume 40% of the world's resources but a lot of what they use lies under their own feet: their enormous wealth stems from the fact that small numbers of eager pilgrims spread into an empty land packed full of natural treasures. They have 25% of the world's coal, 21% of its oil, 25% of its copper, 46% of its maize, 21% of its meat, and so on. The Americans have so many of the world's good things that not until the late '60s, during the Vietnam war, did they begin to know what it meant to be stretched financially, or emotionally. The Great War barely touched them, the Second World War lasted, for them, a very short time, but twenty years later the cost of modern warfare began to reduce even the huge piles of gold in Fort Knox, and the long saga of failure wore away the brash confidence that had been their hallmark.

As they see it, Americans have been obliged to take on the task of defending the free world against the advancing tide of communism, which will eventually overturn the capitalist system which has given the highest standard of living anywhere in the world to its inhabitants. Indeed some Americans believe they have a mission to bring the benefits of their way of life to people who are less well off. Not only are they politically in head-on collision with the Soviet Union, they feel a moral purpose in opposing it because of what is seen as the fundamental difference between communism and other forms of political allegience: that whereas other political concepts can lie alongside whatever spiritual beliefs are already held, to a fervent communist the God most Americans believe in does not exist. While this is true in theory it ignores the fact that millions in Russia, and in the Satellite countries, still worship the Christian God or Allah, that communism is a theory like any other, that people make communism and that human beings are essentially the same whichever side of an artificial political barrier they live.

In America in the post-war years this inflexible attitude led to an unreasonable crusade against any person suspected of having "Commie" views. For a short time there was a type of persecution reminiscent of the zeal of Christian bigots, and though this was short-lived, like the victims of that bigotry, it left a deep-rooted belief that they were right and anybody who veered Left was irretrievably wrong, an outlook which has detrimentally clouded American thinking and foreign policy ever since.

*

In 1988 the European heart of Russia will have existed for a thousand years. In the earliest days Vladimir of Kiev (who kept 800 concubines, give or take a few) chose Orthodox Christianity as the national religion after sending envoys to study the Jewish, Moslem, Roman Catholic and Byzantine Orthodox rituals. When the Golden Horde arrived in the 13th Century they tolerated the Russian church and its monasteries, which were thus able to preserve the culture learnt from the Greeks and Romans. However, Russia was cut off from the Italian Renaissance and did not begin to catch up with West European developments until the 18th Century, and then only in some of its cities.

It was Ivan the Terrible, the first Tsar – the Russian name for Caesar, as is the German "Kaiser" – who in the 16th Century pushed the boundary of Russia south to the Caspian Sea and sent people to occupy the great, almost empty, spaces of Siberia. Expansion and development continued for the next three hundred years: over many decades Russians slowly moved south to Turkestan and Kazakhstan, to Samarkand and the Afghan Pamir, though not without opposition from the inhabitants. As a young officer Leo Tolstoy fought in the campaigns against the Tartars. By 1890 the nation had become multi-lingual and multi-religious and around half its population was non-Russian.

The university in Moscow was founded in 1755 but when a census was taken in 1897 only 27% of children of school age were being educated. Since it began, the peasant society had changed little; scattered small communities with no organisation (and therefore no political power) lived on great windswept plains or in clearings in the vast forests, ill clad, near to starvation and sharing their hovels with the beasts of the field. Today, 90% of people over 15 years of age are literate.

The total population of more than 250 million people live in eight partially self-governing republics, such as Belo-Russia, Georgia, Kazakhstan. The largest is the Russian Soviet Federal Socialist Republic, which covers three-quarters of the total land mass of the Union, including part of Siberia, and alone has around 135 million people living in it. 83% of them are Russians and the rest of them are Ukranians and Tartars. Siberia, two-thirds of which is covered in pine forests, extends over nearly half the territory of the Soviet Union and contains three-quarters of its natural resources, including 55,000 oil and gas wells.

There are a great many similarities between the Soviet Union and the United States: a large, mixed, and to some extent, similar population (Ukrainians, Slavs, Jews, Chinese); intensely patriotic people, most of whom fervently believe in their way of life; enormous manpower and natural resources; gigantic Armed Forces. At first sight though, Russia would appear to have the best prospects.

Because of its geographical position in the centre of the greatest land mass in the world (50 million square kilometres) it can defend itself or expand into Europe on "interior lines", whereas the United States is isolated by great oceans. (Historically, interior lines – the ability to deploy forces at relatively short distances from a strong base rather than having to probe from a great distance towards the enemy's base – have been militarily advantageous: control is easier and re-supply simpler; more can be achieved with less effort; land forces, which must, in the end, decide any war, are more easily deployed on interior lines than those conveyed by naval forces on exterior lines.)

In the last half century it has hugely increased its industrial power and developed the most modern technology, primarily for the production of war weaponry, the manufacture and use of which, unlike in America, is not constrained by public opinion. However, the USSR cannot yet feed itself, relies on the West, especially America, for grain, and its economy, despite great efforts, is still functioning badly. In part, this is due to the fact that the physical size of the nation and its huge population make it extemely difficult to govern from the centre. Americans recognised this fact in the early days of their existence and found the answer by delegating a large amount of control to the constituent states, something which the Soviets feel unable to do for fear that the whole structure will fall apart due to the many tensions that exist because of its oppressive regime and the slow improvement in standards of living.

Russia is a closed society headed by a small caucus of guarded and hidden men who maintain themselves in power by continuing the methods used since the revolution of 1917: censorship of all information by strict government control of the media; a network of commissars throughout society and the Armed Forces who are responsible for the indoctrination and covert surveillance of the population and are backed by secret police; harsh sentencing of any people who oppose the regime – death, imprisonment, banishment to Siberia or detention in mental asylums. Financial inflation, absenteeism, alcoholism and cynicism are said to be endemic in Russia, but because it is a closed society it is difficult for foreigners to know what is going on. Unlike in the West, where democracy demands the publication of nearly all information, the Soviet government publishes only what it sees fit to publish, bans the reading of many books – for example, it is a criminal offence to read Dr Zhivago by Pasternak ("Zhivago" means imprisonment) – jams external broadcasts, prevents its own people from travelling freely, inside the USSR and outside it, and closely watches the few foreigners who come as visitors. Politically, no choice is offered: citizens may vote Yes or No to only one Communist candidate in each electoral area. (The extent of intimidation and social pressures – Ivan next door may tell on them if they don't vote – may be judged from the fact that, contrary to human nature, 98% of the population feel obliged to take part in this travesty of democracy, whereas when populations feel free it is unusual to get more than a 50% turnout in a democratic vote.)

The USSR contains a great diversity of races who speak many different languages and dialects: there is no single unifying language as there is in the USA. Power is held by a small group of White, European, Atheist Communists but more than a fifth of the population are Moslem (the proportion is growing, since they are breeding more quickly than non-Moslems) and the majority are non-Russian in race and culture. While the ethnic groups in the United States are blended together throughout the nation, in Russia most of them are separated by geography and history, and could therefore pose a coordinated threat to the central government.

The favoured ruling elite have a paranoid fear of capitalism in general (which, contrary to communist teaching, contrives to produce a better standard of living for the population as a whole than communism has ever achieved anywhere) and of NATO in particular. They feel surrounded by political animosity and a looming military threat. From their point of view the existence of the United States Seventh Fleet in the China Sea, of the Sixth Fleet in the Mediterranean, of 100,000 US troops and many air force squadrons deployed permanently in West Germany, of American nuclear-capable submarines, aircraft and missiles, which can strike at them from any direction, constitute a massive threat to their regime. The independent nuclear deterrents possessed by France and Britain reinforce, in their minds, the belligerence of NATO.

The mutually antagonistic Russians and Chinese( who also have nuclear weapons) share a 4,800 kilometre border. The Chinese leaders accuse the Soviets of diverging from the true teachings of Marx and of making military incursions into their territory. Periodically they verbally abuse the Russians, presumably in order to keep their citizens aware of the threat posed by people who grow in military power with every passing day. Distrust patrols their frontier with loaded weapons.

Externally, the Satellite states have a Christian heritage and an historical antipathy to Russia; their numerous attempts to to break away from their Communist shackles are the visible eruptions of the boils which continue to supurate under the surface. Materially they are not badly enough off to want Marxism but though they may desperately wish for freedom the obvious presence of Soviet Armoured Divisions on their soil is a reminder that the punishments which followed the uprisings in East Germany, Hungary and Czechoslovakia would be repeated.

Each of the Satellites has an army which is integrated into the Warsaw Pact military structure. The period of military service is used to further indoctrinate young men in Marxist ideology, and to remind them of the need to guard against the threat from the West.

But for all that these soldiers, and the populations they are conscripted from, would be a dubious asset to the Soviets should war ever come.

The Soviet Union cannot afford to release the Satellites from bondage because they would almost certainly slacken centralised political control in response to public demand – say for Trade Unions, now banned – and open their borders with the West. However, with each year that passes it becomes increasingly difficult to prevent them from gaining independence.

*

When the World War ended forty years ago America was by far the richest and most powerful nation on Earth. Europe had been the big battlefield, and looked like one. Russians had united to defend their Motherland against German attack but their nation was devastated. (Had the Germans treated the Ukranians better, they might have welcomed "liberation" and turned against Russia.)

American aid helped the nations of Western Europe to recover and by the mid-'60s the capitalist societies were at the peak of their ascendency. In America the Korean war was long forgotten and the Cuban missile crisis was a cause for some pride; the Russian bluff had been called. Britain had almost finished its inglorious retreat from its empire, the debacle of Suez was a faint scar and the mini skirt was raising spirits. In France they too were uplifted and a new feeling of rebirth was evident: from now on they would go their own way and the rest of the world could go wherever it liked. West Germany's economic miracle was a fact of life; discipline, pride and good order had earned their due rewards; the Volkswagen truly was the People's Car, and millions owned one. On the other side of the Berlin Wall the same virtues had somehow failed to make much difference, except that the East Germans became the most dedicated communists outside Russia.

There had been many developments in medicine, in agriculture and in communications but the field in which most progress had been made was the battlefield. Nuclear powered ships and submarines had been built which did not need refuelling before they fell apart or became obsolete, fighter aircraft flew at twice the speed of sound, bombers could accurately deliver their loads from great heights, tanks had stabilised fire-control systems which allowed their gunners to shoot accurately even when their vehicle was going over rough ground at forty miles an hour, and the atom bomb had been miniaturised. The biggest advances of all had been made with rockets. Inter-continental ballistic missiles, immune from interception, began to supersede aircraft as the chief means of delivering long-distance nuclear warheads.

Having established the ground rules the superpowers began to manufacture all the hardware they might need if it came to a showdown. As the years passed and technology advanced so did the need for more sophisticated weapons. Generation followed superseded generation. Much of the old stuff was sold off to the emergent new nations of the third world. The superpowers, together with Britain and France, became the suppliers of the Arabs, the Jews, the Indians, the Pakistanis, the Vietnamese, the Koreans, the South American and the African republics. One of the stated aims of the United Nations Organisation is to regulate the sale of armaments, but as in so many other things it has proved to be ineffective.

Like the League of Nations the United Nations has no armed forces permanently on call. It is understandable that nations, already fully extended financially with defence expenditure on their own account, should not wish to spend money on keeping troops ready who may never be used, but the present system means that there is bound to be a significant delay between aggression and any response to it by the international forum. In modern warfare such a lapse of time may give the aggressor an advantage which cannot be redressed by subsequent UN intervention. Sometimes the presence of UN troops has stopped the fighting and sometimes it has prevented further outbreaks, but there have been occasions when they have been brushed aside by the combatants.

*

No UN force will be powerful enough to part the two sides in the big battle, if it ever comes.

It has been planned for nearly forty years. Generations of generals have given the problem much thought and then retired to Munchen or Minsk, Oswestry or Ohio to grow roses. Time after time the game has been played on the war maps of NATO and Warsaw Pact operations rooms, with new generation following new generation of weapons. Bigger ships and submarines, faster aircraft, heavier tanks, more firepower; better communications, closer battlefield control, faster response times; increased load-carrying cross-country capacity keeping pace with growing logistic requirements. The one constant has been the obliterating effect of nuclear weapons, though they too have changed over the years, getting bigger, with destructive power equivalent to millions of tons of TNT, or small enough to be delivered by 8-inch artillery shells. The battlefield will be West Germany and knowing it the West Germans put six times as many troops into NATO's front line as the British do.

Red Army doctrine is offensive and NATO forces are defensive: for them to be the aggressors they would have to outnumber their potential opponents, but the balance lies the other way. Russia and the other Warsaw Pact forces out-number NATO in every respect, as the following figures, which change constantly in matters of detail but not in principle, indicate. In manpower the Warsaw Pact could muster 4 million men to NATO's 2.6; 30,000 main battle tanks to NATO's 13,500; 7,430 combat aircraft to NATO's 2,990. They have 515 medium range nuclear missiles to NATO's 59, and 1,600 short range and artillery nuclear weapons to NATO's 1,200. Russia can send to sea three times as many submarines as the Americans: and 945 submarine-launched missiles to NATO's 632. The rest of the nuclear weapons to make up the grand total of 55,000 mentioned earlier would be delivered by aircraft or by multiple warheads on rockets. Or they are land mines. Yes, nuclear bombs designed to be exploded in the Earth in front of attacking formations.

For nearly forty years now NATO has had the capability to annihilate Russia, which has countered by constantly improving its own nuclear potential. The situation has reached the stage where it is totally lunatic; and MAD is the phrase used to describe it – Mutually Assured Destruction: the capability to ensure the total annihilation of the opponent. In nuclear power the Russians could fire 6,000 megatons compared with the American's 4,000 – although the USA has 9,600 warheads against the USSR's 8,000. Both have far more than would be needed for mutually assured destruction.

Because of the imbalance of conventional forces NATO's declared doctrine is to delay a Russian advance until diplomacy has secured a ceasefire, but if that fails, to use battlefield nuclear weapons as the only way to redress the balance: the alternatives are to surrender on the Rhine, which Soviet forces would reach in four or five days using conventional warfare, or to "go nuclear". Either way, West Germany would be totally devastated. In the hope that sanity would prevail before this happened NATO adopted a "forward strategy" some years ago: its forces are deployed as far to the East as possible. The penalty for this is that due to a shortage of troops the NATO line is thinly spread along the front, with little depth and inadequate reserves.

Today, politicians and generals on both sides of the Atlantic urge that NATO's conventional forces should be increased so as to lower the threshold between normal and nuclear war. The problem is that there is no money with which to do so. Even before the recent world recession, which is mostly a consequence of the decision by the Organisation of Oil Exporting Countries to increase oil prices in 1974, NATO nations had great difficulty in making enough of their Gross National Product available for defence. Most of their citizens demanded that there should be no cuts in education and medical and social services, and good politicians must abide by the wishes of the people who elect them. Despite this, many NATO nations have increased their spending by up to 3% per annum during the last few years in an attempt to redress the balance against the massive build-up of Russian and Satellite forces. But inevitably, because they cannot catch up, they have to rely as much as before on the strategy of nuclear deterrence, the balance of fear.

The chess game of checking weapon development by counter-development, of seeing a marginal lead being overtaken and then retrieved, is played by a very small number of men – politicians, generals and scientists – who, in a sense, inhabit the Real world. The civilian populations around them pursue their unrealistic lives in almost total ignorance of the scale of the catastrophe which is being planned on their behalf.

Some people say that there could be no possible reason for the Russians to launch an offensive against the West, that they would gain nothing and would risk unacceptable damage. The Soviets themselves say that their forces are needed only for self-protection against the West or the Chinese. If that is so, then why is their weapon development structured for offensive and not defensive action, and why are their forces far bigger than they need be for defence, and growing continually in size and sophistication? A logical answer is that because of their paranoid fear of the democracies the Russian leaders *do* regard them as being primarily defensive, but that they would be used, in reality or as a means of applying political pressure, to further their long-standing aim of spreading communism if that could be achieved without too great a penalty.

For decades both sides have, from time to time, discussed the control of nuclear weapons and the limitation of conventional forces. In recent years disarmament talks have been held in Geneva, in Madrid and in the UN Assembly in New York. In Vienna politicians and soldiers have been meeting, on and off, for years to try to achieve Mutual and Balanced Force Reductions but like the peace talks in Panmunjon in Korea the MBFR meetings are a charade.

Twenty years ago the main impediment to disarmament was the problem of verification: how could each side be sure that the other was abiding by any agreement? Then, the only way was for very large numbers of observers to be permanently stationed in the other's territory. Not surprisingly, this was not acceptable. Today, satellites can do the job. It needs only three of them, in geostatic orbit 37,000 kilometres above the Equator, to observe the whole of the world's surface. On a clear day cameras carried in other satellites which regularly and frequently travel over selected strips of territory can relay back to their controllers precise details, even the number plates, of military vehicles parked on barrack squares in Brest-Litovsk or Bielefeld; can monitor the building and output of weapons factories; can specify how many ships there are in a harbour; how many shelters there are around an airfield to protect its planes against surprise attack. Technology has given us the means of accurate verification but not the ability to remove distrust from people's minds, as the inconclusive summit meeting of November 1985 showed.

We have very little time in which to establish understanding between the two sides. If we do not, then nuclear war will come. Intentionally, by accident, or by miscalculation.

*

## CHAPTER THIRTEEN

# A PERSONAL COMMENTARY

It is said that nothing in the world is new, that it has all happened before. This statement is not true. The world is in an unprecedented situation.

Never before has it been mentally partitioned, en masse, into two opposed and incompatible beliefs on the fringes of which are quickly-multiplying masses of under-privileged and uneducated people. Never before have successive generations been subjected to constant indoctrination against an openly named enemy under conditions of mass-media communication; after forty years, distrust has become ever more deeply rooted. And never before has the total destruction of humanity and most of the living things on our planet been possible.

This year alone the United States is spending around 300,000 million dollars preparing for a war they do not want. Only a few men in the Kremlin know how much the Soviet Union is spending preparing for a war they do not want either but it is almost certainly more than that. In between the two giants who are squandering these great fortunes are the impotent inheritors of brilliant cultural traditions, and all around them are the ignorant and unfortunate millions in Africa, Asia and South America who, through no fault of their own, have never possessed anything, not even enough to eat. Thousands of them are dying every day of starvation.

Like sleepwalkers, people in the Northern hemisphere go about their business, raise their children, visit the hospital, bury grandad, buy a new television set, hope to God that the unthinkable never comes and try not to think about it. In the East, those who try to protest about the dangers of a nuclear conflict have no voice. In the West some join anti-war groups, such as the British Campaign for Nuclear Disarmament which has existed since the 1950s but has had a new lease of life in the last few years. They march, unfurl their banners, listen to speeches – which, for unexplained reasons, usually castigate the supporters and not the suppressors of freedom – smile and wave at the TV cameras and go home again. Until the other side proves by its actions that it has no aggressive intent we must keep our guard up, they are told by their politicians. That is very true. Freedom to speak, to voice criticisms, to choose a political system, are rare in the world and must be safeguarded. Human Rights are recognised in few places. During the Cultural Revolution in China millions were killed in the name of Marxism. In recent years more than ten thousand people have died because they offended Marxists in Europe. Since the mad Moslem took over Iran more than five thousand people have been executed and during the reign of terror of the Fascist regime in Argentina more than twelve thousand men and women were exterminated. Thousands of Vietnamese died when more than a million of them tried to escape, in mostly unseaworthy boats, after the Communists arrived. More than three million Afghans have crossed the border into Pakistan since Russian liberators arrived in their country. In many parts of the world people are being tortured in prisons because of their political beliefs.

Though freedom must be defended we must find a sensible balance between the shield and the sword, and the intention must surely be to get rid of both as soon as possible. Yet the people who could do so do not. Politicians are powerless, blinded by historical prejudices and enmeshed by international alliances, while under them the mass of people are imprisoned by social pressures. As before in 1914 and 1939 hardly anybody dares to speak out for fear of being thought unpatriotic or deranged. Meanwhile the world totters inexorably towards extinction: from starvation due to over-population, from the exhaustion of its resources, from pollution. And, probably long before these things have had time to take effect, from the detonation of hundreds of nuclear weapons.

*

When the first civilisations evolved the human population of our planet was tiny. While great lumps of rock were being laboriously dragged for miles across Salisbury Plain to Stonehenge there were only two or three hundred cannibals in the whole of Scotland. Only a hundred years ago vast areas of the planet had never been seen by any man or woman. Now most of the Earth is crawling with people. Thousands of millions of the species have quite unconsciously accomplished the fantastically difficult process of becoming alive and have opened their eyes to the beauty of this place – though for some it is hard to see it behind the screens of grinding poverty and dirt that surround them. The growth of humanity through the centuries looks like an express train approaching from a great distance: a speck on the horizon becoming larger and larger until it blocks our whole field of vision and overwhelms us with its size and noise and energy. Now, parts of the Earth groan with the weight of millions of deprived people scratching around for food and withering in the Sun's heat while in other places the gifted ones use seeds from their ancestors' brains to push back the barriers of ignorance in universities built on land where dinosaurs used to tear each other to shreds. It is difficult to believe, sometimes, just how far we have come, but there is still so much that is wrong. Three things in particular are apparent: the ignorance in which we still live; the reluctance with which we discard out-moded ideas; the failure to foresee, comprehend and act upon the dangers which threaten us.

*

After uncounted and unrecorded generations of human beings had lived and died the Sumerians, the Greeks and the Romans made great advances, but their populations were tiny and only a handful of them contributed anything significant. Many hundreds of years passed before other men and women took up the building blocks they found lying around and began to make a bigger and better house to live in. A few talented souls created beautiful pictures to hang on the walls, fine music to listen to and books that took the minds of men and women far far away from the fire which warmed the room they sat in. But this happened only in the last ten generations, and only in some parts of the world. For nine tenths of its existence Mankind has lived in a state of savagery.

Because some human beings have always discovered and invented new things every generation in the developed countries considers itself to be far in advance of its predecessors. In some ways it is right to think so: compare what children learn today with what their mothers and fathers were taught in the 1950s. (It is said that the amount of knowledge available to us has doubled in every decade since the Second World War.) Young people looking back a hundred years are astonished by the outlandish attitudes and clothes then worn, and amazed at how ignorant people were. Two hundred years ago our ancestors are only just recognisable to us as being people who lived, remotely, the sort of lives we live. Three hundred years and beyond they are so distant we feel that they lived in another world: ours is not theirs. Yet though each new generation tends to think that they are on the fringe of knowing everything there is to know, we are still incredibly ignorant about so many things.

When the Great Plague was ravaging England again in 1666 Isaac Newton, at the age of 23, had discovered the mathematical laws of differential calculus and variable quantities and had thought out the basic principles of light and gravity and how to determine speeds. When he lectured at Cambridge University very few people went to listen to him because hardly anyone could understand what he was talking about. That situation applies today: at the pinnacle of the pyramid of knowledge there are some whose minds are reaching out so far that only a handful of other people know where they are going. Yet even they are still only on the verge of discovery. Newton, speaking of his astounding achievements, said, "I was like a little boy playing on the sea-shore, diverting myself by now and then finding a smoother pebble, a prettier shell, than ordinary, whilst the great ocean of truth lay undiscovered before me." More pebbles have been found, and a shell or two, but the great ocean still holds its secrets.

Despite all that has been learnt since the time when the Buddha lived we are no further forward than he was when he said that we do not know enough to understand how the Universe came to be created. Astronomers learn a little more almost every day but more often than not their new knowledge poses more questions than it answers. And our ignorance about the infinite is matched by our incomprehension about what goes on in the infinitesimal. About that we are becoming clearer, but it is going to take a very long time to fathom out what makes cells, genes and proteins function as they do; to understand the reasons for our bodily and mental behaviour; to truly comprehend what life is. For example, even with the technology now available it is going to take thousands of scientists another twenty years or so fully to evaluate the genetic structure of human beings. In medicine and mental health, for all the advances made recently, the blind are still leading the blind. And of dire importance is the fact that we are nowhere near to discovering how to change or control our animal nature; how to eliminate the brutality which is so at odds with our intellectual achievements. The most advanced people have to live with basically the same instincts as the most backward, the most damaging of which is aggression. Almost half the dreams people have involve violence. Our subconscious fights long-dead enemies.

One of the greatest impediments to progress is the fact that our acquisition of knowledge is not matched by a comparably rapid ability to change our attitudes. Real comprehension is lagging behind raw learning. Religion, the cause of so much death, destruction and waste, is the most damaging example of this. The existence of a God or gods, like theories about the origins of the Universe, cannot be proved. Which does not mean that, beyond the limits of our puny comprehension, mighty supernatural powers do not exist, but it cannot be right for educated people in the 20th Century to cling desperately to ideas and myths which were first thought of by their primitive and ignorant ancestors. Less than a hundred years ago some tribes in Siberia believed that human beings were always surrounded by invisible enemies; voracious spirits constantly demanding bestial sacrifices in exchange for the withholding of punishments. Cringing, these people offered up their ransoms: they crucified dogs on trees. Their beliefs, like those of the Aztecs, have gone, but if most of their descendents now scoff at such things why should different but equally irrational superstitions be desperately adhered to by otherwise sensible, informed and cultured people?

Mystery is still the soil at the roots of religion. There is no single unifying belief common to all the religions in the world, no thread which relates them all, except awe of invisible powers. Many religions condemn specific acts which, unrestrained, would destroy society – murder, stealing, lying and, in monogamous communities, adultery – but these are sensible and logical prohibitions which would be necessary even if they were not linked to religion.

Ever since men and women began to think, they have tried to find ways to communicate with powers which they hope are guiding us. So be it. People need comforting but surely they should not be bemused by myths or blinded by hatred.

The profligate spending of Earth's resources despite the fact that the time is fast approaching when we are going to run out of them is a startling example of the lack of foresight shown by the so-called leaders of the world, who cannot raise their eyes beyond their own petty problems and prejudices. Planning continues based on an assumption made long ago: that Earth has an infinite quantity of resources which can be utilised for an eternity of time. It is not so, yet many people still swallow without question theories which presuppose that it is. For example, clever men talk convincingly about colonising other planets.

The ability of human beings to travel into deep space is a science-fiction myth. When the British Astronomer Royal said so a few years ago his words were greeted with great derision: there is no limit to what we can achieve, people said; just see what we have done! They did not, and many still do not, want to accept that there are limits, yet this is surely so.

The velocity needed by a rocket to escape from the pull of Earth's gravity is 6.9 kilometres per second. Space rockets are, of course, achieving this, but not significantly more. Light travels at 300,000 kilometres per second, *forty thousand* times as fast. Even if by some fantastic inventive break-through it became possible for human beings to travel at that sort of speed generations of them would have to live for hundreds of years on a spacecraft, breeding new generations on the way, before it could reach out beyond our own galaxy. Much closer to home the planets in the Solar System, still many years away in time of flight, cannot support human life, being either too hot or too cold and without a breathable atmosphere. We evolved on Mother Earth and cannot live in an icebox or a furnace. Other creatures may do so, indeed the first spark of life here could conceivably have come from somewhere distant (locked deep inside a meteorite and spilt out when it shattered on impact?) but not by mechanical means which are within our grasp. Why then do some people eagerly anticipate the expenditure of vast sums of money on space exploration when most of the human beings on Earth are underfed and many of them are suffering from incurable diseases?

Is our destiny not here, where we live? Are there not enough problems and worthy causes clamouring for our talents and attention? Should we not be looking at brain and body cells rather than trying to build castles in the air?

*

A hundred years after Newton died the entire world population was only 760 million, or thereabouts, and in the whole of Europe there were fewer people than there are in Japan today. Another hundred years on, in 1827, Europe's numbers had nearly doubled and so had the world's. We were on the verge of the great surge forward caused by the industrial revolution yet even in the 19th Century, as had always been the way, warfare, temples and jewellery had the first call upon the money available; the betterment of the lives of the less well-off took a poor second place. Though by the 1960s the masses in the West were benefitting from the general improvement in national wealth, warfare had become the biggest consumer of all. The great inventions of the 20th Century came together and reached their peak of achievement not in servicing humanity but in improving ways to destroy it.

War has filled a lot of the pages in this book but then that is not surprising, since it has always been one of mankind's chief concerns. Nor should it be surprising that some of the most advanced types of human beings now living wear military uniform. For example, the breadth of knowledge, the analytical ability, the physical skills and the destructive power possessed by the captain of an aircraft carrier, whether it sails from Norfolk in the USA or Murmansk in the USSR, are astounding. On the super-structure of his ship there are radio antennae through which it communicates with its base perhaps thousands of kilometres away, and radar scanners which give early warning of approaching aircraft. In its depths are sonars which search the sea under its hull and in the hull are nuclear-powered engines, a hospital in which advanced surgery can be done, gymnasiums, air-conditioned rooms in which men rest, eat and sleep. On its deck and in the hangars under them are up to ninety aircraft. Some carry airborne radars which can reach out beyond the range of the ship's radars. Some are armed with weapons which can shoot down aircraft or sink ships – supersonic missiles which can "home" on to their target automatically, carrying a lethal warhead. Some are loaded with atomic weapons, neat and compact but with explosive power thousands of times that of the Hiroshima bomb – a bucket of instant sunshine, some pilots call it. There are helicopters which can dunk a sonar in the sea miles away from the mother ship to detect an enemy submarine outside the range of her sonar. Other helicopters constantly hover around when the ship is launching or retrieving planes, in case of accidents. Expensive though the aircraft are – each of them costing several millions of roubles or dollars – they are cheap in comparison with the pilots, whose training has cost the nation far more. The planes carry sophisticated, computerised navigation systems. They can fly at around Mach 2 to a target hundreds of kilometres away and when they return will be landed at high speed on a tiny pitching deck by a man who has mastered what is one of the most difficult feats of muscular and mental coordination a human being is capable of.

Who can doubt that the First Prize for scientific progress and mental and physical skills has been won by War and not by Peace?

If the weapons under the control of that ship's captain were ever to be used on the orders of the politicians who control him whole cities and all the human beings in them would vanish from the face of our Earth. If even a fraction of the entire arsenal of nuclear weapons possessed by both sides were to be used nearly all life on Earth would end. The radius of damage caused by even small nuclear weapons is colossal. Half the energy released by the explosion goes into the blast wave, another third follows it in a great flash of searing heat. The rest becomes tissue-destroying atomic radiation, which would spread hundreds of kilometres from Ground Zero, the point on the Earth under which the fireball is exploded. If our atmosphere ever becomes saturated with it, the effects of the prevailing winds caused by its spin will result in all the Earth becoming radio-active, including the Southern Hemisphere. Furthermore, the dust clouds raised by the explosions will be so dense that, as happened once before so long ago, night could come for a hundred years. Nearly all living creatures and plant life would die. In the most primitive and dreadful conditions only a few creatures might survive but even if they did, in time the high level of radiation would bring about genetic changes, creating monsters. Perhaps after a few decades nothing at all that we could recognise would remain alive and the whole process of evolution would slowly start again . . . Perhaps.

*

It looks and sounds as if the old forms of artistic skill are dying. Today, the graphic arts and music are for the initiated only, and beyond the comprehension of other mortals. For a very brief span of Man's existence, just a few hundred years, it was a means by which some greatly gifted people created things which matched, in the senses, the visions other people were having in their minds. The visions have changed and so has the ability to match them with shape and colour and sound. Now it seems that the creative ones are working in other ways. In the United Kingdom thousands and thousands of children (four times as many as in the United States) have home computers. On them some are creating new worlds in the mind.

Already Tchaikovsky or Mahler symphonies could be created with a computer by feeding it with the distinctive patterns of notation and orchestration individual composers used and telling it to write scores using appropriate instruments. The Tenth Symphony of Beethoven may yet give pleasure to millions, though I doubt if it will have that touch of humanity which makes all the difference. Soon a man in Berlin or Paris will be able to pick up a telephone and speak in his own language to a man on the other side of Earth who will hear a voice not in German or French but in the language he uses. What he says in reply, in Japanese or Spanish, will be almost instantly translated by a computer and relayed by another voice synthesiser back to the first man.

The possibilities for the future are far beyond what we can now imagine – a world community working together for the good of all, language no longer a barrier between people, many more diseases conquered, virtually limitless energy produced by tapping the heat which lies in the centre of the Earth, aggression curbed by bland drugs, creativity a part of everyone's life. Utopia. But . . .

There is a limit to the number of people Earth can feed, there is a limit to the resources which can be taken from it to care for them and there is a limit to the amount of damage that we can do to it. We have already reached those limits.

*

"We are breeding a sub-species." These words were said by a harassed Brazilian administrator commenting on the appalling catastrophe which drought had brought to thousands of his people a year or two ago. Television pictures showed skinny, tattered, shoeless human beings raking through great piles of reeking garbage, fighting with vultures for cast-off pieces of anything edible which might be lying amongst the filth; showed little children smiling with pleasure at finding a fly-encrusted mouthful of dubious nourishment in which disease crawled, hungry and waiting to bite. Not even Homo Erectus, Upright Man, a million years ago, had to stoop so low. Surely it is not beyond the wit of man to get his priorities right and do something to help such people rather than spend great piles of gold producing the means of our destruction?

But despite the many reasons for pessimism there are things which give us hope for the future: the ability of the human brain to absorb and use more and more information; the fact that people can go, in two or three generations, from a backward to a much more advanced way of life, quickly adapting to new circumstances; the fact that people of many different races, religions and backgrounds can live together in relative peace and achieve common purposes – if the United States and the Soviet Union can do it then so can the whole world, given time. The problem is that we have very little time. The barbarians changed; after a thousand years they produced Neil Armstrong, the first man on the moon, and all the thousands of people who put him there, but we cannot wait a thousand years.

*

Human beings have truly amazing attributes, in body and mind. Curiosity and endeavour drive us on constantly: to learn more, to improve things, to leave a better place for our children and their children. It is not surprising that we get muddled and do not really know, sometimes, if things are better or worse than they were but if the Sumerians or the Greeks or the Romans were able to return and see our great cities, the quality of life some people have and the beauty of the works of art that have been created they would, I am sure, be in no doubt. They would be struck dumb. But, knowing human nature, not for long.

Perhaps the thing that strikes me most forcefully when trying to sum up this book, to find a key to the whole baffling, often depressing but nevertheless astonishingly stimulating fact of being alive, is the blinding revelation that all living things are related, that we are one creation: that our basic genetic structures are all the same. And that we are immortal: no living thing ever dies, because the combination of atoms which made it exist disperse again and become something else; perhaps land or air or water, but also, almost certainly, in time, parts of other living creatures. Our body cells contain atomic particles which in their time have been many things – other people and animals, plants and chemicals, earth and sea and sky. And even stars. The Buddha was right, though he did not have the scientific knowledge we have to know why.

*

In this book we have travelled along the rim of knowledge to the place where we think we now stand. My aim was to try to comprehend how it is that the world we all share is in such a mess. It has been a worthwhile task. The story is astonishing and though I am no less concerned about things than I was, I no longer feel baffled by it all: to understand is to forgive, someone said.

*

Bristol
England
August 1986.
March 1987.

## APPENDIX ONE

# SOME FACTS ABOUT THE NATIONS OF THE WORLD AND THE UNITED NATIONS ORGANISATION

At present there are 174 nations in the world. The twenty-four nations in the Far East have a combined population of 2,600 million people, more than twice the rest of the world put together. Before the Second World War only China, Afghanistan, Japan, Bhutan, Nepal and Thailand existed independently.

The Middle East, with a population of around 146 million, contains twelve nations which were created after 1945.

There are now thirty-two nations in Europe, with a total population of 470 million. Only fifteen existed before 1800. The oldest is France – 843 AD. (England 927 AD)

Africa has fifty-four nations, of which forty-six were created in or after 1960. Their total population is about 320 million. (It also contains Egypt, the oldest nation in the world.)

There are thirty-three nations in the West Indies, Central and South America. Seventeen were created between 1808 and 1839 and sixteen in the 20th Century, thirteen of them after 1945. The combined population is relatively small at nearly 300 million but is growing quickly.

There are seven nations which have a population of over 100 million: China, India, the USSR, the USA, Indonesia, Japan and Brazil, in that order of magnitude.(China and India have one and a half times the population of the last five put together.) Another seven nations have populations of between 50 and 100 million: Bangladesh, Germany, Pakistan, Nigeria, Britain, Italy and France.

Of the 174 nations in the world only twenty-five are fully industrialised (that is, they can manufacture heavy goods and sophisticated electrical equipment) and another twenty-two are partly industrialised. Of that forty-seven, twenty-nine are in Europe.

The people of 127 nations still live at a basic level of human development, but with technology and modern ways of life influencing them to a varying degree.

The main conclusions to be drawn are that:

> Human beings in Asia vastly outnumber the rest of the world but do not possess the administrative ability, industrial capability and natural resources they need in order to cope with huge and quickly-expanding populations.
>
> Most of the world's industry is concentrated in an area which has only one-ninth of its population.
>
> Of the fourteen nations which have more than 50 million people two are superpowers – that is to say, they have enormous resources and the population necessary to exploit them – another five have fully developed industry and technology but seven are underdeveloped and weighted down by a dense mass of poor, ignorant people.

There has been a progressive creation of new nations. Before 1800 AD there were only twenty-seven nations in the whole world – including Andorra, Liechtenstein and San Marino! More than half of the nations which now exist were created in the last forty years, most of them as the result of the withdrawal of European powers from their empires.

*The United Nations Organisation*

After the Great War the League of Nations was formed to try to avert further wars by establishing the beginnings of world government. Flawed because it lacked the membership of nations vital to its success, thwarted by self interest and without the will or means to enforce its policies, it was a lamentable failure.

In 1945, before the Second World War ended, a successor was founded in San Francisco when the charter for a new organisation was signed by forty-six nations.

All the nations of the world except the very smallest, and any excluded by the democratic vote of existing members, are members of the General Assembly of the United Nations Organisation, admitted by a two-thirds majority of that forum. The five big powers, America, Russia, China, France and Britain, are permanently represented in the Security Council, which is primarily responsible for world peace. The Security Council has a further ten elected short-term members and can make decisions which, theoretically, are binding on the entire Assembly.

The UNO also has a Trusteeship Council, responsible for the monitoring of any nations or groups for which it assumes administering responsibility, an Economic and Social Council with twenty-seven members and the International Court of Justice, which has fifteen judges. A Disarmament Commission was established in 1952, and an Atomic Energy Agency in 1957. Possibly the greatest achievement of the UN was the signing by one hundred members, in 1963, of the Nuclear Test Ban Treaty, which bars the testing of atomic weapons in the atmosphere.

When the United Nations Organisation was created China was represented by the nationalists under Chiang Kai-shek. Though in 1950 China became Communist under Mao Tse-Tung, many years were to pass before the actual government of China was allowed to enter the UN forum; meanwhile the Nationalist government, in exile on the island of Taiwan and kept afloat by the USA, was supposed to represent the hundreds of millions of people on mainland China. The lack of confidence created by this situation, the use of the Soviet Veto and the emotive groupings of Third World nations have resulted in the UN becoming a forum for much talk and little action, and many of its idealistic aims have never been fulfilled.

Nevertheless, its continued existence is a better option than its demise, since the means for improving the world's political and economic situation exists if member nations can be persuaded to take those courses of action which put the good of the majority before the interests of the minority.

*

# APPENDIX TWO

# CAUSES OF WORLD TENSION

*KOREA*

In 1945, two days before the Japanese capitulated, Russian soldiers moved into North Korea. A month later American troops arrived in the south. At the end of 1948, having built up a large North Korean army, the Russians withdrew. The Americans left in June 1949. A year later the North Koreans invaded the South.

The UN Security Council called for their withdrawal, and on members of the United Nations to assist the South Koreans. Because the Soviets had been refusing to attend the Security Council in protest against the presence in the United Nations of Nationalist instead of Communist China, Russia, for once, was unable to apply its veto. On 1st July 1950 American forces returned to South Korea and in August British troops arrived, soon to be joined by soldiers from twenty-one nations. Though militarily they were not in significant numbers, politically they gave much support to the United States.

In October 1950 the North Koreans, heavily counter-attacked, retreated back over their border, pursued by UN forces. The Chinese threatened to intervene and in December did so. By Christmas Day they had forced the UN troops back into the South, where the conflict then dragged on in static trench warfare until July 1953.

In three years, thirty thousand Americans died and more than three thousand soldiers of the other UN forces. There were nearly two million South Korean casualties. In comparison there were an estimated half a million North Korean casualties and nearly a million Chinese. South and North Korea were devastated and ruined economically, took many years to recover and to this day remain divided. A UN Armistice Commission still exists and meets regularly as a matter of habit but it is a long time since anyone expected anything to come of their fruitless formalities.

*

## *VIETNAM*

French traders and Roman Catholic missionaries first went to Indo-China in the 18th Century. When they tried to increase their influence they were resisted by the Annamese, people who had originated in Indonesia and had driven the original natives, the Khmer from Cambodia, away from the Mekong Delta. Nevertheless in the last half of the 19th Century the French established control over a large area of South-East Asia.

In 1941, with the homeland defeated, the French administration in the Far East was obliged by the Japanese to surrender some of its territory to Thailand. By 1944 Ho Chi Minh, a life-long Russian-trained communist, and Vo Nguyen Giap, schoolmaster turned soldier, had established guerrilla forces in the north of Indo-China. When the war ended their small forces moved into the vacuum of power left by the withdrawal of the Japanese but by February 1946 the French were back in control. In 1950, following the communist take-over of China, the USA decided that Indo-China qualified for military aid, which it was hoped would prevent the spread of communism. It was to be the beginning of a long and sacrificial American involvement which ended in their defeat and withdrawal twenty-five years later.

At the beginning of the long war the French deployed Algerian, Moroccan and Tunisian as well as French troops and Foreign Legionaires, a large proportion of whom were experienced German soldiers. By mid-1952 the USA was paying 78% of the cost of the war, General Giap had an army of more than 300,000, a third of whom were professionals, and the Vietnamese National Army, raised to support the French, numbered around 150,000. However only a small proportion of it was effective. For two years the two sides met and fought and separated and fought again inconclusively in the jungles and paddy fields in the north of the country.

The turning point for the French was the loss of Dien Bien Phu in May 1954. They inflicted 20,000 casualties on Giap's forces but lost more than 7,000 killed and wounded and 11,000 prisoners, most of whom were never seen again.(Only 3,000 of the garrison were Frenchmen.) On the day that the Viet Minh broke into the air-supplied fortress in the jungle a conference opened in Geneva which resulted some months later in French withdrawal down to the 17th parallel, said to be a provisional demarcation line between North and South and not a frontier between two new nations. Nobody believed it: nearly a million people from the north, mostly Roman Catholics, moved south.

In the North, Ho Chi Minh and Giap consolidated the new communist state and made plans to push the foreigners out of the whole of Vietnam. It was to take a long time. In October 1954 President Eisenhower committed the United States to the support of the non-communist South Vietnamese regime.(There was much talk in Washington at that time about the "domino effect", whereby the fall of one non-communist state would result in the toppling over into communism of the whole of South East Asia.)

In 1956 Giap deployed what was now called the Viet Cong and started to attack. By 1959 his soldiers, largely equipped and supported by the Russians, were threatening the South Vietnamese with complete disaster. The Americans pushed more and more men into the conflict and by the mid-'60s had nearly half a million troops committed, but to no avail. The effort they made was colossal but the soldiers from the well-fed West were no match for the home side, either in physical toughness or in mental determination. Despite the token presence of troops from other nations such as South Korea, and the use of the most modern military technology in the world – massive high-altitude, radar-directed bombing, hundreds of helicopter gunships, enormous fire-power from the latest rapid-fire weapons, defoliation chemicals which killed the jungles in which their enemies hid, electronic surveillance aids and computer-controlled re-supply – the United States only managed to prolong the battle without ever coming near to winning it. The fact that they had unlimited air support and the Viet Cong had none at all made no difference to the outcome.

Giap's Tet Offensive in 1968, in which his forces attacked nearly all the cities and provincial capitals in the South, cost the lives of 37,000 North Vietnamese soldiers as against the death of only 3,000 Americans and South Vietnamese but the publicity given to the Viet Cong's early successes by the media in Continental USA raised a storm of misgivings and protest. From then on the war did not have the backing of the majority of the American public, who liked it less and less as the air-freighted body bags continued to flow without pause from a battle zone which was thousands of miles away but could be seen in all its close-up nastiness every night in every living room.

In the end, after three years of wrangling negotiations, the USA had to settle for the shameful minimum – the total withdrawal of its troops in exchange for the return of American prisoners of war. "Peace" was said to have come to Vietnam on 23rd January 1973 but Giap had refused to commit himself to the withdrawal of his troops from the South on the grounds that they were not there. In 1975 they attacked again and the beleaguered South Vietnamese government collapsed. It was all over.

Well, not quite. The dominoes fell as Vietnam pushed over Laos and Cambodia. In the latter gentle place a smiling, bloody tyrant named Pol Pot engineered the social re-structuring of his country in accordance with communist principles – he forcibly evacuated most of the people in the towns and cities and put men, women and children to work on the land in order to raise food production. If they protested they were killed, as had been all educated people, including doctors, scientists, administrators; they could think, and organise, and lead, and were therefore a danger. The towns withered and died and so did the crops and the starving people who were desperately trying to grow them. This experiment in political science cost three million lives, or thereabouts. Nobody knows exactly, there were too many skulls to count.

*

## *ISRAEL*

During the closing years of the 19th Century Jews had begun to return from the many places in the world to which they had wandered and settle in what they called their homeland. By 1914 there were 85,000 of them there. In 1917 Balfour, the British Foreign Secretary, told Lord Rothschild, a wealthy Jewish banker, that the British "viewed with favour" the creating of a national home for the Jewish people in Palestine. In 1922 the League of Nations gave Britain the responsibility for doing so, a decision which was a stunning blow to the Arabs who during the Great War had fought off Turkish rule in the belief that when it ended they would be able to rule themselves. Instead the French went into the Lebanon and the British into Palestine, both with League of Nations authority.

During the late-1920s Jewish political and guerilla movements were formed to put pressure on the British to implement the Balfour Declaration, and to protect Jewish settlements from Arab attack. During the 1930s the British were reluctant to allow victims of Hitler's persecution to go to Palestine, in the belief that by adding to the Jewish population there they would only make the problem more difficult. Even so, by 1936 the Jewish population had grown to about 400,000.

When the Second World War ended it seemed to the Jews that the British government was beginning to favour the Arabs. Determined to succeed in setting up their own nation they began to attack the British administration and Armed Forces. By 1947, in response to a bloody campaign of bombing and intimidation, the British had deployed nearly 100,000 troops. They had become trapped in a progression which was to be seen repeatedly during the next thirty years: terrorist action by a small group of fanatics provokes a military response; the military, unable to identify the fanatics, begins to take restrictive measures against the whole population in an attempt to protect them from terrorist incidents and apprehend the trouble-makers; the terrorists increase the intimidation of people who are opposed to their aims – or indeed just want to get on with their lives in peace; the population become antagonistic to the troops but are less frightened of them than they are of their own fanatics with whom they have to go on living; in the end the troops have to withdraw, since it has never proved possible to subjugate for ever a totally alien population.

In 1947 the United Nations voted to establish a Jewish state but before the British withdrew, in May 1948, fighting broke out between Arabs and Jews, the Arabs desperate at the thought of having Jews in what had been for centuries their part of the world and the Jews incensed that two-thirds of the territory of Palestine, including Jerusalem, their holy place, was to be handed over to one-third, the Arab part, of the population. (Because Jesus died and is believed to have been resurrected there, and because Mohammed is believed to have ascended to heaven on a winged horse from the site that is now the gilded Dome of the Rock, Jerusalem is the holy place of both Christians and Moslems.) Fighting continued until April 1949, the Jews defeating the assorted Arab armies deployed against them and enlarging the area allocated to them by the UN by taking over the whole of Galilee west of the river Jordan. The West Bank was to become a bone of contention and the cause of the formation of the Palestine Liberation Organisation, pledged to reinstate Arab refugees there.

In consequence of their decisive victories in the wars fought in 1956, 1967 and 1973 the Israelis have increased their territory and captured Jerusalem. In 1979 one facet of their conflict was eased when their thirty-year war with Egypt was officially ended, but they have no choice but to remain committed to massive expenditure on the armed forces they must have in order to remain in existence. The cost is gigantic financial inflation – currently surging along at around 400% per annum – political instability, and an uneasy way of life for the three million Jews who live surrounded by enemies.

The Home of Peace belies its name, as it has always done.

*

*INDIA*, with its mixed population of Hindus, Moslems and Sikhs, was a dilemma for the British.

For decades during the first half of the 20th Century Indian politicians had agitated the volatile population into demanding self-government, as a result of which there had been a campaign of civil disobedience: a veined undercurrent of antipathy moved barefooted through the country. It was realised by the British that if they went, the many religious groups would be at each other's throats, but on the other hand it was not feasible for them to stay in a country of that size if they were unwelcome: the military commitment needed to ensure the maintenance of law and order would be gigantic. At home, the post-war Socialist administration under Attlee was much concerned with establishing the British Welfare State, to which it gave far higher priority for the expenditure of such money as was available than the preserving of links with India and other overseas dominions.

It was therefore decided, in consultation with Indian politicians, to partition the territory on the basis of its religious majorities: there would be a central Hindu block with a Moslem nation on each side of it – Pakistan. When this was announced there was serious rioting, which spread to the Sikh Punjab. Viceroy Mountbatten, charged with extricating the British as quickly as possible, recommended that they should depart (after three hundred years) ten months sooner than had originally been planned.

As the time for withdrawal drew near there was horrific inter-communal killing as people fled from those areas which were to become alien to them but in which they had managed to live side by side with people of different religious beliefs for generations. Before and after the British left in August 1947 uncounted millions of Moslem and Hindu children, women and men, died in a fever of vicious slaughter. Trains packed with bloody corpses stood stinking in the mid-day sun and vultures feasted as they had never done before.

There had been much cause for both sides to take pride in the transformation of India from a chaotic mass of small states speaking more than eight hundred dialects into a great nation administered by common usage of the English language but in the last days of the Raj nobody had cause for pride. Except perhaps the Indian Army which, also split, maintained its high standards of discipline.

No sooner had independence been achieved than the two new armies were at war over the future of Kashmir – which itself wanted to be independent. The result, in 1949, was a partitioned state, with by far the biggest part under Indian Control. In 1965 the two nations clashed again over Kashmir, this time in a bigger war which was to cost them a total of about 12,000 casualties.

The weakening of West Pakistan brought about by that conflict strengthened demands for independence by the Eastern part of the country, a thousand miles away, to which West Pakistan reacted by imposing a punitive regime. When the millions of refugees who had fled across the border into India became a serious threat to its stability that country intervened militarily, and defeated the West Pakistan forces which were trying to eliminate the rebels. In 1971 yet another new nation emerged, Bangladesh.

As well as its conflicts with Pakistan, India has had two armed clashes with China, in 1959 and 1962, over disputed borders.

*

In *CYPRUS* the population of 600,000 is 80% Greek,(in the sense of speaking that language, having Greek culture and adhering to the Greek Orthodox religion), 18% are Turkish-speaking Moslems and the rest are Armenian, but though the great majority regard themselves as Greek, Cyprus has never belonged to that nation: they colonised it between 1500 and 800 BC but since then it has been ruled by many people, culminating in its conquest by the Turks in 1571 AD. In 1878 they sold it to the British.

In 1955 a small element of the Greeks on the island asked for union with Greece, Enosis. When the British (and the Turks) resisted this demand a terrorist campaign started which, in 1959, culminated in British agreement to withdraw, except from two "sovereign bases". Under a new constitution Cyprus was to have a "Greek" president and a "Turkish" vice-president. In 1964, after civil war broke out, a United Nations force was sent to the island to keep the two sides apart. In 1979 Turkish troops from the mainland (only sixty-six kilometres away) invaded the north of the island and enforced its partition. Now the UN force patrols the border between two new nations, the Turkish Cypriots having declared themselves independent.

*

The *LEBANON* has been at war since 1975, the root of the problem being that the country has long been led by Christians established in power at French and British insistence during the mid-19th Century when Lebanon was under Turkish rule. Maronites have been there for two thousand years, a Christian enclave in a hostile Moslem world, but it was not until 1975 that the place became a battlefield on which rival Moslem sects and the Maronites have fought for power. The Syrians, who have never come to terms with the independence given to Lebanon by the Free French in 1943, backed Druze Moslems after the Israelis intervened to prevent Arabs from turning Lebanon into a Palestine Liberation Organisation base from which to launch attacks on Israel. The country is devastated, a hundred thousand people have died and despite repeated ceasefires the problem remains unresolved.

*

*IRELAND*

The English first took an interest in their offshore island in the 12th Century, when King Henry II became concerned about the activities of one of his enterprising noblemen who had grabbed a piece of land there; he sent some soldiers across the water to see what was going on. For the next few hundred years not a lot happened but then King Henry VIII decided that he wanted to marry Anne Boleyn, in order to do which he had to divorce his Spanish wife. When the Pope declined to cooperate the English people were suddenly excommunicated en masse from the Roman Catholic church by Henry (himself excommunicated by the Pope), who established his own version of a Protestant Christian religion.

In succeeding years England was involved in a series of wars with its Catholic neighbours in Spain and France and was concerned that they might establish a base in Ireland. In order to counter-balance the Catholics, Protestants from Scotland were given incentives to settle in the north of Ireland and Protestant noblemen were given land in the South. Thus people who were racially the same (the Scots had come from Antrim in the north of Ireland in the first place, around the 5th Century) but had developed with a different identity, became mixed with people who had a different religion.

Out of that situation has grown one of the most intractable of political problems, one which has flared up over and over again. In Cromwell's time, when he was the Puritan staunchly-Protestant Lord Protector of the Scots, Welsh, English and Irish, he over-reacted to Irish rebellion and left a legacy of hatred which has been kept alive generation after generation: at the head of his troops he led the massacre of about three thousand occupants of the town of Drogheda. As he put it later, with a touch of pious pride, "Not above thirty of them escaped." (As it was common practice in those days to put to the sword all the occupants of a town which refused to surrender he may have felt that he was abiding by the rules of war.)

The Irish have long memories and many scars remain, on both sides. To quote two, which are the excuse for rioting and bloodshed to this day: The siege of Londonderry, relieved by forces under King William III, King Billy, a Dutch Protestant, the hero of the bowler-hatted men with orange sashes who march every year in the North to celebrate a victory won nearly three hundred years ago. (Derry was given the prefix "London" at the time when merchants of the City of London were being encouraged to support the economy of the grey-stone riverside town.) The Easter Rising of 1916, also celebrated annually by the other side, when Irish Republican rebels seized the Post Office in Dublin, thus demonstrating their contempt for the English administration.

In 1922 Ireland was partitioned, six of the nine counties of the old Irish province of Ulster being kept as part of Great Britain, the rest becoming another nation, Eire. A fairly recent poll indicates that in the North 40% (or thereabouts) of Ulstermen and women think of themselves as British, 32% think of themselves as Ulsterpeople and 20% think of themselves as Irish. The other 8% don't know. Or care a lot.

In the years between November 1969, when the present Troubles started, and mid-1986 nearly three thousand people have died and many thousands more have been injured in mutual violence. Most of the Irish don't really know why they fight, except they cannot abide the people they have been taught to hate.

*

## APPENDIX THREE

# SOME IMPORTANT INVENTIONS OF THE 20th CENTURY

The phenomenal growth in the use of motor vehicles during the last fifty years has transformed world economics and politics. Since 1913 world output of oil has increased thirty times. At the time of the oil crisis of 1973 demand was rising by 12% per annum. In 1936 there were two million vehicles on the roads in Britain; by 1983 the figure had increased seven times, a trend which has occurred all over the developed world, with the way of life becoming geared to the use of motor transport. Because of door-to-door convenience, enormous transport fleets of powerful articulated trucks have taken away from railways the movement of large quantities of goods. Railway engines themselves burn oil in place of coal, or use electricity which may be generated by oil-burning power stations. In terms of tonnage, oil is now the biggest commodity in world trade, the power source that keeps wheels turning and aircraft flying.

Aircraft fly because their wings, curved on the upper surface and flat underneath, rise when they are pushed through the air. Where the airflow leaves the curved upper surface a vacuum is created at the "trailing edge" of the wing; the natural reaction of the under surface to move upwards and fill that vacuum creates lift. The longer the wing, the more lifting potential there is, as with a glider. The greater the power pushing the wing, the faster it will rise, as with an F-16 combat aircraft. The more power there is the more weight can be lifted, as with a Galaxy transport plane. (Seven of them could have done the entire Berlin airlift, which needed more than a thousand of the types then available.)

By 1945 all new aircraft were monoplanes, some powered by multiple, propellor-driving petrol engines, some by jet engines which compress hot gases and exhaust them rapidly. Speeds had increased three or even four times until by the early '50s aircraft were regularly breaking the sound barrier: that is, they could go faster than the speed of sound (Mach 1), which is 760.98 miles per hour at sea level. Now, nearly all military aircraft are capable of supersonic flight and some can reach Mach 3. (The Anglo-French Concorde is the only working supersonic passenger plane.) Between 1939 and 1945 the size and load-carrying capability of planes quadrupled. During the war Britain and America produced great numbers of bombers, adaptations of which became the air transport fleets of the post-war world, changing the pattern and volume of international transportation. In 1954 it cost twenty week's wages – based on average earnings – to pay for a ticket to cross the Atlantic by air; today, it costs one week's wages.

Sea transportation was also revolutionised during the war. Because of the urgent need to replace ships sunk by U-boats the wartime method of building changed from slow rivetting to faster welding. Then the discovery of new alloys enabled engine components to withstand much higher temperatures, and therefore to work more efficiently. Turbines began to replace diesel engines and the size of cargo ships increased progressively; less than two decades after the war supertankers of 250,000 tons had been built and now there are freight-container ships of as much as 100,000 tons conveying sealed loads around the world on the long part of the haul which takes them from door to door. Fewer bigger ships are needed than smaller ones, and fewer men to operate them as new technology is used for ship and load handling; the world's fleets are declining in numbers if not in carrying capacity.

*

In the early 1920s radios were the cat's whiskers; man's genius for invention had reached out into the atmosphere and wireless, conceived by Marconi more than twenty years before, was within the reach of people in Europe and North America. High-frequency alternating currents of electro-magnetic energy were feebly transmitted into the ether to be intercepted, at no great distance, by enormous aerials. These fed the pulses into a circuit which transformed them intelligibly, mixed with whines and cracklings, through earphones or great horn-shaped loudspeakers, back to their original Morse or voice vibrations. (The apparatus was crammed with wires but because there was no direct land-line link to the sender the system was known as wireless.) Receivers began to be made commercially, rather than by crack-pot enthusiasts, and became accessible to more and more people. The power output of transmitters increased, while in receivers a single trembling filament, faintly responding to an electrical whisper, became one valve and then two and then more: signals could be received at a greater distance, interference was subdued, reception was better. Great music entered humble living rooms; the famous became tangible people, listened to with wonder; news was received instantly instead of hours or days later. Quite suddenly, and to most people quite inexplicably, the world was a smaller place. And in the 1920s a Scotsman by the name of Baird took things far further by using transmitted radio waves to produce a picture on a screen. A miracle indeed: how could unseen and untouchable emissions travelling through the air be turned into a picture?

Radio waves are in four bands, long, medium, short and ultra-short, so classified by the measurable distance between the successive waves of electric current. In general, the longer the wave the further it will go, but the more it will be interfered with by atmospheric disturbances. Long, medium and short waves bounce off a natural electrically-charged layer about 70 miles above the earth's surface and can reach out further than ultra-short waves, which travel line-of-sight and cannot bend round the earth's curvature; to extend their range transmitters are erected on a tall mast on the highest available geographical feature. Television signals are similar to radio waves but are of even shorter length, and they too can only travel in straight lines from the transmitter to the receiver. Therefore, in order to provide coverage throughout a region masts have to be spaced about fifty miles apart: more, if the terrain is very hilly. These masts receive the signal, amplify its strength and then re-transmit it on to the next mast or to television sets in the area.

In a television camera the viewed picture is focussed by a lens on to plate which is covered with lines (625, now, here in the United Kingdom) on which are up to 200,000 points, each of which responds electrically in proportion to the strength of illumination falling on it: the brighter the seen picture, the greater the response. An electron beam scans the plate, line by line, every 1/25th of a second, absorbing from each spot an electrical impulse which reflects the strength of illumination on the spot at that instant of time. These impulses are amplified and then transmitted through the ether at specified wave frequencies: the "channels" to which the receivers are tuned. In the early days there was only one, here in the United Kingdom. Now there are several, in Europe many and in a few places hundreds. Using dish aerials to catch signals beamed up to satellites circling the earth and then reflected down again some people in America can tune in to more than a hundred, though the point of that is difficult to see.

Received at the speed of light by the television aerial these impulses are fed to the back end of a cathode ray tube in the set, from where they are beamed by an electron gun in sequence across 625 lines on the viewing screen. Because it is coated with a flourescent chemical which glows when struck by the electrons fired at it, the brightness being in proportion to the strength of the bombardment, the screen mirrors the amount of light falling on the points on the camera plate, which in their turn have captured what is seen by the lens. A pattern of luminous points of varying brightness is formed in rapid succession on the screen but because they are being repeated so frequently they, like the pictures projected by a cine film, are retained by the retina of the eye to form a continuous picture. Thus the viewer's eyes see precisely what the camera lens sees. (The signals, and therefore the image can, if so desired, be sent along a wire instead of through the air – cable television.)

In most colour transmissions mirrors and filters break down the "white light" spectrum seen by the camera lens into a red image, a green image and a blue, each of them masked so as to impinge on separate lines of sensitized points on a plate. Each of these separate images is scanned simultaneously by moving beams which "read" the electric charge on the points which, as with black and white, are a reflection of the amount of light falling on the scene being televised. Three signals are then transmitted simultaneously, received almost instantly by the home TV aerial and "fired" by three electron guns in lines across the front of the tube, which is covered with many thousands of phosphor dots which glow red, green or blue. As before, the strength of the glow is a reflection of the amount of energy being picked up by the scanners from the plates at the camera end of the system. Mirrors in the receiver blend the colours together and because the dots are so small, and the speed of scanning so fast, the eye does not register them separately but sees the image as a blend of colour and a continuously moving picture.

In 1939 wireless sets were bulky, unreliable and rare but by 1945 armies were equipped with sturdy voice-to-voice sets with a range of about thirty kilometres; and the means of powering them had been radically improved.(Only ten years before, many home receivers were still using acid-battery accumulators which had to be taken to the local garage to be charged.) During the 1950s and '60s the invention of new electrical components enabled a greater range of radio communications to be brought into use, for example line-of-sight High Frequency transmissions which are less prone to atmospheric interference and so give a clearer signal at the receiver. For the military, radio interception had always created security problems but during the 1960s new systems were developed which "scrambled" speech as it went into the transmitter and unravelled it again at the receiver, enabling people to speak "in clear".

Radar, a means of measuring the distance of an object by timing the reflected pulse of a radio beam, and of locating it relative to someone looking at a cathode-ray display (that is, at a TV screen) was to prove one of the most important of 20th Century inventions, both for military and peacetime use. Ships and aircraft can now move visually blind but able electronically to "see" what is around them. And can be detected, as can underwater objects by the use of sonar, another wartime invention which pulses sound waves into the sea and measures the time taken for them to bounce back.

*

The first calculating machine was the abacus, a counting frame invented thousands of years ago and still much used in some parts of the world. In 1642 a Frenchman built a mechanical adding machine and in 1694 a German made one which could multiply and divide. In the early 1800s looms were controlled by punched cards: the method of weaving – the lifting or lowering of the vertical threads through which the shuttle carries the horizontal threads – depended on where the holes were in the card. In 1835 an Englishman planned a machine which could be programmed to do arithmetic, compare its calculations and if necessary modify its programme; unfortunately his plans were mislaid for a hundred years and by 1937, when they were found, his mechanical methods were outdated. In 1886 an American developed a machine which could sense the holes in a punched card and make calculations from the information represented by the holes.

By 1944 the first electronic machine had been built in America, at Harvard University. ("Built" is the right word: it was 15 metres long, 2 metres deep and 2.4 metres high and stood on strengthened floors under which hundreds of cables were coiled. It generated enormous heat and needed massive cooling systems. Some white-coated hot technicians actually worked inside the computer!) In 1946 another was made at the University of Pennsylvania which was a thousand times faster – it took two hours to do nuclear-physics computations which would have taken 2,800 hours of calculating by a hundred mathematicians – but it filled several rooms and had 18,000 vacuum tubes, or "valves". It was not until 1949 that a stored-programme computer (one which kept in its memory the basic information it needed to function) was made in Britain, at Cambridge University. It contained 3,800 valves.

In 1957 the first "second generation" computers, which used transistors instead of vacuum tubes, valves, were made, reducing the size enormously and improving reliability.

An electronic valve consists of a positive and a negative electrode inside a glass tube from which all air has been extracted. If the negative is connected to a piece of metal and heats it the metal releases electrons – electrically charged particles – which are drawn towards the positive. If a third electrode is placed in between, changes to its voltage will influence the rate of flow of electrons. In other words valves are a means of varying a flow of electricity. They are, however, quite large, hence the size of the early computers.

The invention of transistors completely altered the prospect for the future of computers. Transistors are made by introducing foreign atoms into a crystal structure, the effect of which is to agitate the structure and "free" electrons. By applying an electric charge to the area where positive and negative electrons meet in the crystal their rate of flow can either be increased or blocked. Transistors therefore do the same job as a vacuum tube but are a fraction of the size. And cost.

The reason why transistors are so important is that computers use binary arithmetic, that is, only the figures 0 and 1, to represent all information. (0 and 1 are binary digits, or "bits"). In such a system 0=000, 1=001, 2=010, 3=011, 4=100, 5=101 and so on. If a transistor is used as a switch, (known as a flipflop) voltage put in indicates 1 (on) and voltage withheld means 0 (off). The number 4 would be stored as On,Off, Off; 3 would be Off,On,On; 2 would be Off, On, Off etc.

Many more binary digits are needed to represent numbers than decimals – ten bits to three decimals – but this does not matter because in a computer calculations are done electrically at the speed of light. Since the computer must be able to use words as well as numbers distinctive combinations, or patterns, of bits are used to represent each character; that is, each number, letter, or symbol such as "*". A minimum set of "alpha-numerics" is 10 numbers, 26 letters (A-Z) and 16 specials – such as $, £, % – and needs 52 different permutations of 0 and 1 combinations to identify each of the 52 characters.(A character, including a space between words,is called a byte. A million bytes are a megabyte.)

Multiple, linked transistors are known as logic gates and are used to control the flow of information, to do mathematical calculations or to open and let in information retained in the machine's memory – the programme. Programming entails feeding the computer's memory units (often banks of tiny iron rings) with patterns: telling it what to do in binary language which is stored on the rings – if they are magnetised it is a 1, if not it means 0 – and called into action when the programme is "run". This must be done in a logical way so that there can only be a No or Yes answer – a shut gate or an open one which will let the current through to the next stage and the next decision.

Since the speed at which a computer works depends on travel time – the time taken for the current to flow – it is important the everything should be compressed as tightly as possible. With third generation computers made in the late-1960s this was achieved by using integrated, printed, circuits – instead of loose wires soldered together the circuitry was printed in a conducting metal on a non-conducting base.

In 1971 the first microprocessor was introduced. It had all its essential electrical components, the equivalent of up to 14,000 transistors, etched on to a single silicon chip only a few millimetres in size. The crystal structure of the silicon is used as the basis for tens of thousands of flipflops, gates and circuitry, miniaturised by photographic compression processes. Not only did the physical size shrink but the power required to work machines was reduced from hundreds of kilowatts down to the output of a small battery.

In 1948 it took about one thousandth of a second to add two numbers together; a modern computer will do it in one "nano" second.(There are as many nanoseconds in one second as there are seconds in 32 years!) Millions of instructions per second can now be processed in a big computer.

Peripheral objects are needed around a computer, to feed it with information and to extract it in an understandable form: for example, magnetic tape or punched cards to input information, a printer to output "hard copy". The dot-matrix printer connected to the computer on which this book is written by a word-processing system writes forwards, left to right, normally and then prints everything backwards along the next line, so avoiding wasted travel time. It prints 120 words a minute and its hammer head which forms the letters strikes the paper 120 times a second.

*

Quantum physics is the study of the structure of atoms. Indications are that physical laws within atoms are related (that is, there are similarities and a common governing logic) to the physical laws at present understood about the construction of the Universe. Unfortunately the laws of quantum physics, in so far as they are proved, are not compatible with Einstein's Theory of Relativity.

In essence this states that at very high speeds – near to the speed of light – the velocity of light emissions measured by two observers moving relative to each other are not the same, whereas to one observer, no matter how fast he moves or in what direction, there will be no difference in the speed of light reaching him. (This explains why, even though the Universe is expanding, light reaching us always arrives at the same speed: Earth is the single observer.) Also, light is delayed when passing near to stars and galaxies because their gravitational pull bends the rays; spacetime is not the same as Earth time. In theory if a manned spacecraft were to reach a great distance from Earth its occupants would be living in a different time-frame from people on our planet and so would age at a different rate; they might return, within their own normal lifespans, to find that Earth has moved on many years.

Through his mathematical studies Einstein predicted the structure of atoms; and that they could be split. From this theory came atomic energy – the nuclear weapon and nuclear power.

Some heavy atoms – ones which have many neutrons and electrons – are not stable. By bombarding them with neutrons their nuclei can be split into other, different, atoms, in the process releasing enormous energy and two fresh high-velocity neutrons. The new neutrons split other atoms, release more energy and more neutrons and so on: almost instantly, in a gigantic disruption of the stored energy that holds the world in place. Nuclear fission.

One of the effects of this unnatural breaking up of atoms is that many are left unstable – that is, there are free particles in the remnants of destroyed atoms which are projected outwards and try to find a stable life for themselves in other atoms. This is nuclear radiation, which continues until all the parts of the disrupted atoms have locked on to new atoms and settled down. However in the process they will have changed them, including those which are in living tissue. When this happens the new atoms may not be acceptable to the living creature and will cause it to die.

In an atomic bomb a conventional explosive is detonated so as to make two unstable masses of Uranium collide; when they do, nuclear fission occurs. In most nuclear reactors a radio-active core is surrounded by water which slows down the speed of the neutron emissions and heats up in the process. That super-heated steam is used to spin turbines and generate electric power. In a Hydrogen bomb the nuclear emissions do not split atoms but fuse them together because they collide at fantastically high speeds, triggered off by the fission of Uranium or Plutonium: an atomic explosion brings about fusion, which produces more released energy than fission, hence the greater power of the H bomb.

*

One of the most momentous inventions of the Second World War was the ballistic rocket, developed in Germany and used against England in 1945. By 1957 these had become intercontinental missiles capable of spanning oceans. The space age began in the same year when the Russians put a dog into orbit around the earth. In 1961 Yuri Gagarin became the first space man.

(Americans and Russians both used German scientists to start them off on the development of their own rocket systems.)

Unlike an aircraft, a rocket functions without the presence of an atmosphere. Its ballistic shape keeps it stable in flight and it carries fuel which burns without air: in other words it chemically supplies the oxygen needed to burn another chemical which turns into a gas at high pressure. When that gas is vented out it creates a reaction force – due to the expulsion of atoms at high velocity from a "closed" system – which moves the rocket forward even if it is in a vacuum: it does not need air to push against. When the propellant has all been burnt the rocket has attained its maximum speed. With intercontinental missiles the upwards thrust of the fuel takes the missile out of Earth's atmosphere in a ballistic trajectory which brings it back in a curved path on to its target.

*

## APPENDIX FOUR

# INTELLIGENCE & GENETICS

In 1904 work first started in Paris to try to find out what intelligence is and how to grade it, in 1916 further studies were begun in America but it was the 1930s before the idea was beginning to be accepted in developed nations and 1958 before an agreed system was widely used.

Intelligence tests are applied to determine mental powers. The so-called IQ (intelligence quotient) of children is worked out by testing them to find their mental age, dividing it by their actual age and multiplying by 100. For example, a child who achieves good results and is credited with a mental age of ten but is actually eight years old would have an IQ of 125. (10/8 = 1.25, x 100 = 125). If the IQ is above 100 the child is advanced for its age, if below, then it is backward. With adults, an assessed average performance of persons in a specified age group is given a score of 100. The results of tests taken by people in that age group determine where they lie in relation to 100. A result of 100 indicates above-average intelligence.

IQ is therefore a figure based on comparing an individual's test results with what is considered to be normal for them. The difficulty is to decide what is normal and to design fair tests.

In an organised society which has detailed records going back over the last forty years or so, and therefore a vast amount of data available, it is possible to assess what the average child or adult should know but in less organised societies there is no base line. Only a very small proportion of the people in the world can therefore be assessed because of the difficulty of compiling tests which relate to their background knowledge.

As to applying a fair test, that too is a difficult problem. Our genes partly determine our intelligence potential but the environment in which we live greatly influences what the genes can achieve. Studies indicate that memory and reasoning are not genetically controlled but that word fluency and numeric skills are. Intelligence tests on identical twins raised together show almost identical results but if they are not then there is less similarity – their environment has a significant effect on their intellect. Social class, education and culture are environmental factors which affect IQ.

Obviously, well-educated people have a bigger vocabulary than the uneducated and have more general knowledge. Children brought up in an "enriched environment", like lesser species on which tests have been done to prove the point, are more enquiring than those raised in a narrow and dull intellectual environment: people learn from what they hear, and sharpen their wits accordingly. Such children are also under more pressure to succeed than children from a social class which sees little prospect of success: or, indeed, may react against success because of inverted snobbery – our Alison thinks she is better than we are! All such factors give people in a higher social class an advantage in achieving good results in IQ tests. Therefore, as an example, to apply the same test written for a middle-class, well-educated white child to a poor, ill-educated black child cannot be fair; and to deduce from results that the black child is inherently not as intelligent would be wrong, as it would be to say that an impoverished white child is by nature less intelligent than the better-off one.

The performance of some individuals from a particular social or educational group will be much better or much worse than that of the average for the group, which indicates that the way in which people's intelligence is regulated by their genes is a highly complex matter which can produce surprising results regardless of inheritence or class. Beethoven's father was a syphilitic drunkard, his mother was consumptive. Of his brothers and sisters one also had tuberculosis, one was blind, one was deaf and dumb and another died in infancy. No betting man would have given much for his chances of doing well at anything.

Taken as a whole, seven out of ten in a tested population will achieve an IQ of between 83 and 116 and only one in a hundred will be at the bottom (52) or the top (150) of IQ ratings. In other words, the great majority are on either side of the average and only a few people are very slow or very clever. As to genius, that is in a class of its own; it is seasoning added to a richness of intellect.

While the great majority of people have much the same level of IQ only those who are near the top can begin to understand what those at the very top are thinking, a situation which will apply more and more as discovery reveals an increasing complexity of existence.

If an organisation in a developed country applies standards of IQ and educational attainment when selecting executive class employees of, say, IQ 120 and six passes in recognised academic tests then it will be searching for people in the top ten or twelve per cent of its population. If it specifies a university degree then the group becomes even smaller.

Though the age-old principle of leadership by dominant people (not just males any more) still applies, weak individuals may find themselves academically qualified for their responsibilities but inept at discharging them, since intellect alone will not supply good leadership. Since leadership is vital to society it is important that all the necessary criteria are applied when selecting people for key positions: that their character as well as their intellect is adequate for their responsibilities.

Genius and madness are not closely related. Amongst very gifted Americans, 90% of whom are professional or managerial White Anglo-Saxon Protestants (they have the best likelihood of good genetic inheritance because they have been well nourished for generations and have also been able to gain the most from environment) the incidence of mental illness and suicide is well below average, indicating that the ability to understand, to control, and therefore to succeed, generally makes a person contentedly able to cope with life. (Some highly intelligent people though find difficulty in reconciling their intelligence with their temperament, which reflects animal behaviour which they feel should be under better control.)

Homo Sapiens would achieve enormous advances as a species if there could be a general improvement in the world environment, achieved by raising the life style of those who have least and by utilising to the full the talents of those who are already fortunate in their inheritance.

*

The human cell contains DNA, RNA, proteins and enzymes. The "D" nucleic acid carries the genetic information and the "controls" inherited from the person's parents, the "R" is a messenger between the "D" and the proteins, and enzymes regulate the interaction between RNA and proteins.

"D" nucleic acids are giant chain molecules, an immensely long (in atomic terms) backbone of atoms along which are strung side-chains of small clusters of atoms at regular intervals. The clusters consist of atoms grouped together in only four different combinations, four "letters". In ascending order of size, in a virus there might be five thousand letters, in a bacteria a few million, in animals several thousand million and in men and women several billion.

Each human cell contains a code which tells it where to be in the body and what to do – though why a particular cell takes up its appointed place as part of your eye or your heart or a hair under your armpit is not yet understood. The nucleus receives information chemically through the cell wall (which has "gates" in it) and decides what action to take: the DNA splits if a new cell is wanted or the nucleus triggers the despatch of a particular protein through the cell wall to another part of the body where it is needed. Precisely how all these things happen is not not known either.

Cells wear out with age and new cells form to replace the worn-out ones but as you get older the process becomes less efficient and worn-out cells have to last longer: skin becomes less elastic, and therefore wrinkled; muscle fibre becomes weaker; bone more brittle.

DNA is formed in a double helix, that is to say it is a chain of atoms folded over and twisted up inside itself like one screw inside another. A link of DNA and its clusters makes up a gene. The way in which the chemical combinations of clusters are set out along the DNA thread determines what a particular gene is for; what it does in the body. Many, many genes, strung together like beads, comprise a chromosome. There are twenty-three matched pairs of chromosomes in every human cell, forty-six in all, except in sex cells, which have half the number, only one from each pair, which have separated at random. The mix of parents' characteristics is therefore a matter of chance. A characteristic, be it a great talent or a great liability, will get left behind during the making of one sex cell though it may be included next time. This explains why brothers and sisters can look and be so different, and why characteristics can skip generations and reappear later – Grandad's nose, or his ability to fiddle.

Cells multiply by dividing. The DNA splits in half, each half taking a complete set of chromosomes, and a new cell forms with a nucleus of RNA and proteins. Body cells therefore contain the same hereditary instructions, which are a blend of father and mother: skin colour, facial and body characteristics, talents, temperament. Half of them came from your father at the instant of conception and the other half came from your mother. (If you can't stand your father, it's too bad: he is you, whether you like it or not – which could be why you don't like him.)

Because there are about six *billion* clusters of atoms in a complete set of human genes the mating mixture produces a unique human being – except in the case of identical twins (or triplets etc). They carry the same set of instructions and therefore look almost exactly alike – though they develop their own personalities and do not generally act alike.

Genes with exactly the same job to do in the same position on a pair of chromosomes work together, but they may not always pair off. If not, then one will be more dominant than the other in determining the outcome of inheritance – for example, if there is a brown-eyes gene from the mother in the eye-colouring position and the other is a blue-eyes gene from the father the offspring will have brown eyes. Brown-eye genes are stronger than blue-eye genes.

Proteins consist of at least two thousand atoms strung together in a chain which has side-chains attached to it (consisting of the same four "letters" as those which make up a gene) and is folded on itself to make a compact bundle. The way in which the bundle's chains and side-chains (the amino acids) are strung together identify it and its job in life.

The proteins in cells make the body live: they change food into energy, burn up energy in muscle, remove poisons out of the system, discard used chemicals through the organs, create new cells and so on, keeping life in balance. Other groups of atoms, enzymes, act as agents between the RNA and the proteins; like jailers they too carry keys which unlock doors and allow specific chemical actions to take place.

There are two types of sex chromosomes, the "X" and the "Y". Women have only X and men have X and Y. If a male X sperm implants a female X then a girl will be born; if a male Y sperm invades a female X then it will be a boy. Whether the sperm is X or Y is a matter of chance.

The ability to breed generations of small rodents very quickly in laboratories has enabled scientists to produce very pure strains. Because the same cell structures from many donors can be studied under a powerful microscope, it is easier to try to plot the genetic formation. By altering or removing genes and then culturing new cells and putting them in the womb of a female to make the next generation scientists are able to identify the function of particular genes. They have done this with monkeys, the nearest creatures genetically to Homo Sapiens, (specifically, the chimpanzee, which is very closely related) and have begun working on human cells. This is termed genetic engineering, other branches of which are concerned with the creation of variations to existing cells such as viruses. While there are great possibilities for good, such as the altering of cells which cause genetic malformations in new-born human beings (for example, Down's Syndrome) there are also frightening possibilities such as the creation of new cells which can cause killing diseases or which might reproduce themselves out of control.

*

## APPENDIX FIVE

# POPULATION CONTROLS

Government controls can be effective only if the message is properly understood; in other words if the crisis situation can be put across so compellingly that people will realise that they must not reproduce more than one person each – or, better still, less than one each. However, this pre-supposes education, self-control and prophylaxis: an understanding of the problem, the will to do something about it and the means of preventing conception. At present, world-wide, this is not a starter. In some Third World countries 40% of the population are under fifteen: the fertility potential is gigantic. Between 50% and 95% are illiterate: the education potential is next to nothing. In some places 65% of births are illegitimate: self-control is almost non-existent. As to prophylaxis, with high fertility, abysmal ignorance and rampant self-indulgence the chances of people successfully using pills, barrier methods or the rhythm system are minimal.

There are other difficulties. It is not practical to compulsorily control copulation. Since it is also impossible to legislate against conception, the alternative is to ensure abortion, but in primitive places this is extremely difficult, due to administrative problems, people's antipathy and the lack of hospital facilities. Persuasion and inducement may be quite effective but much depends on the nature of the people concerned. In Japan, with its educated, receptive and disciplined society, it has been possible to stabilise the population by making cheap barrier and chemical contraceptives available, by ensuring that there are facilities for safe abortion and by creating the mental attitude towards it which makes it socially acceptable.

India is very aware of the problem and is trying to educate its people in birth control. In the 1970s it embarked on a programme of mass sterilisation of women; in one period more than eight million operations were done but due to poor surgical conditions hundreds of women died. Unless there is a breakthrough in tackling their problem in a few decades from now there will be more Indians than there are Chinese.

In China, since 1979, families have been banned from having more than one child because if they do the population will increase to 1,400 million by the year 2000. The Chinese government have therefore laid down rules:

> Couples must get permission to marry and once married must have permission to start a pregnancy.
>
> They must be over 24 years of age before they marry.
>
> They are given bonuses and benefits if they adhere to the rules but lose them if they do not. For example all workers in a factory get a 5% 'non-production' bonus but if any of their members become pregnant without permission they may lose the bonus; there is therefore great pressure on individuals to contribute to the collective good by obeying the rules.
>
> Couples get family benefits (money, a guaranteed job for the child, a place at university if it is bright enough) but will lose those benefits – and as much as a year's pay – if they have a second child.

The system depends on controls being exercised by elder citizens – the "Granny Patrol" – who look out for women feeling broody, showing lassitude or having morning sickness. If there is doubt and a pregnancy test proves positive the woman must have an abortion. Prying and pressure are an unavoidable part of the new way of life.

In many parts of China the government's policies are working, largely because the people have lived under a communist system for forty-five years (that is, they have become used to complying with regulations), because anyway they are historically attuned to close family life and communal living and because they fully understand the consequences of failure: if the population reaches 2 billion then the nation will starve; if they can contain it then the possibility of a good life remains.

However, even in China there are many traditional reasons why the rules are not being obeyed everywhere. More than 80% of the population labour on the land and sons are needed to carry on the work; girls are not welcome for that reason – and because the family name dies out unless there is a son – so if the first child is a girl, despite the penalties there is a strong incentive to have a second who may be a boy. Also, children are needed to look after the old people – so if the government decrees that there must be few children then adequate state pensions will have to be provided instead, with all that that means in terms of a large financial drain on the nation.

Though there are problems it seems there is a very high probability of success in restricting the population in China. However, such measures would be very difficult, if not impossible, to apply in most parts of the world because of local attitudes or religious objections. For example, out of fear those Moslems who remain in India are encouraged to have more children in order eventually to redress the balance against their Hindu neighbours. In South Africa the measure of a negro man is the number of children he has, quite often by more than one woman. And in many places religion is strongly against contraception.

South America is more than 90% Roman Catholic and that church remains adamant that there must be no interference with the natural consequences of coupling other than by utilising the rhythm method (that is, limiting intercourse to those days in the month when the woman's egg is still in the ovary and has not yet moved to where it can be fertilised by the man's sperm.) Large parts of Europe are also Roman Catholic and there too, even where the whole population is educated and has the means of contraception available to them, the taboo applies strictly. Since 1945 25 million Roman Catholics have been born in the developed parts of the world who, during their lifetimes, will consume as much of the world's resources as will the combined populations of India and Pakistan.

Hindus and Moslems, as well as Roman Catholics and some other Christian sects, are opposed in principle to abortion so that even if practical difficulties could be overcome there is a mental barrier which cannot. There is no doubt, however, that the time will come when a reduction of population must be achieved. If Man does not do it then nature will.

*

# INDEX

# BIBLIOGRAPHY


| *Title* | *Author* | *Publisher* |
|---|---|---|
| History of the Modern World | Johnson | Weidenfeld & Nicholson |
| Language, Truth & Logic | Ayer | Gollancz |
| Emerging Cosmology | Lovell | Columbia Univ Press |
| The double-edged helix | Liebe Cavalieri | Columbia Univ Press |
| The story of Mankind | van Loon | Publishers' Guild |
| Great turning points in history | Snyder | Reihnhold |
| Nature of Truth in religions | Reischauer | Tuttle |
| The contemporary world | Major | Methuen |
| The Last Two Million Years | Several | Readers Digest |
| Man through the Ages | Bowle | Weidenfeld & Nicholson |
| The book of key Facts | Several | Paddington Press |
| Enc of Ancient & Medieval History | Several | Larousse |
| The Greatest Thinkers | de Bono | Weidenfeld & Nicholson |
| Cosmos | Sagan | Futura |
| Book of the Physical World | Several | Penguin |
| Econ History of world population | Several | Harvester |
| Man & the Vertebrates | Romer | Pelican |
| Lifetide | Watson | Hodder |
| History of Land Warfare | Macksey | Guinness |
| Be fruitful & multiply | Fremlin | Hart-Davies |
| A matter of people | Moraes | Deutsch |
| History of Europe | Brooke | Methuen |
| Weather facts & feats | Several | Guinness |
| Life on Earth | Attenborough | Collins |
| The World | Hodgkison | Preece |
| How to save the World | Allen | Corgi |
| Man in Africa | Turnbull | David & Charles |
| Greek & Roman Architecture | Robertson | Cambridge Univ Press |
| Mechanics of the Mind | Blakemore | Cambridge Univ Press |
| Future Shock | Toffler | Bodley Head |
| World History 1900–1968 | Browse | Cambridge Univ Press |
| Psychoanalysis | Freud | Penguin |
| Principles of English Law | Redmond | Macdonald |
| Psychological aspects of society | Rowan | Davis |
| The Humanist Outlook | Ayer | Pemberton |
| Economics of everyday life | Williams | Pelican |
| War since 1945 | Carver | Weidenfeld & Nicholson |
| Civilisation | Clarke | Murray |

| | | |
|---|---|---|
| Sex in History | Tannahill | Hamilton |
| Europe in the age of Imperialism | Gollwitzer | Havill Press |
| Armageddon 1918 | Falls | Weidenfeld & Nicholson |
| China | Butterfield | Hodder |
| Postwar | Mayne | Thames & Hudson |
| Rise & Fall of the 3rd Reich | Shirer | Secker & Warburg |
| The Mighty Continent | Terraine | Hutchinson |
| The Battle for Oblivion | MacQuitty | Harrap |
| Prophecy & Progress | Kumar | Lane |
| The machinery of the brain | Wooldridge | McGraw Hill |
| Mankind & Mother Earth | Toynbee | Oxford Univ Press |
| An Outline of History | Wells | Collins |
| An unfinished history of the World | Thomas | Hamish Hamilton |
| Memoirs | Montgomery | Collins |
| Encyclopaedia of useful facts | Several | Stroud |
| Science Fact | George | Topaz |
| Psychology | Hall & Thompson | Worth |
| Computer Science | Atkin | Macdonald/Evans |
| The Struggle for Europe | Wilmot | Collins |
| The double helix | Watson | Weidenfeld & Nicholson |
| History of the Eng Speaking Peoples | Churchill | Educnl Book Company |
| There and Back | Pyke | Murray |
| Life Itself | Frick | Macdonald |
| Ten novels & their Authors | Maugham | Heinemann |
| Our Planet Earth | Several | Ward Lock |
| Life that lives on Man | Andrews | Arrow |
| The Ascent of Man | Bronowski | Book Club Assoc |
| The Sword & the Scimitar | Bradford | Gollancz |
| The Mysterious World | Clarke | Book Club Assoc |
| The Common Stream | Parker | Collins |
| Third World War | Hackett | Sidgwick & Jackson |
| The World at War | Foster | Book Club Assoc |
| Britain & her Army | Barnett | Lane |
| Sociology | Robertson | Worth |
| The restless years | Paustovsky | Harvill |
| The Industrial Revolution | Ashton | Oxford Univ Press |
| Natural Selection | Fisher | Clarendon |
| Introduction to the study of man | Young | Oxford Univ Press |
| Defeat into victory | Slim | Cassell |
| The Theban plays of Sophocles | Warling | Penguin |
| Psychoanalysis | Stewart | Allen & Unwin |
| Study of History | Toynbee | Oxford Univ Press |
| Mastering computer programming | Gosling | Macmillan |
| The Micro Revolution | Large | Fontana |

*